Piracy in the Motion Picture Industry

Also by Kerry Segrave
and from McFarland

Jukeboxes: An American Social History (2002)

Vending Machines: An American Social History (2002)

Age Discrimination by Employers (2001)

Shoplifting: A Social History (2001)

Movies at Home: How Hollywood Came to Television (1999)

American Television Abroad: Hollywood's Attempt to Dominate World Television (1998)

Tipping: An American Social History of Gratuities (1998)

American Films Abroad: Hollywood's Domination of the World's Movie Screens from the 1890s to the Present (1997)

Baldness: A Social History (1996)

Policewomen: A History (1995)

Payola in the Music Industry: A History, 1880–1991 (1994)

The Sexual Harassment of Women in the Workplace, 1600 to 1993 (1994)

Drive-in Theaters: A History from Their Inception in 1933 (1992)

Women Serial and Mass Murderers: A Worldwide Reference, 1580 through 1990 (1992)

By Kerry Segrave and
Linda Martin

The Continental Actress: European Film Stars of the Postwar Era; Biographies, Criticism, Filmographies, Bibliographies (1990)

The Post Feminist Hollywood Actress: Biographies and Filmographies of Stars Born After 1939 (1990)

Piracy in the Motion Picture Industry

by

KERRY SEGRAVE

McFarland & Company, Inc., Publishers
Jefferson, North Carolina, and London

Library of Congress Cataloguing-in-Publication Data

Segrave, Kerry, 1944–
Piracy in the motion picture industry / by Kerry Segrave.
p. cm.
Includes bibliographical references and index.

ISBN 0-7864-1473-1 (softcover : 50# alkaline paper) ∞

1. Copyright — Motion pictures — United States — History.
2. Piracy (Copyright) — United States — 20th century. I. Title.
KF3070.S44 2003
346.7304'82 — dc21 2002155763

British Library cataloguing data are available

Manufactured in the United States of America

McFarland & Company, Inc., Publishers
Box 611, Jefferson, North Carolina 28640
www.mcfarlandpub.com

Contents

Preface

This book looks at the history of film piracy in the motion picture industry, domestically and in foreign countries, from the early days of the business up until 2001. Also examined are other types of stealing from Hollywood that have been practiced by exhibitors over the years. Mainly they have been the under-reporting of box office receipts and a type of unauthorized exhibition known in the trade as "bicycling." Against that is a briefer examination of the opposite side of the coin: examples of Hollywood stealing from others. If the film capital expected its copyrights to be respected, and it did, it failed to extend that courtesy to others. Emphasis in the book is on the Hollywood studios that were known as the Hollywood cartel, the Hollywood majors, or just the majors—Paramount, RKO, United Artists, Columbia, Universal, MGM, Warner Brothers, 20th Century–Fox (hereinafter Fox), and Walt Disney.

Opening the book is a brief summary of piracy in vaudeville in the first decade or two of the twentieth century for it was in that environment that films often got their start. Piracy is defined as the unauthorized reproduction or use of motion pictures. Examples include a person who steals a print of a movie, or "borrows" it for a few hours from a projectionist to make copies and then distribute them. Another example is a cinema owner who screened a film for an extra day without paying for it, although he legally had the print for his earlier authorized screenings. Piracy could range from elaborate organizations mass producing videocassettes in a 24-hour-a-day factory operation with worldwide distribution networks to a video shop owner who bought a legal tape and then made a couple of extra copies for his rental stock. Hollywood pursued all it identified with equal vigor. Over the years the majors developed an elaborate system to deal with the problem, a network that reached around the globe.

Research for this book was conducted at the University of British

Columbia, Simon Fraser University and the Vancouver Public Library. Online databases and hard copy periodical indexes were searched, as were books on the film industry. The back files of *Variety* were one of the more useful sources.

1

Vaudeville and the Copy Act

"During our act he [Al Fox] stood in the wings and stole word for word, and complimented us on being so good."
—Beecher and Maye, 1907

"It is far better to do a bad, but original act, and to continue to improve it, than to do a stolen or partly stolen one."
—White Rats of America, 1908

"My business is piracy, pure and simple..."
—Alexander Byers, 1909

Motion pictures arrived on the entertainment scene at a time when vaudeville was the dominant part of that industry, having its own heyday from, roughly, 1880 to 1920. As people would soon come to attend the movies every week—usually several times per week—so did they first patronize vaudeville just as heavily. Piracy was a regular part of life for the vaudevillian. While copyright law existed and offered some protection, that law was somewhat vague and still in the process of being defined by the courts. Artists were more likely to try and act together to limit piracy by bringing pressure to bear on theatrical bookers, using trade papers to inform each other about infringements and to shame alleged lifters and copyists and so on, as opposed to launching copyright lawsuits.

The trade journal *Variety* was one that opened its pages as a forum for artists to complain about copy acts and any and all problems about life as a vaudevillian. In a January 1906 letter to this forum, A. McAllister, manager of vaudeville singer Ida Rene, complained that May Belfort was performing material created and owned by Rene. Grumbled the manager, "Miss Belfort's deliberate purloining of Miss Rene's property cannot be looked upon by any healthy-minded person as being anything short of contemptible, she is actually living, moving and having her being on the results of another's brains." A couple of weeks later Belfort responded by criticizing the character of both Rene and McAllister before declaring that Rene did not write the two songs in question but had only obtained the singing rights for England, not America.[1]

Then McAllister wrote again to complain of Belfort's "silly and inane attempt at defense of her abominable conduct in purloining ... Miss Ida Rene's property." Rene co-wrote both songs, he stated, and if Belfort paid for her copies they were stolen. He also declared he had a letter with information from a friend of Belfort, stating that Rene's work was taken down in shorthand for Belfort while the former was singing.[2]

That generated another response from Belfort who insisted that an A. J. Morris wrote those songs by himself. She denied the existence of the letter McAllister mentioned, or if it did exist she called it a lie. And so this exchange ended. Although it lasted longer than most such exchanges, what it had in common was character assassination and allegations, but no resolution.[3]

One letter with no specific complaint came from Herbert Ashley, of the artist team Matthews and Ashley, who praised *Variety* for publishing letters and articles about piracy. Ashley thought the problem was pervasive and applied equally to all performers, from the small fry to the headliners.[4]

In a June 1907 letter the team of Beecher and Maye complained that the team of Al Fox and Nellie Carber had stolen their act and were working it on the Ammons circuit and in other vaudeville houses. During the summer of 1906 when they were playing in New Brunswick, New Jersey, explained Beecher, Fox (then with no partner) came on to work and "During our act he stood in the wings and stole word for word, and complimented us on being so good." Soon thereafter Fox had teamed up with Carber.[5] The team of Rawson and Clare complained that a team had stolen their act and had also used the name Caire, to be close to Clare. They laid the blame on that team's manager, Adolph Neuberger, whom they described as "a kind of nondescript dancing teacher up in Harlem who had been trying for years to place his pupils in vaudeville, and has at last succeeded with a couple through stolen property."[6]

W. Harvey complained he had been informed by several artists that a team known as the Parker Brothers was doing his act — he balanced and juggled articles of bedroom furniture. Another team, De Cortet and Rego, warned performers to beware of pirates if they went South. They had opened a new act in New York City in March 1908. Not long after that they played Atlanta where another team played on the same bill for a few days.

The latter pair, the Cottings, stole their act completely and were doing it by the spring of 1908.[7]

Walter C. Mack wrote to the trade publication to state that a former assistant of his was playing the small houses in the West infringing on Mack's act and title. Mack billed himself as "The Original Svengala" while the assistant performed as "Svengali." To try and stop the copyist, Mack had written to different managers along the circuit, warning them the man was an imposter and was infringing. However, Mack had to report that "it is evident he is working cheap, for they continue to play him."[8]

An example of how confusing the situation could sometimes get was seen in a letter from Carleton Macy who complained his vaudeville act "A Timely Awakening" was being pirated under the title "Hubby Realizes" by William Abrams and Agnes Johns who were then touring in the West, Macy was Boston-based. Also, this was reportedly the second time Abrams and Johns had done this. The first time they claimed they had bought the act from a newspaper man in San Francisco. A resolution was reached that time when Macy made arrangements with the other two for them to use the act "for a certain time" and, of course, for a sum of money. However, that time had expired and Macy leased his act exclusively for that territory to Alexander Von Mitzel and Iris Maynard. At some point after that Abrams and Johns wired Macy to again lease the act but Macy had to inform them it was already taken. Apparently they went on to use the act anyway. Macy's informant told him they were using his act word-for-word and had recently played in San Francisco. Illustrating the cooperation among artists that often existed, Macy commented that "Each time this pirating of the act happened to me I have been informed by brother artists."[9]

Another common practice by vaudevillians early in the twentieth century to try and protect themselves was to publish advertisements in those same trade journals. These were meant to stake out the performer's territory and to warn away potential lifters. For example, in February 1906, Tim McMahon (leader of troupes known as McMahon's Watermelon Girls and McMahon's Minstrel Maids) took out a full-page ad to list 11 songs he had written and copyrighted and to warn that any infringement would be prosecuted to the full extent of the law.[10]

Artist Harry Radford complained in his ad that a team in America was using his name and had simply appropriated it. In passing, he noted that name appropriation was fairly common and that in Germany fakes used the names of Harry Houdini and W. C. Fields, among others. The team of Palmer and Gilbert took out an ad in which they complained about pirating in general in the form of a poem. They urged the names of pirating artists be publicized and that the lifters be publicly shamed.[11]

Weber and Rush printed an ad to warn potential pirates away from their act. They went a little farther than most in threatening to sue not just the pirates but also theatrical managers and others who permitted pirated acts to be produced in their theaters. Apparently fed up with having his material stolen, performer Knox Wilson asked readers of his ad to write to him with answers to the question of "What should be the just punishment?" for pirates. He promised a reward of $10 for the best answer.[12]

In his 1907 ad, performer Leo Carrillo asked theater managers to afford him protection against imitators and copyists. He explained he had spoken to alleged pirate Art Fisher in the Keith vaudeville circuit booking office and asked that all material belonging to him be eliminated from Fisher's act. Both Fisher and P. F. Nash (with the Keith office) promised compliance, yet a week later, said Carrillo, Fisher was still working the Keith circuit and had not changed his act.[13]

Famed performer Houdini placed an ad in November 1918 in which he warned theater managers and potential copyists that the "Vanishing Elephant" illusion was his property and was fully protected by law. He decided to place the ad when it came to his attention that "certain magicians are contemplating buying baby elephants."[14]

Accounts of pirating were not limited to self-reports in the form of letters to the editor or advertisements from aggrieved performers. They were also a frequent topic in the news articles found in those publications. An American acrobat team, Rice and Prevost, had both their act and name (slightly varied) stolen by a German pair (calling themselves Price and Revost). Rumor had it, in 1906, that the Germans had been booked for America on the Keith circuit and would soon appear in New York or Philadelphia at a Keith house. That idea caused the reporter to fume, "The furthering of this base-faced attempt by the Keith management does not guarantee safety for any producer." However, a year later pirates Price and Revost, then playing in London, England, had not made it to America, although their arrival was still rumored. Commenting on the theft, it was reported that "They neglected nothing belonging to the originals, having taken the music also."[15]

On the petition of showman Gus Hill, the U.S. Circuit Court for the Northern District of Illinois granted a perpetual injunction in 1907 restraining Charles J. Tyler of Chicago, from producing a play called "Hooligan's Troubles" on the ground that such a title, as well as much of the material contained in the show, encroached upon Hill's property rights in his musical show "Happy Hooligan." The court held that Hill paid for the use of the Opper cartoon name. Also held was that the name "Hooligan" was in the nature of a trademark and that Hill was entitled to protection in its use.[16]

Jean Bedini (of Bedini and Arthur, a juggling team) reportedly intended to produce an act similar to the Fred Karno troupe's "A Night in an English Music Hall" over the Keith circuit in the houses where the Karno company had not played. Bedini had secured two members of the Karno group, the property man and the magician, and claimed he was advised to do this by the Keith office. That claim was believed to some extent by the reporter who commented, "It is generally doubted if the Keith office suggested that an act be stolen bodily.... It is admitted, though, that the Keith people may have intimated that should an act resembling Karno's be offered at a lesser figure than the Englishman receives, it would receive their favorable consideration."[17]

That rumor caused Karno manager Alf Reeves to take out an ad warning artists not to pirate from "A Night in an English Music Hall" or from "Mumming Birds." In turn, that prompted Bedini to take out a full-page ad in which he went into a convoluted, unintelligible explanation of why he was not a pirate.[18]

Later in 1906 Karno asked the court to stop Bedini from producing "A Night in English Vaudeville," alleging it was an infringement of his own production, "A Night in an English Music Hall." Bedini's defense was that the Karno act was not copyrighted and that a similar scene was found years earlier in a production called "The Jersey Lily." Karno argued that no one appreciated the value of "The Jersey Lily" scene until Karno first produced his act and, he told the court, in any event, Bedini had taken his production "A Night in an English Music Hall" in its entirety. The U.S. Circuit Court decided in favor of Karno, granting him an injunction against Bedini.[19]

E. F. Albee, general manager of both the Keith booking office and the Keith circuit of vaudeville houses, met with Alf Reeves shortly after the court decision, and promised that if Reeves would allow Bedini's "A Night in English Vaudeville" to play the week out at Keith's Union Square Theater in New York without taking any further legal proceedings, the Keith booking office would not give it any more time, thereby causing the dissolution of the act. Albee expressed surprise to Reeves that his office had entertained a copy act; he said he had never seen it and knew nothing of the affair. A cynical journalist noted that Albee did not inform Reeves why he had waited until the court intervened before he assumed "the lofty position of the abused one." Also commented on was that had the Keith office not "patted Bedini on the head and told him he was a good fellow because he was cheap, and would steal an act," Bedini would not have become "the mountain of regret" the Karno theft made him, nor would the Keith organization "be placed in the position of an accessory to an unsavory business transaction." Around the same time another infringer on the Karno rights, back-in-the-news showman Gus Hill settled in cash for $3,000 for using a copy of a Karno sketch in the third act of Hill's production "Around the Clock." The settlement gave Hill the production rights to the sketch for another season.[20]

A few months later Hill was preparing a lawsuit against the Empire Circuit Company (Western Burlesque Wheel) charging that it was playing in the houses of its circuit an act that infringed upon his exclusive rights to that Karno sketch (from "A Night in an English Music Hall"). Hill, after litigation, purchased from Karno the exclusive right to use the piece in the United States with the proviso that he could not show it in a vaudeville house. In the suit which preceded Hill's purchase of the act, the court laid down the legal principle that it was Hill's duty to protect himself against piracy, rather than Karno's. One of Hill's employees saw the Will N. Drew burlesque show "Tiger Lillies" in Chicago and reported to his boss that the purchased piece was being shown almost exactly as it was in Hill's "Around the Clock."[21]

At the height of her popularity, vaudeville superstar Eva Tanguay complained, in 1909, about people copying her act. Complaining there were at least 20 imitators of her then on stage she did a rant against copyists and then declared, "I make this whole statement to the public because only the public can protect an originator, and that would be by hissing the imitator."[22]

Checking out her story, a reporter went to the Manhattan Theater (in New York City) where a large sign proclaimed that Billee Seaton was imitating Eva Tanguay. When asked if she didn't know that instead of imitating she was "copping an act," Seaton replied, "Oh, I know I am 'copping an act' all right. But that ain't nothing. Don't they all do it? I have seen fifty with acts of others. I don't like it, just the same, and I hear Miss Tanguay doesn't like my doing it." She added, "I don't want to do this, but the managers want me to. This week there have been people here from every big agency, and they told me to go ahead and do the whole thing." Manager of the Manhattan, William J. Gane, said he engaged Seaton as a business proposition. "Everybody is imitating everybody else," he explained. "I can not afford to engage Miss Tanguay at our prices of admission, so I have signed Billee Seaton for a run. She pleases my audiences immensely, and has proven a drawing card." In some of the press material sent out that week by the Manhattan, the following appeared regarding Seaton: "Every slight detail of Miss Tanguay's work has been copied by Miss Seaton, even to the costumes, which are the exact duplicates of the ones worn by the original." Down the street at Keeney's Third Avenue theater there was another imitator of Tanguay billed for the following week. Lobby photos of Gertrude Lynch showed her wearing outfits identical to those worn by Tanguay.[23]

One week in September 1907, the Ward Brothers put on a new act under the title of "There's No Place Like Home." After the first performance there was much comment within the profession that the brothers had lifted pretty much all of Eddie Leonard's "In the Land of Cotton." The pair declared the Leonard act was their property as they had financed the original production. Leonard stated it was a deliberate steal and he, along with a backer, had originally financed his act. A week later the Wards cancelled 36 weeks of vaudeville time with their new offering but denied the Leonard situation had anything to do with it. Rather, they said, the cancellation was because they got an engagement in a legitimate stage production. This case seemed to be an example of fellow performers rallying around a victim of theft and more or less shaming the perpetrators into a change.[24]

Through her attorneys, Ida Fuller, the fire dancer, notified the United Booking Office that Rialto, a dancer then playing in New York, was infringing upon her dance and the management would be held accountable if it continued. She cited a 1902 case in which she successfully sued an artist and manager for infringing on her material.[25]

A complaint was lodged with the National Association of Theatrical Producing Managers by Cohan and Harris against Charles B. Arnold's "Serenades." Attorney for Cohan and Harris, Denis O'Brien, happened to be in Buffalo on business. To pass a little time one afternoon he went to the theater to see the "Serenades." On seeing the show he discovered it used the business of, and the song "I Say, Flo," from the Cohan and Harris production "The Yankee Prince." The "Serenades" called the number "Flo." When he caught the pirates, O'Brien threatened to sue upon his return home to New York. In response, the show took the number off. Penalty for the offense committed by the "Serenades" was $100 for the first performance and $50 each time thereafter. O'Brien was eligible to collect after the Association passed judgment on the case.[26]

One self-described, and very open, pirate was Alexander Byers, who operated the Chicago Manuscript Company in that city in 1909. For a consideration, he claimed he could supply the manuscript of any dramatic production, musical piece, vaudeville turn, blackface act, monologue, and so on. A reporter observed that "His thievery is cheerfully brazen" while Byers stated, "My business is piracy, pure and simple.... I have in my possession the manuscript of practically every play or playlet which has achieved any success." Material came to him in various ways. For example, an actor with a manuscript might come to him to sell it. There was always a leak somewhere and he waited for material to come to him, rather than going out to try and get it. Byers said he would never send a stenographer to a show and take it down in shorthand. Cheerfully he admitted to being a party in a number of lawsuits, some of which he won and some of which he lost. Mostly, though, he described the suit outcomes as draws—which he defined as continuances in which event the lifting went on. Also, he published catalogues in which he openly listed products for sale, at prices ranging from $2 to $10. Readers of those catalogues were advised to ask if what they wanted was not listed. Questioned about some of the vaudeville sketches by well known performers listed in his catalogue, Byers admitted he didn't have all of them on hand but could get them if necessary. "We stick in a good many names of established vaudeville acts as an advertising dodge," he explained, "when we haven't the 'script' on hand." When the reporter visited Byers at his office the pirate had several stenographers all busily at work.[27]

Producer Jack Singer claimed various burlesque shows had lifted many of the bits, jokes and lines bodily from his "The Behman Show," for which Singer had paid money. When he saw "The Sweetest Girl in Paris" in Chicago, he noted that it had 19 comedy bits that were exact duplicates of those used by the Singer company. He also complained that producer Barney Gerard signed Joe Barton, formerly of the Singer troupe, for no other reason than to have him perform a bit he had done for Singer. Barton said that in his tenure with Gerard (then over) he declined to use any lines, bits, comedy, and so forth, from "The Behman Show." However, he did acknowledge that Gerard asked him to do a particular bit he had performed when Barton was with Singer.[28]

Nat W. Wills was a monologist who paid a large sum of money for his material—he paid Vincent Bryan $100 weekly and had recently paid another writer $500 for some material. Wills was furious when a Chicago newspaper printed nearly the entire monolog he had been using while the *New York American* repeated many of Wills's jokes in its Sunday edition.[29]

Performer C. E. Lindall saw the act of Fitzsimmons and Cameron in Charleston, South Carolina. On the road himself, he later wrote to the orchestra leader, G. Muller, at the house where the pair was playing to offer him money if the band leader would copy the act. "I wrote down many of their jokes but neglected to take the first ones down," Lindall explained. "If you will write them down and send to me I will send you at the least $1 for your trouble. And will make it two or $3 if you get a good lot of it down." Lindall added that "If I should write direct to them they would probably want $10 or more and it isn't worth that to me.... If you get the words of the song for me that will be worth another dollar. I know the tune."[30]

In Harrisburg, Pennsylvania, in January 1913, at a matinee performance at the Orpheum theater, Nixon, a magician who was to have opened with a piece called "The Fantom Pictures," announced from the stage he would be unable to give a performance due to interference by Clive, another illusionist who did an act called "The Spirit Paintings." Clive, who was in the audience, stood up to denounce Nixon as a copyist. Nixon had contracted with house manager Walter Vincent to appear for $250 a week, half of what Clive had agreed to at the same house for the same week. Sometime earlier Nixon started his copy act under the name of "The Spirit Paintings." Clive protested in the pages of *Variety*, which caused Nixon to change the title to "The Fantom Pictures." Nixon's agent emphasized his act was as good as Clive's and could be had for half the money. Vincent heard about this and sent someone to catch Nixon's act. Then he cancelled Clive (whom he had signed just two days earlier), even though Clive offered to reduce his contract terms from $500 to $300, on the ground that Clive misrepresented himself in having the exclusive rights to the illusion. "The Spirit Paintings" was first presented in America two seasons earlier by the English performer P. T. Selbit. Clive arranged with Selbit and his agents to obtain the U.S. rights. *Variety* lashed out at manager Vincent, who, in an attempt to save money, it said, "deliberately and knowingly encouraged a 'copy,' besides canceling a valid contract they had made with the original act before the latter was to open."[31]

Tom Barnes was informed by the manager of Keith's Louisville (Kentucky) circuit he could not play the Barnes and Crawford act as J. Francis Dooley (Dooley and Sayles) had used considerable of Barnes's stage matter in that theater. That was a salary loss to Barnes of $500 a week. He had been out of vaudeville for seven or eight weeks doing a legitimate show. Barnes wanted to do vaudeville for a couple of weeks while waiting to go into rehearsal for another legitimate stage show. During his absence, however, Barnes said nearly all of his material had been stolen by various acts. One of those pirating acts was Spencer and Williams. They had promised to stop using his material when Barnes brought it to their attention but then ignored that promise.[32]

Performer Charles Kenna took an unusual approach to the problem in 1915 when he announced in a trade ad that the vaudeville profession was at liberty to "choose" such material as it wished from his original material. In return, he requested only that acts taking advantage of this offer inform him what had been taken and where it had been used. That was to obtain advance information in order that Kenna could substitute material when following an act into a city where the act used some of Kenna's turn. He admitted he had grown tired of having local people inform him of other acts employing Kenna (billed as "The Street Fakir") material and hearing another act was claiming stolen material as its own. Not sure what to make of the ad, *Variety* commented that "Whatever the real purpose of the Kenna advertisement, also whether it was written seriously or in a sarcastic version, Mr. Kenna has exactly hit on a vaudeville condition doubtlessly many other standard artists of the Kenna caliber feel as bitter about."[33]

Nor was piracy limited to within the borders of America. There was much international piracy, especially between the United States and Europe. Julian Eltinge, a well-known American female impersonator playing abroad in 1906, complained that a Parisian artist had pirated his act in total and was presenting it in Paris cafes using the name Altinge.[34]

Vaudeville producing team Lasky and Rolfe learned that John Kurkampt (an American orchestra leader then living in England) and Alice Raymond (an American artist then also in England) had stolen the formers' piece "Quintet," calling the lifted version "The Harmonious Fairy Shell," which was then playing in London. Jesse Lasky recalled Kurkampt was a musical conductor whom he knew and met while in England. "I invited him to dine with me one evening. During the dinner, I explained the various productions we had made and intended making," said Lasky. "This [pirating] is one of the results." Lasky and Rolfe's options for redress were limited to retaining London attorneys to act for them.[35]

When the performing act Spissell Brothers and Mack returned to the U.S. in 1907 after a tour of Europe, a pirate act quickly sprang up there, calling itself Spissell, Spissell and Spissell. They even advertised the theft in foreign theatrical journals that, fumed a journalist, "have abetted this form of piracy for a long time, especially those on the continent." He added that no American act could be successful abroad "without leaving copies behind it." According to the report no account was taken of those thefts by the German theatrical trade papers: "If the 'copy' act is sufficiently far-sighted to place a page advertisement, costing about ten dollars, in the paper, it travels along with immunity."[36]

In the following year, 1908, a review appeared of an act performed by a Mr. Hymack. It was the first American appearance for the European whose act was described as an "lightning change novelty" turn. It was an act performed earlier in America by Mystic, later called Mysticus. Reviewer George M. Young observed that "the act shown by Mystic is a direct copy of Hymack's. The latter's changes are cleanly made, while that of the copy act were bungling, slower and a poor imitation of the original, though the attempt to follow the original as closely as possible was at all times discernible."[37]

An American team, Cameron and Flanders, had a sketch they did called "On and Off." In London, an English act, Amy Anderson and a Mr. Anderson, was presenting a sketch called "On and Off the Stage," in January 1909. It was viewed by Paul Murray of the Morris [talent agency] London office and a *Variety* representative. The *Variety* man told Murray the Cameron act had been wholly copied. Murray proceeded to interview the Andersons during the course of which he bawled the pair out. The male Anderson reportedly had the "nerve" to ask Murray how much he would pay to have them take the piece off. With the Andersons then performing on the Moss-Stoll tour, Murray wrote to Oswald Stoll, calling his attention to the theft. Amy Anderson and her English company had opened in New York City in August 1908 with a sketch titled "The Bandanna Queen," which *Variety* called "the worst in every way that ever occupied the stage, before or since." Some managers refused to let the company play at all while most of the others had them open the bill (the worst spot in vaudeville). During the week of September 14 the two companies played the same house and one of the English group was observed to watch each performance of the American pair.[38]

Another *Variety* reporter stated that a trip he made through just three or four English music halls in June 1912 revealed no less than five steals perpetuated by English acts. He added that "It is probably only fair to surmise that some American acts coming back from England do the same thing regarding the taking of bits which they think will do nicely over here; in fact, almost every season Wilkie Bard [UK performer] suffers because someone returns [to America] with some of his material." A particularly brazen steal was said to be the theft of "In 1999" by the English group the Meymotts, who presented it in England as "In the Future," according to Jesse Lasky, who put on the piece in the United States. When the Lasky show played in New York in February 1912, the Meymotts (then touring in the U.S.) asked him for the English rights, offering to pay a royalty of $15 weekly. Lasky turned down the offer. Then the Meymotts visited the house daily, taking down the dialog and business of the sketch. Another English performer, Carlton (a comedy magician), was said to be "notorious" for stealing material. After performing in America Carlton had dinner with some other artists the night before he sailed home for England. One was Johnny Neff, who said sarcastically to Carlton, "Have you made up your mind yet what act you will do on the other side?"[39]

Edmund Hayes had arranged to open his act in London in the spring of 1913. It was to be the initial foreign appearance for the American whose stage character was a piano mover. However, before his engagement his agents cabled him to immediately send over his manuscript for copyright registration as the agents had learned a pirate planned to introduce the piano mover before Hayes opened. Immediately Hayes cabled the entire script, including stage instructions and "business," a total of 2,218 words—this was the fastest way to send it. The cable company gave Hayes the benefit of a "block rate" but his bill for the wire was still $246. Also, the telegraph company requested his permission to advertise that the message was the longest private cable ever filed with them for transmission.[40]

At the Palace in London, Toby Claude and Jack Strauss opened in "The Little Cabaret," an "exact reproduction" of the show of the same name by Valeska Suratt that had been staged in New York the previous season. Claude had been rehearsing an act for English vaudeville with Jack Mason coaching and staging it. Mason then hired Strauss, but suddenly quit as manager. Immediately, Strauss, who had appeared in America with Suratt in "The Little Cabaret," stole the act and produced it for Claude. Speculation was that Mason (who had staged "Cabaret" for Suratt in the U.S.) walked out when asked to put on the former Suratt piece. *Variety* went on to give the Claude pirated piece an excellent review.[41]

A scenic "train effect" was first employed in a vaudeville stage piece in New York. The creators copyrighted or patented the effect in England and on the European continent, then leased or sold country rights. In Berlin the Metropol theater used the effect without permission. The lessees of the effect in Germany took steps to prevent the Metropol from further use of it in the revue at that house. A settlement was reached whereby management of the Metropol agreed to pay 10,000 marks compensation.[42]

Piracy even extended to the trade publications themselves. In a September 1907 editorial, *Variety* expressed outrage that a rival entertainment publication, the New York *Clipper*, had stolen *Variety*'s "New Act" department feature. Dripping with venom the editor declared, "The latest 'copy act' in vaudeville is the New York *Clipper*, the fossilized, mildewed sheet, whose editor's most aggressive action is the drawing of his salary, and whose chief executive lacks the force and originality to take the initiative in any undertaking more important than the opening of the morning's mail."[43]

Just one week later the editor was back to hurl invectives at the same publication, this time for stealing its "New Acts for Next Week" feature. *Variety* published its list of new acts for the coming week on the Saturday previous while the *Clipper* published on Wednesday, simply giving the same information that *Variety* gave four days earlier. If the *Clipper* had any sense, thought the *Variety* editor, it would print the acts for the coming week, thereby coming out three days before *Variety*. "Do you catch the idea, you slumbering, sublime misfit of an editor?" On the previous Saturday *Variety* listed that Jeannette Melville would appear at Pastor's the coming week in a new act. However, between the time the journal went to press and publication day Melville had to cancel her engagement due to illness. Yet on Wednesday the *Clipper* listed Melville as a new act at Pastor's, leaving *Variety* convinced the *Clipper* was simply stealing its listings.[44]

Half a year later the irate editor was back to complain that another rival publication, the *New York Dramatic Mirror*, had not only stolen the "New Acts" feature but was also stealing *Variety*'s reviews from that department. To prove its claims, the journal set up a sting operation. In its May 16, 1908, issue *Variety* ran a review of an act called "The Undertaker" by the team of Pleasant and Newburg. The *Mirror* ran a briefer review of this new act in its May 23 issue. *Variety* had made up both the act and the performers—neither existed. *Variety* declared its lawyer would prosecute the *Mirror* on "this indisputable evidence of theft."[45]

Throughout this period, various solutions or preventive measures to the problem of piracy were attempted, or at least discussed. Back in 1906 Will M. Cressy, president of the Vaudeville Comedy Club, sent out letters to all vaudeville managers and agents requesting that protection for originality be extended to artists who originated material, after such claim had been proven. Favorable responses were said to have come from almost all vaudeville circuits that pledged to render assistance in bringing pirates to justice. Typical of replies was one from John W. Considine, president of the Sullivan-Considine circuit, who said in his letter to Cressy, "I will stop any one playing my house that you assure me is using stolen material."[46]

A short-lived trade union of vaudeville artists, the White Rats of America, issued a circular in 1908 called "A Little Good Advice," which dealt with the problem of piracy. Performers were urged to be original, to not steal from other acts, and to prosecute and put to shame any and all who did pirate. It said, in part, "It is far better to do a bad, but original act, and to continue to improve it, than to do a stolen or partly stolen one."[47]

The publisher of *Variety*, Sime Silverman, wrote a lengthy article in 1908 in which he argued the copy act could never be eradicated. He saw two remedies, either of which could be a preventive but not a cure. The first remedy was that if a strong artists' association existed then a copyist could be barred from playing on the same program with a member of the association through the latter issuing an edict that a certain artist had been adjudged guilty of copying and that no member should appear in the same theater with him while he remained under the bar. The second remedy was to use publicity. That is, publicity was said to be the surest stopper to copying or, if started, to the continuation of it. Silverman thought the White Rats were sincere in their efforts to stop piracy but he felt they were not strong enough to be effective. A copyist, he said, was "just as much of a thief as the burglar who may steal the valuables of a family at night." Either the pirate reduced the salary of the original or he took away good engagements. It was very disheartening for an act to hit town and hear that so-and-so played the same material there the other week. Moreover, the pirate often argued it was actually he who had the original act. Silverman claimed that *Variety* always disclosed in reviews that a copy act had been presented; he was proud of that. Returning to his idea of using publicity, he argued it was all-important and items such as copyrights, injunctions and pleas to artists or managers had no effect compared to that of a review exposing his act. "The notice in the first place is certain to be unfavorable, and in the second place, it stamps the thief." Silverman concluded; "Although the managers have promised to crush the 'copy act' wherever discovered, there has been no serious or concerted effort by them."[48]

A new copyright law went into effect on July 1, 1909. It contained a provision that any person who willfully and for profit infringed any copyright covered by the statue and who knowingly aided or abetted such infringement was guilty of a misdemeanor and upon conviction could be imprisoned for up to one year and/or fined not less than $100 and not more than $1,000. This made it possible, for the first time, for an artist to bring a criminal proceeding against the owner or manager of a theater in which a pirated work was performed. Under the old law that had not been possible. Previously the manager of a house could not be proceeded against and the only way a victim of piracy could get redress from him was to appeal to his sense of honor and decency. Another section of the new law specified the penalty that could be recovered for an infringement of a dramatic work as $100 for the first and $50 for each subsequent infringing performance — assessed against the pirating performer.[49]

Leader among the "small time" vaudeville circuits was Loew's Consolidated Enterprise. General booking manager for that company, Joseph M. Schenck, was asked by a reporter about his stand on the playing of copy acts on the smaller time circuits. He replied, "I am positively opposed to it.... The Loew houses never play a 'copy' if advance information is furnished. When we discover that a 'copy' has gotten on our time, we close the turn just as quickly as our contract will allow us to do so." Copy acts on the small time were reportedly a source of much worry to the standard acts on the big time circuits. For the previous two seasons the smaller vaudeville houses, declared a journalist, "were apparently indifferent to what was played, provided the price was satisfactory." Those acts on the small time either bought material from other pirates or literally copied acts they witnessed in regular vaudeville houses. "Nothing in vaudeville spreads as quickly as the news that an act has been stolen. An agent who lends himself to these transactions takes the risk of becoming proclaimed as the practical receiver of stolen goods."[50]

Solutions were even discussed internationally. At a convention of artists' societies from around the world in Paris, France, in 1911, a resolution was passed whereby a member convicted of having taken the material of any other member could be fined, suspended or expelled from a proposed world federation of artists' societies. Reportedly most adamant on that point were the English delegates. Little could be done to non-members but it was proposed to bring both moral and legal "influence" upon them.[51]

One outcome from the Paris meeting came a few months later when the Internationale Artisten Loge (IAL) of Germany decided that a well-known performer (unnamed) who had copied material from Charles T. Aldrich be ordered to discontinue his pirate act and that he be suspended from the IAL until he stopped producing it. Aldrich was an American who brought his act of "lightning" costume changes and comic juggling to Europe a couple of years earlier. The copy was obtained in Vienna where Aldrich's dressing room was burgled in the middle of the night. The man who committed that act sold his illegally obtained material to the German who had just been expelled from the IAL. There was said to remain in England "one performer who has been guilty of an equally blatant acquisition of the same act."[52]

A few months later the artist suspended from the IAL of Germany (it had members from all over the world) was identified as Jennings Bray, also named as the person who broke into Aldrich's dressing room. Bray had been booked in England for the coming autumn but all those contracts were cancelled after his suspension. Aldrich was described as "one of many to suffer through their turns having been 'copied' by foreigners, who either play the 'copy' before or after the original has left Europe — sometimes even before leaving the country it is copied in."[53]

A few of the vaudeville people in New York who were the greatest victims of material stealers came up with a suggested plan in 1914 for the protection of the artist. It was proposed that an association be formed with dues fixed at $100 or more yearly, payable in advance. From that money an office would be maintained with an "inspector" in charge. His duty would be to continually visit theaters in New York. When he uncovered a copyist the new association would go to the head of the circuit then employing the pirate and demand that the lifter be notified to discontinue the use of the stolen material immediately. Also, each lifter caught would be exposed in the pages of *Variety* through the report made by the association's inspector. It was believed those two sanctions would be able to reduce thievery to a minimum: "It is now quite prevalent."[54]

William Cline, of Los Angeles, wrote a vaudeville sketch called "Between Towns." He leased it to Dan Flynn for a cash amount and a royalty payment for each use. That royalty was paid for a short time but then ceased on Flynn's statement that he was no longer going to use the piece. Later Cline heard Flynn was appearing in the east in a sketch called "Between Trains." A comparison disclosed that it was Cline's original with a few very minor changes. When Flynn arrived on the West Coast while touring on the Sullivan-Considine circuit with the act, Cline had him arrested under the criminal clause of the copyright law. When the case came up for trial he pled guilty and was fined $100 and costs. Prior to the arrest Cline notified the circuit of the infringement and requested they not play Flynn and the stolen piece on their time. Sullivan-Considine refused. Cline notified the circuit three different times but all requests were refused. It was then that Cline took the more drastic step of having Flynn arrested.[55]

Believing publicity was the best protector for the theatrical player through the possible notoriety that could attend exposure of material theft, *Variety* announced in 1916, with great fanfare, the installation in its New York office of a "Protected Material" department for the sole purpose of protecting an originator of stage dialogue, business, title, and so on. There was no charge of any kind to the artist involved. Said *Variety,* "The curse of vaudeville is the theft of material. Theft discourages, disheartens, and depresses an originator or creator of anything new to the vaudeville stage, whether it be dialogue, 'business' or title." A creator of material was to send his original material in a sealed envelope that *Variety* would not open unless a dispute over material arose. When a complaint of piracy was made to the publication it would investigate and open the sealed letter (only with the owner's permission) if it would help resolve the dispute. Refusal to allow the envelope to be opened, or its withdrawal, would be considered by *Variety* to be an admission of guilt. Following its investigation *Variety* "will thereupon print all the facts in the case, stamping the 'lifter' as a 'material thief,' detailing all matter that may have been stolen." This idea of a protected material department was not new with *Variety*—several other trade journals featured something similar. *Variety* admitted the New York *Clipper* started such a department a couple of years earlier, called a "Registration Bureau."[56]

An example of the department in action in a case that year involved an act called "The California Orange Packers," playing on the Loew circuit. *Variety*'s Protected Material department received a complaint against this act filed by the original California Orange Packers. Ray Adams (one part of the original group who left to form his own unit) headed the copy act which first called itself the Four Orange Packers and later the California Orange Packers. That act played only the small time, using an exact duplicate of the original act. After adjudication by *Variety*, Adams was given a short period of time to change his stage act. When he did not change it *Variety* notified Joseph M. Schenck of the Loew circuit who, backing the trade journal, immediately ordered the copy act taken off the books. Also, Edgar Allen, booking manager for the Fox circuit, who had the pirating Packers act booked on his time, stated he would take the turn off the Fox books.[57]

Another group doing similar adjudication was the Vaudeville Managers' Protective Association (formed in 1900) that acted as prosecutor, judge and jury in cases where a vaudevillian was accused of stealing from another. Many vaudevillians registered their acts in the Protected Material department of the National Vaudeville Artists (NVA — a part of the Protective Association) by enclosing their material in a sealed envelope and handing it in at the NVA office. Those envelopes were opened whenever one act accused another of stealing. When an accusation was made, "court" was called into session. Officially the court was known as the Joint Complaint Bureau of the Vaudeville Managers' Protective Association and the National Vaudeville Artists. Both management and performers sat on the bench and handled various types of complaints, not just the stealing of material. During its first eight years of existence this body heard some 14,000 cases, of which only four ended up being referred to regular courts of law.[58]

An example of that body in action could be seen in a 1916 case wherein Jimmy Lyons was charged with doing an act that was a copy of one by Lou Anger. In a hearing before the Joint Complaint Bureau it was determined that he was indeed doing a copy act. Lyons agreed to pay Anger $100 as a royalty for past use and to immediately get a new act.[59]

According to vaudeville historian John DiMeglio, Bob Hope pirated from the magazine *College Humor*, changing its jokes to suit his style. Hope admitted, "I did anything just trying to get material to do." George Burns also resorted to taking his jokes from *College Humor*, and other magazines including *Whizz Bang*. Like Hope, he adopted the jokes to suit himself. At any Palace theater opening matinee many small time performers reportedly sat in the audience, on the prowl for new material. Small time bookers were said to condone lifting material from headliners since it afforded their theaters topflight material. As performer Benny Rubin described it: "Mel Klee did Al Herman, Marty May did Jack Benny ... Sid Marion did Jack Pearl [and] there were more." Among those who lifted from the Palace headliners were the Borscht Belt comics, those who served as social directors for the hotels in the Catskills. When Fred Allen learned that Al Jolson used one of his lines, he wrote Jolson a letter. Though Jolson's reply stated that Allen could have his joke back, Jolson kept using it. Even John and Bert Swor, brothers headlining in separate acts, had a dispute over material. When a line he delivered fell flat, Bert asked the theater manager about it and was told that the same line had been used the week before by his brother. Bert angrily informed John that he had better drop the line from his routine. John did.[60]

Performer Ben Blue was once accosted by W. C. Fields, himself "notorious for lifting lines," and accused of stealing a routine. Blue called Fields a liar and other performers intervened to finally convince Fields that he had originally stolen the material from Blue. In an open letter to *Variety*, Bert Lahr once accused Joe E. Brown of having stolen the Lahr character. Brown never replied but an old-time comic named Sam Sidman did, with anger. He claimed that Lahr had stolen the character from him and not only that, but Sidman had stolen it from Sam Bernard. "I admit it, why don't you?" demanded Sidman of Lahr.[61]

Bill Smith, another vaudeville historian, in discussing the various protected material departments, recalled that the Protective Association's Joint Complaint Bureau was headed by Pat Casey, who acted as arbitrator. Smith thought it unlikely that many vaudevillians would ignore a cease and desist letter from Casey since the Association was an arm of the United Booking Office, the Keith-controlled booking agency, and an offender could be refused bookings. Some performers did not use such departments, preferring to take direct action. To make his point to a new comic using his material at the Palace around 1928, W. C. Fields hired two strong-arm men, to discuss the matter with the offender in the backstage alley. Apparently the newcomer never used the disputed material again. The birth of the stage name Jack Benny was the result of one such complaint letter. Ben K. Benny had appeared in vaudeville from about 1910 until the early 1920s. He had achieved enough recognition to cause Ben Bernie, a famous bandleader, to complain that the two names were similar enough to cause confusion. Benny got a Pat Casey letter, and substituted Jack for the Ben K.[62]

Smith recalled that some theater owners, familiar with one performer's material, would stop another from using it under threat of cancellation. Other owners, however, "preferred the imitator because he usually could be hired for less money than the originator." Singing comic

Billy Glason entered show business sometime before 1920. He said the Protective Association system worked for him because through it "I got gags taken out of Jackie Osterman's act, Georgie Jessel's act, and others. We would get notes—'Report to the Office' notes—and be told to take out material because it belonged to somebody else." George Burns remembered that a performer could do the same act year in and year out without making any changes. All a performer needed was 15 to 17 minutes of good material. "In those days there was something called the Pat Casey office. You had seventeen good minutes and it was your life savings. You would write it down, put it in an envelope, and put the envelope in the Pat Casey office," explained Burns. "If somebody stole a joke, they'd open up that envelope, and if it proved you were the first one to do the joke, they'd make the other actor take it out."[63]

Looking at early copyright law and protection, author Jeanne Thomas Allen concluded there was little indication that a vaudeville act enjoyed much legal protection at any period in its history. Federal copyright could be acquired only through the registration of a description of the act with the Office of Copyrights. Until 1909, when the law offered protection to dramatic-musical compositions (sketches), vaudeville acts had to qualify under the provisions for dramatic or musical copyright. It meant an act had to have enough dramatic substance to qualify for copyright protection. As late as 1914, the courts ruled that the noise, motions and postures of an actor and mere "stage business" possessed no literary quality and could not be protected by dramatic copyright. As a result, a vaudeville act could be protected only if it used an original piece of music delineated by a published notational system or if it relied upon a script sufficiently to qualify as a dramatic composition. Allen declared that it was "very difficult for vaudeville performers to qualify for federal protection."[64]

Legitimate stage productions were also victimized by pirates in the early years of the twentieth century. Just before World War I there was no copyright protection in Canada against the theft of American plays. As a result, Canada had become "notorious" for lifting plays that had achieved success in the U.S. Reportedly there were over 500 cases where American plays were reproduced in Canada, mostly in stock, without permission or payment of royalty. Some of those traveling pirated plays in the Canadian provinces had been routed into the American northwest territory, where they had played "until discovered."[65]

Around the same time, a prominent Pittsburgh play producer and broker said there was wholesale pirating of plays by various stock companies within a 40 mile radius of that city and elsewhere in Pennsylvania. He said that managers of houses running the stolen material were unable to pay the royalties demanded and in order to produce them resorted to lifting whatever they wanted. Over the previous 15 weeks, this producer added, nearly all of the most successful plays had been produced in pirate editions, under different titles.[66]

Russell Henrici wrote the legitimate theater management in Worcester, Ohio, to solicit bookings for "his" production of "Buster Brown," then playing in Mansfield, Ohio. Suspicious of the solicitation, the Worcester managers sent the letter on to the New York office of Leffler Bratton, whom they knew owned the show. That company confirmed that Henrici had no right to product "Buster Brown." Leffler Bratton also said that the production "Let George Do It," which had recently opened in that area, was also unauthorized.[67]

In 1915 the Mid-West Theatrical Association (Chicago) was taking steps to stop the Bonner Producing Company from mounting productions of "The Deep Purple" and other pieces without paying for the rights. A year later Ligon Johnson, attorney for the United Theatrical Managers' Protective Association, acting with the attorney for the American Play Company, ascertained that John R. Price had been pirating the play "Within the Law." They informed Assistant U.S. District Attorney Hershenstein of the facts and the latter secured the indictment and arrest of Price in New York City. Thus, Price reportedly became the first play pirate to be indicted and arrested in that city.[68]

Around 1923 play piracy was said to be done openly on the West Coast. "The Broken Wing" had played in Oakland under the title of "Across the Border" and "Mister Antonio" was presented there as "The Organ Grinder." A reporter commented that "The pirating producer has grown so bold he seldom changes names of characters and all of the sure-fire dialog is retained." Farces and comedies, all pirate, were given at regular intervals. They were apparently taken by local showmen or any of the several theatrical associations.[69]

In Regina, Saskatchewan, in 1926, two members of a stock company and the lessee of the theater in which they played were convicted and fined for presenting a pirated version of "Abie's Irish Rose." Alfred T. Layne, the leading man of that stock group that bore his name, Ellis Goodman, general manager of the company, and J. Graham, lessee of the Grand, in which the company was housed, were fined. The arrests were made after the troupe had played its full scheduled week. Author Anne Nichols had been notified in New York that her play was being pirated. She sent her agent Harry Lambert to Regina. He sat through two performances to assure himself the play was being copied word-for-word. A warning was issued to the three named individuals that they were pirating, but that warning was ignored. At the trial Goodman testified to having bought the script in good faith from a Sacramento broker for $50, believing he had also purchased performing rights. He was fined $25. Layne said he had nothing to do with the choice of plays and that was all the responsibility of Goodman. However, the court held that after the warning, at least, Layne had knowingly committed piracy. He was fined $10. Graham claimed he told Goodman to drop the play in the middle of the week, after the warning was received. The court, though, said Graham continued to draw his 50/50 split of the profits after that time and that therefore some of the responsibility was his. Graham was fined $20. Although the fines were not large the case was considered to be an important legal and moral victory for Nichols, and other foreign authors, as Canadian copyright law by this time held that foreign material was protected.[70]

In a different area of entertainment Arthur Casey of Philadelphia was arrested there in 1922 by the local U.S. marshal and charged with infringement of the copyright law on the complaint of the Music Publishers' Protective Association (MPPA). Casey was alleged to have caused the words of a number of compositions copyrighted by MPPA members to be printed on song sheets and selling those sheets in front of various Philadelphia theaters at five cents each to people passing in and out of the shows.[71]

Performers in vaudeville appear to have had material pirated regularly. In many ways the organization of vaudeville made pirating easier. Artists were on the road for months or even a year or more at a time. It was hard to keep track of things on one coast when the artist was touring on the other coast. Copyright laws offered some protection but were rudimentary as the courts were still engaged in interpretation and definition. Legal protection outside of the performer's own country was even more problematic. Copyright holders at the start of the twentieth century—within the dominant medium of vaudeville—were almost all individuals, many without the funds necessary to hire lawyers to seek redress, if such a solution seemed possible. That was quite different from the end of the twentieth century when the copyright holders—within the dominant medium of motion pictures—were almost all huge conglomerates. Of course, they did not lack funds to pursue legal remedies but they also had enough influence to direct the government to do at least much of their bidding in the piracy area. Vaudeville managers sometimes encouraged piracy and sometimes did not. Some of that was split along small time versus big time vaudeville lines. A large, big time vaudeville circuit, such as Keith, could not openly encourage or allow much piracy in its own houses because it would likely have led to a rebellion amongst the originating artists on that circuit. To the extent that vaudevillians controlled or lessened piracy it was the result of banding together, of solidarity, and of the use of shaming techniques. When a performer saw someone doing John Doe's material he would write to Doe to alert him. That observing artist, and others in on the situation, would complain to the theater management and perhaps also to the circuit's booking office. Also, they might confront and reproach the copyist. At least that was what happened some of the time, with a degree of success. Piracy in vaudeville in the period 1890 to 1920 was, however, rampant. Motion pictures arrived in this atmosphere of pervasive copying and lifting of material.

2

The Silent Era, to 1929

"Any parties advertising the possession of such pictures not obtained from the Gaumont Company are fraudulent liars."

—Harry Lauder, 1908

"The picture people steal with impunity, seemingly feeling secure from damage action."

—*Variety*, 1925

"For years all of the Chaplins, Lloyds, etc., were shown long before the authorized exhibitors could secure them."

—Julian Gillespie, 1927

The emergence of film in America in the late nineteenth century was closely tied to the mass theatrical entertainment from which it was launched. Motion pictures were first introduced into the vaudeville program around 1896. They would continue to be part of various vaudeville programs for decades, in addition to being presented in stand-alone programs and venues. As audiences grew tired of rival film versions of Niagara Falls, fire engines, and so forth, producers turned to comic episodes and then began to steal each other's plots. Louis Lumiere made a film called *L'Arroseur Arrose* or *Watering the Gardener* (1895), in which a boy stepped on a hose, the gardener looked into the hose to see what had caused the water flow to stop and got a soaking as the boy walked away. An Englishman reproduced the episode and it was said that before long, according to film historian Kenneth MacGowan, "there were ten versions in circulation. Producers not only pilfered plots. They stole prints, made 'dupes,' and sold them under new titles."[1]

Film historian Andre Gaudreault described piracy as "a practice that was extremely common in the film world between 1900 and 1906, and one in which all the major production companies partook in England, France and the United States." He added that all producers at the time enthusiastically pirated by duping the films of competitors who had not taken the precaution of copyrighting them with the Library of Congress. A letter from Frank L. Dyer, Edison (a production firm) lawyer, to William Gilmore, production manager, dated January 22, 1904, stated: "The Pathé films are not copyrighted and therefore you can make and sell as many copies thereof as you desire without molestation from him, just as copies of uncopyrighted books can be made in this country without infringement." In that fashion numerous hits were duplicated and fortunes made from the creative work of competitors. Georges Meliès' *Trip to the Moon* (1902) was one example of a film that was widely distributed in America where it was very popular "without Meliès ever being able to collect a single cent." Because of that experience Meliès sent his brother to the United States to look after the copyrighting of his films. After his arrival, in his first catalog in 1903, Gaston Meliès chided U.S. studios that lacked the ingenuity to produce unique work and "found it easier and more economical to fraudulently copy [our films] and to advertise their poor copies as their own original conceptions." When he opened the New York branch office he declared "we are prepared and determined to energetically pursue all counterfeiters and pirates. We will not speak twice, we will act."[2]

Another historian, Arthur Knight, observed that in the period 1905 to 1909 films were not rented but sold outright by the foot. Anyone with a print could easily strike off a new negative for a few dollars and sell dupe prints for far less than the amount charged by the original producer. It was a practice, said Knight, that persisted until authorized film rental exchanges were set up.[3]

In the days of the one-reelers, the first decade of the 1900s, when movies were unlikely to be exploited on individual merit and did not have the built-in appeal of star value, they were literally sold by the foot. That gave the exhibitor what amounted to rights for perpetuity, wrote author William Everson. Buyers were attracted by the trademark, not the star, director or story — to Biograph the producer, not Griffith the director. Biograph knew their one-reelers could be made for around $500 each, and by estimating how many prints would be sold at so much per foot, they could then fairly reliably calculate the profit. It was a safe system. However, it both minimized potential income from unusually popular films, leaving the bulk of the profits to the exhibitors, and offered the producer very little legal protection. There was nothing to prevent an exhibitor from making a duplicate negative of a film that he had bought, noted Everson, and selling copies himself. Income would be diverted from the producing firm and the often poor quality of the duped prints could reflect negatively on the original producer. That happened frequently and, since many of the pictures being offered for sale had not been copyrighted, there was little legal recourse. Even if a film had been copyrighted, obtaining proof of illegal duplication was usually difficult. Biograph, Vitagraph, Edison, and other producers tried to overcome that problem by incorporating their trademark into the décor of their sets, usually as a somewhat unobtrusive wall decoration. The reasoning was that the trademark offered proof of manufacture, and any person buying a print from a source other than an official one would recognize immediately that he was being offered an illegal print. Everson added that "The infringements of copyright in this period were many, but basically the industry was still too small for the losses or profits involved to be worthy of lawsuits."[4]

Another who commented on trademarks was film writer Eileen Bowser. Bowser observed that to prevent the "piracy rampant in the early days of the industry," the producing companies started to place their trademarks on the sets of nearly every scene, on the walls of the set, or even on trees when the scene was shot outdoors. It was a practice that started in American films, she estimated, around 1907. So important was the practice of showing the trademark that it was required by the licensing agreement that producers signed with the Motion Picture Patents Company (the dominant film cartel of the era) at the beginning of 1909. According to article seven, the licensee agreed "to photographically print the licensee's trade-mark in each picture of at least one scene of each subject." That rule was changed somewhat in the renewal agreements signed on June 6, 1912, which still required the trademark to be printed on the film, but not on the image. Trademarks, stipulated the new regulation, had to be placed on the title of each positive print, a practice already then being widely followed. However, the use of trademarks in the scenes did not prevent determined individuals from committing piracy. Fred Balshofer began his career in the film business in the basement of Lubin's Philadelphia store, carefully brushing out the trademark from every frame before proceeding to duplicate films from such producers as Georges Meliès. Placing trademarks on the image was a practice that lasted until around 1912. While it was not overly distracting when it appeared on the wall of an artificial set, the effect when the trademark appeared nailed to a tree for an outdoor shot was very obtrusive. At the beginning of 1913 a trade journal remarked "some manufacturers have not as yet eliminated their trade-marks from the doors, walls, trees and other settings in the pictures. Some way should be devised to forego this custom, which so frequently spoils an otherwise artistic setting."[5]

The Motion Picture Patents Company was described at the start of 1909, by one account, as having established a "dictatorship." It effectively abolished such practices as exhibitors purchasing films. When the MPPC sent a contract to someone who wished to acquire a film to distribute or exhibit among the many clauses included were ones that the renter deal only with licensed film manufacturers (producers in good standing with the cartel); that his possession of all films be in the nature of a lease and not actual ownership; and that he return all films to the office at stated periods (six months); that "renters may not sell or rent licensed film to each other; that no 'duping' shall be engaged in or permitted."[6]

Piracy in the film industry through the period lasting until near the onset of World War I was rampant. Most of it was committed by one film production company against another. Relatively little seems to have resulted from those outside the industry stealing and duplicating and selling prints. Partly that was due to the industry itself—it was still developing and still very small. However, as the industry grew, and after a cartel formed, producers became less likely, and less able, to steal from each other. Other factors such as the arrival of the star system and the move to longer and longer feature films also made it more difficult for producers to steal from each other. These same things, though, also lay behind the rapid expansion of the industry, with greater and greater sums of money involved. By the early to middle 1910s individuals and groups outside the industry were being attracted toward it—with a view to piracy.

Three major film producing and distributing companies, G. F. (General Film), Universal, and Mutual, made a joint announcement early in 1914 that they were starting a crackdown on thefts from their premises. This effort was said to involve a "secret service staff" to be maintained equally by the three big producers to reduce the loss of reels through theft. Martin Hilbert, a G. F. reel boy (an employee who took film reels back and forth from the producer's premises) was then under $5,000 bail for allegedly stealing an unknown number of G. F. reels. Employees of producers, at the clerical, warehouse or messenger levels, were often involved in film theft, usually with outsiders also involved. William Brown, a truck man (apparently not a producer's employee) said to be implicated in the charges against Hilbert was also named in the case. G. F. claimed it had lost 250 reels in the previous two months and believed such thefts had been going on for a year or longer.[7]

Later that year film thieves in Chicago made off with a large number of films by posing as theater owners. James Gordon was arrested and charged with obtaining eight films, valued at $800, illegally. Charles Danziger was also arrested in the case. Although he admitted having bought the pictures from Gordon, he asserted he did not know they had been stolen. Several of the larger film exchanges said they intended to place special officers in uniforms in their offices to protect films from being stolen. G. F. was already doing that. However, one account claimed that most thefts had been made from reel boys who left their cases, with film inside, unattended for a moment or two, long enough for a thief to operate. The New York Motion Picture company, which held the copyrights on a number of the Keystone movies that featured Charlie Chaplin as principal comedian, made several successful raids in 1915 on smaller film exchanges and managed to recover several of their copyrighted movies. On those raids they were "accompanied" by a U.S. Deputy Marshal.[8]

The theft of six reels of film from the front of a streetcar in St. Louis revealed the presence of a gang working in that city and in Minneapolis, Chicago, Kansas City, and Oklahoma City, with its headquarters in the east, according to police. Motion pictures worth $50,000 were said to have been stolen in Oklahoma City and in Minneapolis.[9]

Around the same time, 1917, the theft of films from New York exchanges and delivery wagons reportedly kept on at a high rate. Over the previous 10 days the following were stolen and not recovered: Merit Film, four features; Metro Film, one feature and three Sydney Drew comedies; World Film, two features; Kleine, one feature; Vitagraph, one feature; Bluebird, two features; Pathé, one feature; and numerous other reels and parts of features. A special meeting on the problem was held and every film exchange in the city was represented. As a result of that meeting a special delivery letter was sent to every exhibitor in greater New York declaring that the exhibitor would be held responsible for any further loss if the film was stolen after it left the exchange. Also, the letter requested exhibitor cooperation by having them ship their films back by an official carrier appointed by the exchange who was in receipt of a bond guaranteeing the loss of film while in transit. Film company officials believed there was organized traffic of stolen film between the U.S. and South American countries, with New York City being the receiving point of pictures stolen all over America. Once in New York, the title cards on those movies were replaced with Spanish ones and the prints then shipped out of the country. Chicago was another city said to also be suffering from a high rate of stolen films.[10]

Two former employees of a film exchange, Alex Wolfheimer and James McSorley, were seized as they were leaving the premises of World Film and arrested and charged with the theft of a feature film. Meanwhile, in Chicago, Herman Abramovitz was convicted in the criminal courts on a charge of film piracy preferred by the Mutual Film Corporation for having received and sold three stolen Charlie Chaplin comedies.[11]

Sometimes thefts weren't even discovered right away. After doing a inventory in 1917 several New York film exchanges reported high amounts of missing stock. Pathé reported six Gold Rooster features and two complete serials missing, Universal was short some 300 reels, Mutual was also missing 300 reels, and other exchanges were short varying numbers. A print of *Wild and Wooly* had recently been stolen from the lobby of a Brooklyn theater while awaiting shipment. After several days absence, it was returned by express. Several duped prints had been made from it.[12]

Some of the piracy included sending the material out of the country. Morris Cohen of Detroit was arrested in 1919 for receiving stolen property. Released on $5,000 bail, he disappeared only to be found years later and be arrested again. He pled guilty. D. A. Barton, an assistant prosecutor, determined the stolen material was sent to San Francisco and from there shipped on to Japan and other countries of the Orient which had, at the time, "a large traffic in stolen American films." A common practice among thieves then was to eliminate all identifying marks on the films to make identification more difficult and to substitute new titles. Because of that problem, and at the suggestion of Barton, serial numbers were placed on films thereafter and "the traffic in stolen films immediately came to an end."[13]

Thomas B. Spry, an executive with the producer First National in Boston, missed six reels of a Chaplin film from the company's office (he valued the loss at $3,000). Assuming they would be exported, he went to New York City to tell the police. In due course three men were arrested there and charged with bringing stolen property into the state. One of them was Henry Pasqual, who told police he owned a theater in Havana. When he came to New York City to obtain films, he said, he met the other two men who told him they had the films he wanted.[14]

United Artists had a print of *The Nut* (Douglas Fairbanks) stolen from the UA exchange in Cleveland. Also, because of continued reports that stolen films were being sold in Mexico— not just UA movies but those of other producers as well—the firm sent attorney Laurence L. Cassidy to Cleveland to investigate. That led to three men being arrested on charges of using the mail to defraud film companies. The trio confessed to sending out letters that represented them as being in the position to sell various movies and to receiving money from Mexican exhibitors without sending them any motion pictures.[15]

The major industry trade group of the time for motion picture producers was NAMPI—National Association of the Motion Picture Industry. In 1921 NAMPI began a campaign to prevent the pirating of U.S. films destined for the Orient. Leading that campaign was NAMPI's Film Theft

Committee, formed in 1919. One result of the campaign was the arrest of Gustave Lanzke of New York City on a charge of receiving and disposing of stolen items. Two movies recovered in San Francisco were First National's *The Kid* (Charlie Chaplin) and UA's *Suds* (Mary Pickford). *Suds* was stolen from a Brooklyn cinema when thieves entered it in the middle of the night. All this was brought about by Wilmot C. Hawkins, chief investigator for the Film Theft Committee. It was found that a brisk traffic in stolen films for the Japanese market was going on. Hawkins's investigation disclosed that the stolen prints were shipped by a Japanese film concern on Broadway for forwarding to Japan. Lanzke was accused of having sold the stolen print to that company. NAMPI said the duping of stolen prints in Japan had caused heavy financial losses for some film producers and that those dupes were exhibited not only in Japan but were sold extensively throughout the Orient.[16]

United Artists was conducting its own intensive campaign against piracy in 1921, with the help of the Burns Detective Agency. After some six months UA stated it had made inroads into a national piracy ring that had been exporting films to Japan and South America. Richard Baron (doing business as Progressive Motion Picture Supply Company, New York) was indicted for receiving stolen property, namely a UA print stolen by Morris Taitus from the UA Buffalo exchange. Taitus, said the Burns operative, was an old hand at the game. He pled guilty and awaited sentencing. Originally he secured a position as a shipping clerk with the UA Buffalo exchange. After he resigned it was discovered that nine different films were missing. UA general manager Hiram Abrams offered a reward of $500 for Taitus. Soon thereafter Abrams received a wire from Sweetwater, Texas, announcing Taitus's arrest.[17]

Taitus's confession implicated William Pearson of Chicago who was described as the "master mind" of this piracy ring. He confessed to receiving a print of D. W. Griffith's *Way Down East*, a UA release. Harold Goldberg, who worked for Pearson, was also arrested and also pled guilty. Two Japanese pirates, Joseph Kubey and Frank Sara, who operated on the West Coast, exported the stolen films to Japan after they had locally edited and retitled them. Both of them were arrested and released on $20,000 bail. They also worked with Pearson. Laurence Cassidy, the UA attorney involved in the anti-piracy campaign, appealed to the Japanese consul to stop the circulation of illicit films in the Orient. In Latin America, a major stumbling block was that no reciprocal copyright laws existed between the South American nations and the U.S., leaving the American producers with no legal redress. Because the Douglas Fairbanks style of action "appeals so much to the excited Latin temperament," UA was said to have been a prime target of pirates, wanting movies such as *The Mark of Zorro* and *The Three Musketeers*. It was for that reason that UA was compelled to start an intensive anti-piracy campaign at its own expense, "although the NAMPI takes care of such matters for all producers." The pirates had been known to photograph a negative directly from one print and then make any number of other prints: "This method is not of the high standard demanded by American film fans, but for the foreign countries it serves the purpose much to the producers' loss."[18]

Early in 1922 William Pearson was sentenced to a prison term of three to seven years for his part in the thefts. Taitus got four to 10 years while Goldberg, a minor figure, was sentenced to six months jail time. Market value of those stolen films was $1 million although on a per-foot basis the value would have been only about $50,000. Because of its experience with film pirates in this case, UA decided to open film exchanges in the Orient and in South America, starting with Tokyo, Buenos Aires and Rio de Janeiro.[19]

Other gangs of film pirates also reportedly operated from the U.S. to the Orient. San Francisco police were looking for one such gang in 1922. In one week two cinemas in San Francisco were broken into by members of the gang and two movies were stolen from each. Also, the All-Star Feature Film Exchange in San Francisco reported to police that its offices had been burglarized with 33 reels of film stolen. During the previous month similar film thefts had occurred in cities along the West Coast from Seattle to Los Angeles.[20]

George Mooser traveled to Japan in 1922 on behalf of the film industry to pursue the piracy problem. Upon his arrival, he said, Japanese and foreign newspapers commented on the fact that almost all UA products had been sold or used in Japan in the form of stolen or duped prints and ventured to hope that legislation would be passed to effectively stop that traffic. He said he traced the source of stolen or duped prints and found they were shipped from Los Angeles, Seattle and Honolulu to Hong Kong, and that an exhibitor in Shanghai was the chief receiver. In Japan the main receiver was said to be the Oriental Serial Film company, headed by Danjiro Ohta and Haruo Takamura. It was a film gang reported to have operated "long and freely" in Japan. When Mooser finally contracted for the showing of *Way Down East* in Japan, the thieves surfaced to claim copyright on the pirated film by virtue of a Japanese translation of the story of *Way Down East*. They also warned they would take legal steps to prevent the showing of the original and sent word to the exhibitor contracted that 50 "Black Hand" men would be at the theater to prevent the opening. Mooser hoped such behavior would help spur the government to press anti-piracy legislation. For the present he suggested concerted action by all producers and a refusal by them to deal in any way with exhibitors in the Far East who used stolen or duped film.[21]

After several weeks of investigation in the film studios, in 1923, Los Angeles Deputy Sheriff J. B. Fox reportedly broke up a gang smuggling movies to the Orient when he made two arrests. Taken into custody were D. K. Reed and Robert Marley, a shipping clerk at the Ince studio in Culver City. The operation was based on the interception of films at local express offices. Marley sent films to an express office with instructions that he would later come to that office and inform the office of the final destination. However, when he arrived he took possession of the movies and delivered them to Reed who turned them over to a Los Angeles-based company, Orient Film. There, duped negatives were made from the prints and shipped to Japan.[22]

Back among the domestic pirates, Robert Miller, a Chicago film broker was arrested on a charge preferred by H. C. Igel of Universal Film. Miller was arrested after an individual appeared at the Universal office asking for publicity material and a poster for one of the studio's movies, *The Scarlet Drop*. When asked where he obtained the print of the film, he said he had purchased it from Miller. Miller was not authorized to deal with the producer's product. An investigation revealed that eight or nine other prints were missing from Universal's office. One other of them was found in Miller's office.[23]

With film thefts in New York State alone said to total some $1,250,000, an investigation of those thefts was placed in the hands of Rochester attorney John J. McInerney in 1919 by the National Association of the Motion Picture Industry (NAMPI). He was authorized to conduct a statewide probe into the matter. Those movies that were stolen each year in New York State had a reported annual earning power of $12,900,000. In connection with that probe, a sting operation was set up with two private detectives, Charles Jordan and Irving Brown, posing as men who wanted to buy stolen films. That led to purchases and to the arrest of two men, John Van Arnam and Hans Frohman, on criminal charges of receiving stolen property.[24]

Over the summer of 1919 Brown conducted raids and seizures of film in many upstate New York cities, including Rochester and Syracuse. Raids generally were conducted with the "active aid" of the police departments. One raid was on the Rochester Film Exchange. Films worth $22,000 were seized and said to be the property of World Films and of Famous Players-Lasky. Exchange manager Eugene A. Westcott was charged. When the grand jury met to consider Westcott's case the District Attorney's office was unable to locate Brown, so the matter was held over. When Brown still had not been located some months later, Westcott launched a suit against Brown and NAMPI. In addition to raiding the exchange, Brown searched the Westcott home, allegedly without a warrant. Mrs. Westcott said Brown and the Rochester police broke into the home and generally made a mess. Van Arnam and Frohman were also suing.[25]

Chief Assistant District Attorney of New York, A. J. Talley, announced in the summer of 1919 that his office had recovered 300 sets of stolen films valued at $100,000, although it was not reported what time period was involved.[26]

After arresting three men on charges of stealing movies valued at $50,000 from an exchange near Times Square, the New York City police said that the total thefts of films reported stolen from the theatrical district in the previous six months was valued at over $500,000. It was customary practice for theaters and film exchanges in New York to employ contractors to transfer reels of film — instead of using their own employees. In the case of this particular theft, the van driver parked outside a building and when he returned to the truck the films were gone. Police traced the thieves and eventually found several hundred reels of films stored in the basement of a garage.[27]

Three young males (two were 16, one 18) were arrested for film theft in Boston. Two were employed in the shipping departments of the Goldwyn and Pathé offices in Boston and were alleged to have stolen films from their employers, which they gave to the third person who canvassed cinemas in Rhode Island and Connecticut, renting the films in the usual fashion.[28]

NAMPI's Film Theft Committee reported it "made" 17 arrests in the last half of 1919 for film piracy and "comparatively few" for the first half of 1920. It attributed the decrease to a lessening of traffic in stolen films in New York.[29]

A number of film thefts in Cleveland at the start of the 1920s led NAMPI investigator Hawkins to believe it was an inside job so he followed Julius Watt, the night watchman in the Cleveland Film building, who had his own keys to each exchange and who was alone in the building. Hawkins tailed Watt and arrested him in possession of UA's *The Mark of Zorro* and Universal's *Beautifully Trimmed*. Around the same time, the arrest and conviction of John Mikolina and John Ferns in Chicago put an end to a long series of film thefts from delivery wagons there. The first clue came from Clyde Eckhart, a Fox exchange manager, who reported a cinema owner in St. Ann, Illinois, was screening Fox's *The Skywayman* even though the management had no contract with that venue. It was learned that the theater rented from Ferns, a former resident of St. Ann. In the basement of Ferns's home was found a large number of stolen films, which he said he had bought from Mikolina. Both men pled guilty in court; Mikolina was sentenced to three months in jail on grand larceny charges and Ferns was fined $250 and costs for receiving stolen goods.[30]

Another insider involved in piracy was Leon Gorman, local manager of Metro Pictures in Portland, Maine, who was arrested for the alleged theft of $12,000 worth of movies from Metro in 1922. Details of the charges were again supplied by Hawkins. It began with the arrest of a man, John Doe, in New York with 35 reels of stolen films in his possession. They had been shipped to him by Gorman. Doe said he first met Gorman at a national convention of Metro Pictures in New York where Gorman claimed he had 2,000 films in Maine that he wished to sell. The 35 were part of the 2,000. At that point a sting operation was set up. Doe was told to keep writing to Gorman. During the correspondence he told Gorman he had found a prospective buyer. Hawkins arrived in Portland and entered into negotiations to buy some movies. When a price of $3 to $5 per reel was established, police, hidden on the premises, emerged to arrest Gorman.[31]

Boston police arrested two men there in 1927, convinced they had broken up a gang that duped films and sold them through mail order lists. Authorities believed both men had local film connections that gave them access to films long enough to make copies. Acting on a tip, film industry representatives posing as potential buyers visited a Boston laboratory where the two men worked and were shown samples of film. According to investigators the two men offered to reproduce any motion picture desired.[32]

NAMPI disappeared as an organization in 1922 when the major film studios hired Will Hays to oversee the industry and be the film "czar." Created to replace NAMPI was the Motion Picture Producers and Distributors Association (MPPDA), the cartel's main lobbying organization. Paralleling the piracy issue of this period in the United States was film piracy abroad, which did not seem to involve Americans in the theft and duping process but usually, although not always, involved U.S. films.

UK film producers were described as being aroused over the "wholesale" piracy in 1913 of UK-made films. One method involved making dupes of movies in the UK and then shipping them to Canada and the U.S. for exhibition. Around the same time, film dealers in Europe complained of the large amount of film duping going on, not just of European motion pictures but also of American films shipped abroad. Usually only negatives were shipped abroad with the required number of positive prints made overseas, in the case of legitimate movies.[33]

London, England, was the site of the theft of the negative and several positive prints of the film version of R. L. Stevenson's *Treasure Island*. British dealers found the asking price for screening the film to be too high so it was decided to send the preview prints back to America. After being packed into boxes the prints were put into a van headed for a shipping company. While the driver was temporarily absent from the van, the boxes disappeared.[34]

Sam Blair had spent several seasons booking movies in Australia and he contended, in 1915, that much piracy went on in foreign locales. Many pirate films, he declared, were bought in London and shipped to Australia from Barcelona, Spain.[35]

During World War I, piracy was still going strong in Latin America. According to the laws of several South American nations, the first person appearing on the scene with a movie and registering it was regarded as the rightful owner and entitled to prevent anyone else from exhibiting it. When some U.S. film people tried to sell the rights to their films in Argentina they found their features had already been registered there.[36]

After a 1925 tour of several countries— Egypt, Greece, Bulgaria, Turkey, Palestine, and Syria — a Cairo-based *Variety* correspondent declared there was much smuggling going on. Pirated movies such as Charlie Chaplin's *Pilgrim*, and many others, were sent from place to place, sometimes with different titles. The correspondent added that it was difficult for the smugglers to introduce Universal or Famous Players product in Egypt because those two producers, besides their distributors, had their own representatives in the country. Smugglers preferred dealing with those films issued by producers with no agents in the country.[37]

Even in this period the motion picture industry usually turned to the federal government to do its bidding in its war on piracy in foreign locations. Although the film industry was not as big and influential in the 1920s as it would later become, it could usually still count on taxpayer-funded assistance. Beginning in 1919 a number of the major producers launched a concerted effort to check the "notorious" practice of smuggling duped prints of American features and serials into Mexico. One thing they did was send a petition to the Secret Service in Washington asking for drastic punishment of all offenders, based upon the rights guaranteed by the international copyright law. Film executive Louis Burston estimated that copyright owners of American movies lost at least $100,000 per year through piracy perpetuated by a band he said was headquartered in Mexico City. Pleading they were unable to prosecute their rights in Mexico because of a lack of "amity" between the two nations, film men were asking for the cooperation of the U.S. government. Those pirated movies were re-cut and given Spanish titles and subtitles. Also, the Film Theft Committee of NAMPI had agents along the Mexican border. Through the arrest of a Mexican who had several reels in his possession, information was picked up implicating employees in the distribution offices of film producers in New York City.[38]

A 1925 account reported that the U.S. government was helping American movie companies to stamp out piracy in various foreign countries, although no specific details were provided. The U.S. government was said to have assisted in running down piracy cases in Turkey, Venezuela, Colombia, other countries in South America, and in several parts of Africa.[39]

According to a report from Richard May, American Trade Commissioner with the Department of Commerce, the pirating of pictures in Palestine had reached the point where the original producers could not dispose of their product to exhibitors. Through the American Consul in Jerusalem, May, acting upon instructions from Washington, had interviewed the Attorney General of Palestine and "It was soon shown that it was necessary to give the film producers protection." During that interview a representative of an American producer was present with May. While pirates had literally been "cleaning up," the question had never before been brought officially to the attention of the Palestinian government for, said May, it was found that motion picture rights could be fully protected there by the fairly recently passed Palestine Copyright Act of 1924. A journalist remarked that "Recent developments indicate that since the picture interests have appealed to the Government in the matter of pirated films abroad that rapid advancement is being made in cleaning up the situation, according to representatives of the industry in Chicago."[40]

Cuba's government was said to have cooperated with the American embassy in Havana in breaking up the illegal sale of copyrighted U.S. pictures in Cuba. Cuban authorities prevented the exhibition in Havana of two American movies brought into that country by importers who had not purchased any rights.[41]

Instructions to make all "proper efforts" to prevent the showing of pirated films were sent out in May 1924 by the U.S. State Department to all its representatives abroad, acting on the request of Will Hays, president of the MPPDA. Hays explained the pirating of movies had become a common practice. Stolen products were smuggled into foreign countries where they were not protected by U.S. copyright laws and exhibited on a wide scale. State Department agents were also "directed to cooperate" with representatives of U.S. film producers abroad who, in turn, had been directed by Hays to prosecute such violations to the full extent of the law prevailing in the nations to which they were assigned.[42]

Movie exhibitors in Turkey were said to have formed an association to protect themselves from the printing of American films, according to a report to the U.S. Commerce Department from James R. Mood, Assistant Trade Commissioner at Constantinople. The pirating of product in Turkey had been the cause of much concern for several years to the U.S. industry. Native exhibitor Kemal Bey headed that local organization, which was still in its infancy. It was through the efforts of Bey that a recent victory had been recorded. A U.S. feature was purchased, advertised, and ready to be screened when a pirated version with nothing but the title changed was appearing at another cinema. A court, in a case initiated by Bey, issued an order stopping the screening of the pirate version. Still another report to the Commerce Department covered the situation in Japan following the suit over a U.S. movie that dragged through Japanese courts for three years before a compromise was reached. An agreement was reached whereby protection was granted to U.S. producers and their films allowing an injunction to be obtained anywhere in Japan without lengthy formalities. It also meant a pirated film could then be seized in Japan without the necessity of a civil suit.[43]

Eighteen months after the above account about Turkey, it was reported that the pirating of films in Turkey had "practically been stopped," according to Julian E. Gillespie, commercial attaché at Constantinople, then in Washington, D.C., on leave. That was due to the native exhibitor organization, which Gillespie claimed had been formed at his suggestion. Still, there was internal squabbling in the group and it was in some danger of an imminent collapse. If that happened, Gillespie hoped that a newly adopted Turkish civil code could be used to prevent piracy. Financial losses to U.S. distributors had been, thought Gillespie, "exceptionally large" over time. Comedies had the greatest appeal at the Turkish box office with the result that "for years all of the Chaplins, Lloyds, etc., were shown long before the authorized exhibitors could secure them."[44]

A gigantic case of piracy through which American film companies and music and book publishers were being robbed of millions of dollars in 11 nations was reportedly uncovered in 1926 by the efforts of American Esther E. Rosecan, who was in Warsaw representing the Pathé Exchange of New York. Although the entire situation had been laid before the U.S. Commercial Attaché, film companies were said to be unable to stem those wholesale losses themselves due to the fact the U.S. had no copyright treaties with any of the 11 countries then being "flooded" with pirated American films, books and music. Centered in Warsaw, the ring "borrowed" movies that were being legitimately shown in Vienna or other cities, made duplicate negatives during the night, and replaced the films before morning. Next, they made sufficient prints in Warsaw to supply the Baltic States, Russia, Bulgaria, Greece, Turkey, Persia, Romania, Poland, and Egypt. Rosecan found that legitimate buyers of United Artists and Paramount movies were being beaten to the screens by at least several days by rival exhibitors who purchased through the bootleggers. On behalf of her company, Rosecan brought a criminal action but the courts ruled that since there was no copyright law in Poland, the U.S. firm had no grounds for action. One attorney for the pirates declared, in the local papers, that while the practice was "not strictly ethical" the Poles were forced to take such measures to combat the American "invasion" and that "America might be stealing Polish films at the same time." Also, he laid blame on the Americans who had refused to sign on to the Copyright Convention in Berne, implemented back in 1886.[45]

Tying the Turkish and Polish situations together was Julian Gillespie, who reported to the Department of Commerce that a Pole representing himself as the agent of a Polish concern had openly sold a pirated copy of Harold Lloyd's *Girl Shy* to a Turkish exhibitor. To make matters worse, that exhibitor was a member of the exhibitors' organization, formed at Gillespie's urging, to eliminate piracy. Loyal members of that association "convinced" the local police chief he should confiscate the pirated film, and he did. That official later returned the movie, however, when the exhibitor "convinced" him his initial seizure was wrong. The Pole in Turkey had further strengthened his position by securing from the Polish Consulate there a letter representing himself to be the agent of a legitimate firm. That letter advised cinema owners that the agent could furnish them with "copies of celebrated films." With no legal means of relief available hopes rested with persuading exhibitors not to screen pirated material. Other remedies would be for the U.S. and Turkey to sign a copyright agreement or for America to join and adhere to the Berne copyright convention, of which Turkey was a member.[46]

A lengthy report to the U.S. Commerce Department in 1926 detailed the work of the Polish pirates in Romania. American Consul at Bucharest, J. Rives Childs, explained the first attempt by the two Poles to dispose of a pirated print was frustrated when film producers inserted a warning in the motion picture trade papers. Persisting, the Poles located an exhibitor who would screen their pirated Charlie Chaplin's *Gold Rush* (it was retitled). When the U.S. Consulate sought to stop the screening through the police the film people were met at the police station by the exhibitor, the importer, and a number of lawyers and representatives of the Polish legation. Using Polish diplomatic personnel for assistance was said to be a tactic used regularly by the Polish pirates. Police officials were faced by an apparently bona fide bill of sale on the pirated print while the U.S. officials were without documentary evidence that the movie was U.S.-owned. As a result, the police did nothing. Finally, the Americans got the necessary documentation and succeeded in securing an order for the film to be seized, after it had screened for three days. A sheriff sent to carry out the seizure order was talked out of doing so by the exhibitor and his lawyer. Another order was secured the following day but the film was gone by then. Later it was learned the movie had been sold to another Romanian exhibitor for $250. After several months—during which time the film was screened occasionally, and all efforts to stop it blocked—it was finally seized by Romanian officials with diplomats in Berlin, Paris, Constantinople, and Bucharest involved along the way.[47]

Reports reaching the U.S. Commerce Department in 1927 indicated that pirated copies of Harold Lloyd's *Girl Shy* had been screened in Greece while Warner's *Sea Beast* was being shown in China. They learned of the latter following a request from an Italian firm of exhibitors in Harbin asking for assistance from the American consul to prevent the showing of *Sea Beast* by a Japanese exhibitor. Although they did succeed in stopping it in Harbin, after a one-day screening, U.S. officials learned the print had been passed over to a Chinese company for presentation in still another theater.[48]

Producer First National made protests to the State Department in an attempt to protect a Caracas, Venezuela, company that held a three-year distribution contract for its movie *The Sea Hawk*. Instructions were sent by wire from the State Department to Henry W. Wolcott, American consul at Caracas, directing him to make every possible effort to stop unauthorized showings of this movie. Wolcott had reported, prior to the instructions, that Bernardo Herrera, "who has shown innumerable unauthorized pictures," had already been exhibiting *The Sea Hawk* for over three months. It meant that almost no market remained for the legitimate print. Wolcott also noted that on several previous occasions the consulate had endeavored to use its influence to prevent the exhibition of pirated films, only to be advised by Venezuelan officials that nothing could be done.[49]

Another Commerce Department report, in 1927, stated that India was being used as a distribution center by a New York company for the sales of pirated American-made films to other foreign countries. Accordingly, American officials abroad were again instructed to do everything possible to stop the admission of unauthorized copies.[50]

Domestically, little was attempted in the way of organized, systematic efforts at implementing solutions by the major film producers in this period. In some cases ads were used, as they had been for vaudeville artists. UK comedian Harry Lauder took out an ad in a trade paper in 1908 to declare that the only film work he had done was for the Gaumont Company. His attention had been drawn to the fact that certain other parties had been, and were, selling his film work. Lauder said that "any parties advertising the possession of such pictures not obtained from the Gaumont Company are fraudulent liars." Author Jack London felt compelled to take out a trade ad in 1913 to explain that only *The Sea Wolf* film made by Bosworth was authorized by him and to warn readers that unauthorized films of *The Sea Wolf*, and other works by him, were making the rounds.[51]

Efforts were sometimes made to have laws passed that would benefit the industry against the pirates. Congressman Joseph Walsh (Mass.) introduced to the House of Representatives in 1922 the Film Theft bill, which made it an offense punishable by up to five years imprisonment and/or a fine up to $5,000 to transport in interstate commerce a stolen film, or to transport a film "without ascertaining by diligent inquiry that the person delivering or selling the same has a legal right to do so." That measure was introduced on behalf of NAMPI and was drawn up by that organization, after a conference with Department of Justice officials. Prosecution of film thefts under state penal codes for larceny was considered unsatisfactory by the organization. NAMPI chairman H. Minot Pitman remarked that when a film was stolen it was usually at the instigation of a receiver of stolen goods. But often the actual thief, a young boy not subject to harsh justice, received from $10 to $50 for his work, whereas the receiver stood to gain between $500 and $1,000. Walsh's measure did not pass.[52]

NAMPI's own piracy unit, the Film Theft Committee, formed in 1919, disappeared, along with NAMPI itself, in 1922 when the motion picture industry restructured under Will Hays. The cartel's new lobby group, the Motion Picture Producers and Distributors Association (MPPDA), was formed in 1922. A few years later, in 1927, the MPPDA established it own unit devoted to stopping film piracy, the Copyright Protection Bureau.[53]

Toward the end of this period the U.S. Department of Commerce, through Bernard A. Kosicki of the Division of Commercial Law who was directly charged with this task, had secured an interpretation of article four of the Berne Copyright Convention from Fritz Ostertag, Director of the International Bureau of Artistic and Intellectual Property at Berne, as to the protection of films. Ostertag advised that non-published films whose authors (copyright holders) were nationals of one of the union countries were protected by the Convention, as well as all films published for the first time in a union country or simultaneously in a union nation and a non-union nation. A film was defined as being published when it was on the market, when the producers had offered it for sale to the motion picture trade. Whether or not the film had been screened was irrelevant. Most European countries, and many others, had singed on to the Berne Convention, but not the U.S. Kosicki had been looking for some way to use the Berne treaty to help U.S. motion picture producers, despite the American status as a non-member. Around the same time the U.S. had copyright agreements— either through proclamation or convention — with all the Latin American countries, except Argentina, Bolivia, Colombia and Venezuela.[54]

Another group the motion picture producers had to watch out for were the exhibitors, the theater owners and managers. For the most part they engaged in a different kind of stealing from Hollywood than that performed by the print stealing pirates, although cinema employees were often key access people in those rings. At the level of theater owner and management, the stealing was different. One of the most popular scams engaged in by exhibitors was the practice known in the trade as "bicycling." An exhibitor who had rented a film legitimately for a specified period of time, say, for one week at a fixed sum of dollars, would try and screen the print for an extra day or two at the beginning or end of his run. Or the cinema owner would rent the movie for one of his theaters and then screen it illegally at another theater he owned. Or two exhibitors would each rent half as many films as they needed for a full program and then swap the movies back and forth each night, giving each a full program for half the price. In some cases reels of films were sped one by one to a second theater after they finished screening in one venue. Sometimes this was done by bicycle messenger. As early as 1915 exhibitors were reported to be engaged in bicycling. Several New York City exchanges, according to one account, tolerated the practice — if they were informed before the event and consented. In those cases they charged 25 percent over the contracted price.[55]

Erwin Huber, a film exchange executive in Rochester, New York, started a movement there after he held a meeting of film exchange people in upstate New York. Instances of managers who made it a practice to bicycle a picture "for all it was worth" and of stolen films being shown in various cinemas were cited. A vigilance committee was formed to investigate and present specific reports on these problems. Just a week later that committee reported it was having success in western and central New York State and in adjoining territory in Pennsylvania and Ohio. One arrest had been made when a man tried to sell a stolen film and several houses had been placed under surveillance. A private detective had also been hired.[56]

Huber's Interstate Vigilance Committee declared that its success was verified by the statement of several film exchange people who said that the film bookings from certain suspected theaters had increased dramatically. That is, these cinemas had to fill all the time formerly taken by the bicycled or stolen prints. The man arrested for trying to sell a stolen film skipped town and forfeited bail of $500 rather than face trial.[57]

Just one year later, in 1920, bicycling and other "criminal practices" among certain exhibitors in western New York State (around Rochester) were reported to have flourished to such an extent that drastic measures had been decided on by the Buffalo, New York-based Motion Picture Exchange Managers' Association. No mention was made of Huber or his group. At an upcoming meeting of the Rochester Motion Picture Exhibitors' League, several of the Buffalo executives planned to confront the cinema owners with the charges and the amounts of their bills for the illegally used movies. Detailed evidence was said to include days and dates for weeks past on which bicycled and stolen films had been shown in various venues. A group of investigators had hit the towns, visiting each cinema night after night and compiling lists of what films were screened. According to an account, "It is believed that the moral force of the thing [public accusation, shaming, and so forth] will be so great that practically every accused man will immediately hand over his check."[58]

About 15 exchange managers did indeed show up unannounced (except through the pages of *Variety*) at the Rochester exhibitors' meeting where they publicly accused the wrong-doers. "Somewhat stunned by the blow, the guilty parties were compelled to admit their wrongdoing," said a reporter who was present. Given the option of paying or facing the law, "They paid, or agreed to do so." One exhibitor offered the excuse that when his film did not arrive in time he was forced to bicycle in order not to disappoint his patrons. Why then, he was asked, had he not paid for the picture thus used?[59]

A few years later, in 1924, an account had it that smaller film houses in the out-lying districts had reverted back to a practice "more or less permissible in the early days, but long since prohibited"—bicycling. "It is that of interchanging films and giving double bills without the formality of renting the additional feature." Film exchanges were then, in some cases, employing "spotters" to check up on screenings. Also, they were of the opinion that offenders could be prosecuted under the same laws as pirates. Prior to this time, went the report, film exchanges had been content to charge regular rental fees and ignore the incidence of bicycling.[60]

At a meeting before the Washington Film Board of Arbitration, William Laninger, owner of three movies houses, was the loser in a 1928 action brought against him by Paramount, MGM, Fox, and Educational for violation of film contracts. Plaintiffs claimed Laninger rushed films from one of his houses to another by bicycle messenger, in direct violation of their contracts. Laninger claimed he had an oral understanding that he could use any film he rented for one house in all his houses and that it had existed for 15 years, thus "amounting to a trade custom." It was an argument that failed and the plaintiff producers were awarded a total of $1,589 in damages.[61]

Later in 1928 two findings were made by the New York Film Board of Trade in which the board awarded damages in full to distributor plaintiffs, each one against the Hildinger Booking Company of Trenton, New Jersey. Producer Metro charged Hildinger sub-rented three of its films to a school and was awarded $2,000 damages for each picture. Hildinger got $50 for each film from the school, which screened them at times Hildinger was not exhibiting them. In the second instance United Artists charged Hildinger with taking seven of its films and bicycling them from Trenton to Hightstown, New Jersey, to play a second and unauthorized time. UA was awarded total damages of $4,900.[62]

Another practice exhibitors engaged in was the cutting of films. In later times the major producers would never defend their products from cuts for, say, television broadcasting. Nor would they ever pay much attention to their creative people such as directors and writers who decried indiscriminate film cutting. In this period, however, the producers were indeed annoyed when exhibitors took it upon themselves to make cuts in movies. These major film producers and distributors announced in 1914 they had had enough of "film vandals." Upset by that declaration were the exhibitors who had been making a practice of snipping parts of films from reels before shipping them back to the exchanges. That declaration came after several major producers had done their books for 1913 and discovered, after a conference, that 10 percent of all reels issued came back unfit for the screen. A quiet investigation by the producers among their customers discovered some exhibitors had collected as many as several hundred feet of certain subjects and were using them for exhibition. One Bronx cinema owner had 600 feet of cabaret subjects pieced together for screening, something he had done many times. It was made up of pieces of film from this picture and that he had clipped from reels before returning them. He even rented his cabaret film out at commercial rates. With the combined companies circulating 100 reels weekly at an average value of 10 cents per foot (films were rented them to cinemas for so many cents per foot), the 10 percent loss was said to amount to more than half a million dollars yearly. One suggested solution was that the producers establish a blacklist of offenders. The clampdown was implemented not just to save money but to preserve for each audience "the integrity of their output." That is, producers were sometimes criticized for presently half-baked or hard-to-follow material in films when those disjointed stories, they felt, may really have been due to exhibitors cutting their pictures.[63]

By the beginning of 1917 the issue of features being cut by exhibitors, mainly managers of large houses on Broadway, had been a cause for concern for some time, not only to production companies but also to well-known directors. Discarded footage represented a loss of time and money to the studios—most film rentals were then still made on a per-foot basis, although some producers were then levying a flat-rate rental rate based on "quality." Directors claimed the cutting by exhibitors was done so the time of the performance could be held to a maximum of two hours, and as there were other films shown besides the feature (various shorts), cutting was applied to the feature. Those directors wanted the practice stopped and suggested that instead of cutting a feature when it ran over the allotted five reels, the exhibitor should do away with one of the single-reel shorts. Maurice Tourneur, who directed Mary Pickford in *The Pride of the Clan*, said that film was turned over to the Strand Theater with a footage of 6,600 feet but only 5,500 were exhibited. He called it a reckless cutting that caused the feature to lose coherence and that reflected poorly on him as a director. He pointed out the injustice of tampering with features and called attention to the fact that publishers would not change the text of a book manuscript without the author's permission. As far as Tourneur was concerned, only the director should be able to cut a film. "There is some justice to Mr. Tourneur's claim," remarked a reporter, "but that he is altogether correct is questionable." Harold Edel, Strand manager, denied any injustice had been done to the film. "It is true that the Pickford picture was cut [by us], but by so doing we improved it at least twenty per cent," he explained. "It is true that our show is confined to about two hours but that we injure a feature by cutting has never been maintained." Edel added that "we must be the judges of what our patrons want ... if by cutting we can improve a picture there surely cannot be any objection raised." In *The Pride of the Clan* the portion removed, Edel explained, "concerned the character of an atheist who meant nothing to the picture or concerned the story in the slightest. And as the film was too long we eliminated that character." When a reporter spoke to other directors and producers about the issue of exhibitors cutting films they all "protested vehemently against the practice." *Variety* felt there was only one way to put a stop to the practice: the insertion of a prohibition clause in the agreement between distributor and exhibitor.[64]

Just one month later that suggestion was adopted by an unnamed film producer when one of its executives announced that henceforth his company's contracts for the exhibition of its films would contain a clause to the effect that no exhibitor had the right to alter the film, as it was delivered to him, without written consent. That action came about after the executive had occasion to see one of his films in two different houses. In one case the movie was so badly cut and mutilated that its lack of coherence drew comment from the audience.[65]

Apparently no one else followed suit for in 1920 it was reported that a movement had started, backed by many prominent actors, directors, screenwriters, playwrights and producers. Its object was the insertion in all film rental contracts of a clause imposing a substantial money penalty on all exhibitors who cut out scenes or in any manner or form mutilated movies rented for screening. Those behind the idea planned to present a resolution to NAMPI with a request that the national association embody the rule in a standard film rental contract. Actors claimed the practice affected their prestige; directors declared exhibitors knew nothing of film construction and when a picture was cut, "as is frequently the case to shorten up a show," the continuity was ruined. Film production companies were said to have been reluctant to complain — although not happy with the practice — because it might have meant the loss of a Broadway showing for the movie. In small towns and in smaller houses in big cities, the cutting was often not even done by the house owner but by a manager or even a lower-level employee. Distributors added the complaint that often, when scenes were cut out by exhibitors, those "edited" parts were not returned causing the distributor to have to go to the extra expense of obtaining them from the head office. Hugo Riesenfeld, manager of New York City film houses The Rialto and The Rivoli, explained that when he edited films he often improved their quality. However, much indignation was expressed by directors whose films had been "edited" by Riesenfeld. A celebrated, but unnamed, playwright reportedly saw one of his movies screened at a Broadway house. Seeing a key scene was missing, he called the studio to complain — it had been there when he first saw the film screened at the manufacturer's office. The studio phoned the theater only to be calmly informed by the manager that he thought the scene in question was unnecessary and had eliminated it.[66]

At a 1924 convention of the Motion Picture Theater Owners of Eastern Pennsylvania, Southern New Jersey and Delaware, a strong protest was made against film censorship (ordered by state agencies) on the ground that censors "no matter how intelligent or capable, cannot revise pictures without injuring them from an artistic point of view." Yet many exhibitors seemed happy enough to cut films on their own.[67]

When the owners of a cinema in Toronto decided in 1926 that *Wings of Youth* was a better name than *Broken Souls* for a Fox movie, they changed it. Fox sued and was awarded $907 in damages. However, the appeal division of the Supreme Court of Ontario reversed that decision declaring, in effect, that a motion picture exhibitor could change the title of a film if he wanted to.[68]

While there was much stealing from Hollywood (actually, mostly New York in this period) the film capital of the world was engaging in thievery of its own. If it wanted its copyrights honored and respected it did not always extend that courtesy to the copyrights of others. Nor was Hollywood above the practice of trying to fool both exhibitors and the general public by releasing reissues and pretending they were new features. A 1908 suit brought by Klaw and Erlanger, Harper Brothers and Henry Wallace against the film producing firm Kalem sought an injunction preventing the further manufacture and sale of their motion picture *Ben-Hur*, for copyright infringement. Giving some idea of the longevity of a film at this time was *Variety*, which noted in its March 21, 1908, account of the suit that "The film has long outlived its usefulness, having been first made in December [1907]." Kalem had no plans to use it again and no damages were demanded by the plaintiffs. Kalem admittedly had employed a writer to read Lew Wallace's book of the same name and to write up a scenario. From that the film was produced. No permission was sought nor were any royalties paid to the copyright holders of the book. In the suit, Harper (the book's publisher) sought to have a motion picture declared to be a dramatic presentation and therefore subject to the restrictions of the copyright covering books and plays. If the decision went against Kalem it would be impossible to reproduce scenes from copyrighted books or dramatic performances without consent. Kalem had nothing to lose but defended the case in the general interest of the film industry whose lobby group, the Motion Picture Patents Company, underwrote Kalem's defense costs. Said a Mr. Marron of Kalem, a film "is neither a book nor a drama, but is a photograph coming clearly under the provisions of the copyright law, which provides protection for photographs."[69]

Marron was probably referring to a 1903 case, Edison versus Lubin, which extended the 1870 copyright law's protection of photographs to film, ruling that the film as a whole, rather than its individual frames, could be copyrighted.[70]

In May 1908, in U.S. District Court, Judge Lacombe handed down a decision in which he declared that motion pictures came within the copyright law and that the exhibition of films of scenes from copyrighted plays or books were violations of copyright. Therefore the restraining injunction was granted. Klaw and Erlanger were plaintiffs because they held the stage production rights to *Ben-Hur*; Henry Wallace was the grandson of the late author. Commenting on the case, the *New York Times* said, "Down to the present moving picture concerns have never troubled themselves with royalties."[71]

On November 13, 1911, the U.S. Supreme Court affirmed the lower court's *Ben Hur* ruling. Two days later the *New York Times* ran an editorial which celebrated the *Ben Hur* decision as a vindication of the rights of authors.[72]

When historian William Everson discussed the film piracy of the first decade of the 1900s when producers sprinkled their products with their trademarks to protect their work from each other, he observed that no matter how great the losses, the greatest losers were the writers whose work was "pillaged, borrowed, altered, or literally stolen." Some writers, like Peter B. Kyne, reportedly took that stealing in stride.[73]

Another historian, David Bordwell, commenting on the *Ben Hur* decision, remarked that "Up to this point, manufacturers had freely adapted anything...." Prior to 1911 crediting sources was an economic tactic to improve profits; afterwards, crediting sources, at least by purchasing rights, became a legal necessity. Kalem had advertised *Ben Hur* extensively and it enjoyed great theatrical success. It was around this period, 1907 and onward, that the motion picture industry began a strong move away from one-reel movies to multi-reel features. In that period up to the 1911 Supreme Court affirmation of the Kalem case, Bordwell declared, "With little attention to copyright, directors and others in the companies 'borrowed' plots for their movies."[74]

Prior to 1912, motion pictures were not referred to specifically in copyright legislation. That year, films were given the same specific protection as other items such as books received—protection for 28 years. Copyright laws also provided that copies of motion pictures be deposited with the Library of Congress, but from 1912 to 1942 the Library did not enforce that as part of the copyright process. As a result, much of America's early film legacy was lost with no existing prints surviving of many movies because producing studios were too cheap to make one extra copy for the archives and because the Library of Congress allowed the industry to convince it to waive that part of the process. In later years the Library would enforce the deposit condition.[75]

Ligon Johnson, attorney for the United Theatrical Managers' Protective Association, announced in 1915 he would soon commence a campaign against motion picture producers who had been picking bits and scenes from copyrighted plays and incorporating them in films. During the previous few weeks a number of instances of "lifting" had come to light, and on the complaints of some of the theater managers the Association's attorney conducted an investigation. Johnson declared there were a number of producers who, "while they will not lift a play bodily, will pick the big dramatic punch and the idea of the general plot and rewrite it to suit themselves."[76]

Charlie Chaplin was granted a restraining injunction in 1917 by the District Court of the U.S. for the Southern District of New York to prevent the Motion Picture Film Company from releasing three films he was featured in. Motion produced all three with the principal role in each played by a "low" comedian in make-up and dress resembling Chaplin with the ringer imitating all Chaplin's mannerisms. Then Motion assembled and patched together isolated scenes taken from discarded Chaplin productions and added to the three features to make it appear that Chaplin really participated in each of the movies. Theatrical posters were printed containing the plaintiff's name and picture and misleading statements that Chaplin was featured in each film. Based on this action, Chaplin's lawyer uncovered enough information to commence lawsuits in the same court against several other people and firms for producing fake Chaplin films in the same general way as done by Motion.[77]

Around that time the Authors' League of America announced it was watching for cases of story and scenario piracy. The League published what it called a "white list." Any names of film producers not contained in the list were considered untrustworthy. "A recent list issued is minus the names of several of the biggest picture producers," observed a journalist, without identifying the missing. Much like *Variety*'s Protected Material department, the League had a bureau for registering scenarios and manuscripts.[78]

In 1923 that same Authors' League of America announced it was going to start a campaign with the film studios on the ground that the works of its writer-members were distorted and mutilated in being transferred to the screen.[79]

An injunction was granted in London, England, in 1925 against the showing of Famous Players's *Feet of Clay* on the ground the last two reels had been lifted bodily from Sutton Vane's "Outward Bound." William Harris, who produced "Outward Bound" on the New York stage, happened to see the film and then began legal proceedings.[80]

Nor did vaudeville escape from pilfering by Hollywood. Artists in that area suffered especially from film comedians and gag writers stealing their stage material. "The picture people steal with impunity, seemingly feeling secure from damage action," remarked one observer.[81]

According to the Screen Writers' Guild, complaints about the appropriation of original material by motion picture producers were "pouring" in to the Guild in 1928. In the past such complaints had come in from "illiterate but ambitious amateurs who offered nothing worth stealing," or if they did come from experienced writers, those complaints were lodged against "small bootleg" producers. However, the complaints of piracy then being received by the Guild were from "writers of unquestioned ability and integrity, and involve some of the largest producing organizations in the industry. This thievery is being done by adept crooks deliberately employed for that purpose and no other."[82]

In the wake of the Kalem case affirmation in 1911 the motion picture industry made an unsuccessful effort to pressure the government to pass a law that would essentially save it from the ramifications of the Kalem decision. Representative Townsend (New Jersey) introduced in the House in December 1911 an amendment to the copyright laws that would limit the recovery of damages if a film infringed a copyrighted play to the sum of $100 "if the infringement could not reasonably have been foreseen." It was an amendment that sought to permit motion picture concerns the privilege of paying a single, small fine for the use of copyrighted material and to eliminate the possibility of substantial and subsequent fines as then permitted. Townsend represented the district in which the property of the large and powerful producer Edison was located. In response, the National Association of Theatrical Producing Managers formed a committee to fight the Townsend proposal.[83]

One of those who spoke in favor of Townsend's amendment, at a House Committee on Patents hearing, was Representative Moon of Philadelphia. "A story is written and copyrighted and the right to publish sold for, say $50, and the author is amply paid," explained Moon, bizarrely. "That story, while of no particular literary merit, may suggest a scenario available for a moving picture film. The filmmaker has no means of knowing of the existence of copyright in the story."[84]

Motion picture producers also did not want to pay for the music they used — not, of course, on the silent screen but in the film houses where music was an integral part of the ambience at virtually every cinema. While it was the exhibitors who complained about this aspect, through this period the major studios were acquiring more and more theaters which they owned outright as the cartel sought to control production, distribution and exhibition. Sole licensor of music in that period was ASCAP (American Society of Composers, Authors and Publishers), which had formed in 1914 and was thereafter in the business of licensing its members' musical works. ASCAP took out a full-page ad in *Variety* in February 1918 to explain that exhibitors who played ASCAP-controlled music in their theaters had to pay for a license to do so. Many of them were not; they were stealing the ASCAP material.[85]

Apparently the ad was not particularly successful for in 1922 ASCAP announced it was starting a legal drive against motion picture houses (and restaurants) that used its members' musical numbers without being licensed to do so. Organization attorney Nathan Burkan said he was prepared to proceed against over 20 cinemas in New York City. Damages sought in each case would be the minimum of $250 allowable under the copyright law of 1909.[86]

That same year, Frank Rembusch, who controlled 12 cinemas in Indiana, sent out a form letter to 1,000 exhibitors urging them to oppose the payment of a licensing fee to ASCAP. He was then being sued by the performing rights society for playing unlicensed copyrighted music in his Royal Grand theater in Marion, Indiana. He cited the usual arguments used by groups (such as radio) that opposed paying ASCAP. For example, he said that the money collected by ASCAP did not really go to the musicians, it went to attorneys, spies, administration, and so forth; cinemas (and radio, and so on) popularized the music and that meant ASCAP should pay film exhibitors, or at least give it to them for free. Rembusch urged exhibitors to band together and stand together to oppose ASCAP and refuse to pay its fee, what he called a music tax.[87]

The Motion Picture Theater Owners of America (MPTOA—the exhibitors' national lobby group) then announced they were actively engaged in creating a music department to have music to issue to cinema owners free from taxes or license fees. An excerpt from their circular declared, "Theater owners have been imposed upon and thousands of dollars improperly exacted. The same process has been imposed on ... the proprietors of hotels and restaurants where music is part of the daily routine." MPTOA invited all composers in the U.S. to use this proposed new service as a means of getting their musical works before the public. MPTOA said it could also arrange with music stores to sell those compositions and that it could advertise those compositions in the cinemas, giving wide possible exposure. Calling ASCAP demands "unfair and prejudicial to the rights of theater owners," MPTOA proposed to use "every legitimate effort to circumvent these methods and give the American people as free a use of good taste as is possible." Putting some perspective on costs was the Capitol Theater in New York, said to be the largest cinema in the world in 1922. It paid its house orchestra $2,000 a week in total. For the license it held from ASCAP it paid the performing rights society a weekly fee of $5.85 to use its catalog.[88]

A year later at its Chicago convention MPTOA vowed to fight to the finish to defeat the ASCAP "tax," as speaker after speaker denounced the fee. Yet another year later, in 1924, at its gathering, the Motion Picture Theater Owners of Eastern Pennsylvania, Southern New Jersey and Delaware denounced ASCAP and its fees. Organization president M. J. O'Toole stated that bills were then being prepared for Congress to relieve theater owners from ASCAP costs.[89]

In federal court in Philadelphia in 1924, Judge J. Whittaker confirmed that cinema proprietors were required to pay publishers a license fee for using copyrighted music. A total of 31 movie theaters in Philadelphia had been taken to court two years earlier when they refused to pay a performing rights fee of 10 cents per year per seat to ASCAP (the group's standard charge to cinemas). Hotels, restaurants, cabarets and dance halls paid ASCAP a fee ranging from $5 to $15 a month. Some of the defendant theater owners contended they had no control over the music their house pianists chose and if one of those musicians dashed off a copyrighted song the employers were not responsible since they had told the pianists, they insisted, not to play copyrighted music. Of the approximately 15,000 film houses in the U.S., 7,000 had obtained licenses from ASCAP. The remaining 8,000, according to a 1922 report by Will Hays of the MPPDA, averaged 507 seats—meaning an annual fee per house of $50.70. Royalties from those 8,000 venues, which did not go to ASCAP, therefore amounted to over $400,000 annually.[90]

Films in this era were considered to have next to no rerun value. After a movie had made the rounds once it was usually quickly forgotten. When reruns were released, for various reasons, attempts were often made to pass them off as new movies, never before seen. A large number of old films were reportedly being issued by U.S. studios in late 1914. One reason was that the outbreak of World War I had drastically reduced the number of foreign films coming to America. Usually those reissues were given new titles and captions, and while some of the producers were truthful about informing exhibitors that certain releases were reissues, some were not.[91]

Mayfair Film president M. A. Schlesinger reported that an unidentified UK actress was found by a major U.S. studio and brought to America where she became a star. That studio bought up the rights to all of her earlier UK films just to shelve them so they could not be placed in competition by others against her "better" American work. However, she completed her U.S. contract and then severed all her ties to the American studio. At that point the studio released the old English productions under the guise of being American-made and of a recent date. Said Schlesinger, "It would spell fraud in any other industry, but in the present state of the film's business little or no objection is raised to this condition." He felt a law was needed to compel studios to conspicuously mark each positive print with the date of copyright and the date of production.[92]

So pervasive did the situation become that the federal government had to step in. After a 1919 investigation, the Federal Trade Commission (FTC) issued a cease and desist order against Lasso Film over its practice of changing the names and titles of movies which had been previously exhibited. Lasso was ordered by the FTC that if it should rename films in the future that action had to be "clearly, definitely, distinctly and unmistakably" shown to lessees of the items. Also, the film-going public had to be informed that the renamed pictures were old films reissued under new names and titles.[93]

A few years later, in 1922, the FTC started a campaign designed to prevent exhibitors and the public being imposed upon by film studios using any reissue scams. It began with an FTC complaint against producer Fox Film alleging the concern selected several movies previously produced and exhibited and gave them new names—neglecting to inform both cinema owners and film-goers about the situation. Fox general manager Winfield Sheehan responded to the charge by complaining angrily that news reports made it appear only Fox engaged in the renaming of old films while, in fact, he argued, many other studios were involved.[94]

Fox released three features in 1916-1917—*The Love Thief, The Silent Lie* and *The Yankee Way*. During 1919-1920 they were re-released as, respectively, *The She Tiger*, *Camille of the North*, and *Sink or Swim*. No one was informed these were re-releases. The FTC issued a cease and desist order against Fox in June 1923 to not issue old films with new titles unless exhibitors and the public were clearly informed. Fox appealed to the U.S. Circuit Court of Appeals asking the order be reversed and set aside. However, the court upheld the FTC.[95]

In a 1925 order against four distributors in New York, Philadelphia and Boston, the FTC ordered that movies, when reissued with new titles, had to bear their old titles as prominently as their new ones. While *The Three Musketeers* (Douglas Fairbanks) was being shown in New York, the defendants reissued an old Fairbanks film, *d'Artagnan*, under the name *The Three Musketeers* using confusing ad material and other means to mislead the public into believing the reissue was the same as the new release.[96]

Huge numbers of plagiarism suits were filed against film studios in this era by individuals claiming their ideas and/or scripts had been stolen by studios who then turned them into films. Most of such suits failed. A large number of them were groundless and little more than fishing expeditions against the majors in the hopes that they might settle for a specific sum rather than spend even more in the defense of even a baseless claim. It was one of the reasons that studios began to return all unsolicited manuscripts to the sender, unopened. That being said, someone with a valid claim of plagiarism had difficulty establishing proof in court. The odds favored the studios. Things got a little tougher in 1927 when Charlie Chaplin was acquitted of plagiarism. Federal Judge Winslow spelled out a tougher standard. In order to prove plagiarism the plaintiff had to produce evidence that the plagiarized work was actually seen by, and known to, the defendant personally. *Variety* commented that "Companies have experienced considerable vexation through piracy charges in the past and with the original test of proof placed upon the complainant it is anticipated that there will be fewer claims of 'stolen' ideas." At the time, producers protected their material by registering scripts and ideas with the Hays office (MPPDA) while authors filed their material with the Authors' League of America. When disputes arose, arbitration was employed.[97]

Even at this early point in film history, creative personnel, such as actors and directors, were complaining studios altered films without their input or permission. In 1916 Charlie Chaplin brought (and lost) what was probably the first lawsuit by an actor objecting to changes in one of his films when outtakes and new footage were used to expand his two-reeler *Burlesque on Carmen* into a four-reeler.[98]

Douglas Fairbanks sued Triangle Film in 1922 to prevent it from editing his films or changing them in any way in its plans to re-release them. Triangle had leased 11 old Fairbanks films to Hyman Winik, with the right to "re-edit and reconstruct." Fairbanks argued that an actor had the same property rights in a film as did an author in a book and therefore, changes could not be made without his permission. Triangle responded that an actor was an employee engaged in making a product over which the manufacturer had absolute control. Siding with Triangle, the courts held the actor to be an employee with no property rights in the films he made.[99]

Over the course of this period film piracy shifted from being an internal problem of producer stealing from producer to one of mostly outsiders—with some studio employee contacts—stealing prints and then causing them to be exhibited, often in foreign countries. Even then the Hollywood cartel was setting up separate units to deal with the problem. First, the Film Theft Committee, from around 1919 to 1922, then the MPPDA's Copyright Protection Bureau, was established in 1927. Federal government assistance was called upon regularly by the film industry in dealing with offshore piracy while domestically, the industry seemed to like to see itself as working in partnership with law enforcement officials, or perhaps even in a lead position, one of directing local police. Exhibitors were only beginning to engage in shady practices against Hollywood as they tried to deal with what were often onerous terms imposed by the Hollywood distributors. On the other hand, while Hollywood demanded its rights be respected it regularly denied that courtesy to others—individuals, groups and industries—even sometimes denying the existence of those rights.

3

Jackrabbits and Star Stealing, 1930–1945

"The film salesmen ... assured them [the exhibitors] that ... a little gypping wouldn't be amiss."
—*Variety*, 1931

"Directors protest editing of pictures by $40 cutters."
—*Variety*, 1933

"The decision is one of the few handed down in this district in years favoring a plaintiff in a plagiarism action."
—*New York Times*, 1936

Major film-producing studios were said to have been so alarmed in 1933 over a "marked increase" in film thievery that they had launched a nationwide campaign to get legislatures to amend state penal codes. Investigators for the producers reported that first-run product could be bought for as low as $50, and that $250 would buy a print of the most prestigious road show feature before its general release. So well-organized was the piracy racket that a prospective purchaser could buy any print he wanted "from a half hour to 3 hours after he has turned in his order." (This was obviously an extreme exaggeration.) Not enough information was available to the industry for it to determine how many prints were struck from stolen films so the motion picture industry found it "impossible" to calculate losses in financial terms. The market for stolen movies was largely in countries where American exchanges and offices were few, chiefly Central and South America. Amended as the industry would like it, penal codes would make the seller and purchaser of pirated films liable to criminal prosecution. Yet the estimate given here was that "almost" one percent of all the major features produced in a year were being stolen. Given that approximately 500 features were released by the majors, the estimate meant that about five movies were being stolen annually, a very low figure.[1]

Three years later the bootlegging of old prints was called a "major racket" in the industry, with a scope that was international. Hundreds were said to be employed in the activity, domestically and abroad, which was directed from New York. Most of the bootleg product was sold offshore: "This illicit trade garners many thousands annually." The Hays office had private investigators and public officials investigating the situation and the MPPDA member firms had been approached about a possible fund to be used in financing criminal prosecution of multiple suspects. Among the more effective ways to reduce piracy was reported to be for distributors to mutilate prints before sending them to the junk pile and reclamation plants. Pirated prints were sold outright on a flat-rate basis ranging from $7 to $15 per reel, or $150 per feature for the more important releases. Virtually all of the bootleg material came from the major studios; none or very little of the independent studio production was pirated. In this account bootleggers were estimated to be marketing from 30 to 40 of the most popular releases annually.[2]

One source of domestic difficulties lay with what were called "jackrabbit" exhibitors. These were itinerant exhibitors operating off the beaten track. Sometimes they acquired prints legitimately; sometimes they relied on bootleg material. Jackrabbits were a phenomenon limited to the 1930s and 1940s. During the 1930s traveling showmen generally created a small circuit of towns in a given area with perhaps six towns involved so that they could book a print from a film exchange and retain it for a full week, screening it one day in each town. The honest ones told the exchange all the details while the jackrabbit overlooked certain facts. He might have told the exchange he had booked screenings for Tuesday, Thursday and Saturday only and then exhibited off-the-record on Monday, Wednesday and Friday. Often they were caught because a legitimate exhibitor found out and reported them to the MPPDA's watchdog agency, the Copyright Protection Bureau (CPB). Similar violations occurred when a regular theater in town arranged a special screening at a local institution for a stipulated fee but did not tell the distributor. Hospitals, penitentiaries, reform schools, public and private schools, colleges, town halls, sanatoriums, and private homes were some of the places where exhibitors could get $15 to $20 per feature for a Saturday morning showing.[3]

During World War II there was a reported increase in the number of jackrabbit operators, due to several factors. One was the rapid growth of war industry communities that had a smaller number of cinemas than they needed. Another factor was the inability of regular rural theater patrons to go more than a few miles by automobile because of restrictions on rubber tires and gasoline. Warnings were sent out to all exhibitors in 1942, by CPB, urging them to report all jackrabbits they found screening unlicensed films. Some 19 states were rationing gasoline that year. Jackrabbits had to depend on bootleg prints, either "borrowing" an original to make a dupe negative or by stealing a print from an exhibitor or an exchange.[4]

One unusual case of piracy involved the stealing of soundtracks from motion pictures for use as background effects on radio programs. Reportedly those effects cost film producers "hundreds of dollars" but were being used by radio stations all over the country at virtually no cost. Airplane sounds from *Hell's Angels* had been used by radio stations hundreds of times. The same was true for "expensively" obtained mob noises, football cheers, trains, and so forth. Another example was the Universal film *Spirit of Notre Dame* with its "authentic cheering." In that case a cinema exhibitor ran off the movie following the regular show and re-recorded the sound track of the picture—charging the radio station $40. Animal sounds heard on the radio, said the account, most likely came from the various recent movies featuring such creatures and for which some exhibitor pocketed $25 for running the print off privately for the purloiners.[5]

In Chicago, in 1939, R. E. Gregg pled guilty before Judge Philip Sullivan to a charge of copyright infringement involving *The Cat's Canary*. Bringing Gregg to justice involved cooperation among exhibitor organizations, major studio home offices, distributor branches, the Copyright Protection Bureau, local and state police, censorship boards (because fake seals were used), the U.S. District Attorney's office, a grand jury, a federal judge, and the FBI.[6]

By the end of 1939 it was reported that the bootlegging of films for foreign markets had again become a widespread practice since the outbreak of World War II in Europe. An investigation revealed that in the previous two months about 50 prints had been stolen from theaters or exchanges for duping purposes. Police took into custody one man with 33 prints of movies that had been duped. It was also believed that some of those pirate prints had been sold domestically to jackrabbit exhibitors. European markets were particularly inviting to pirates then because it was assumed that bootleg items could be screened without check-up from officials of the major studios, all of whom by then had been withdrawn. Of course, just as the war made it difficult and then impossible to ship in and exhibit legitimate American movies, so did it effect the pirate material.[7]

Charging duplication and fencing in stolen films, the office of the U.S. District Attorney for Manhattan indicted three men for having infringed film copyrights. The trio rented duped films for exhibition in churches and schools and to charitable groups who accepted them in the belief the men had been licensed to distribute them. Originally the films were either stolen or "borrowed" surreptitiously from persons engaged in legitimate film business. Defendants secured 35m prints and reduced them to 16m, which were then sold. Movies involved included MGM's *Ben Hur*, Fox's *Littlest Rebel* and *A Connecticut Yankee*, and Warner's *Dinky*.[8]

The MPPDA's anti-piracy unit, the Copyright Protection Bureau, was maintained by Hollywood's eight major film producers, which contributed $200,000 annually, in 1940, toward its upkeep. With prevention as important to it as detection, part of its mission was to educate American cinema owners. CPB general counsel Edward Sargoy declared that the majors were being cheated out of millions of dollars each year by fraudulent theater practices until the bureau achieved its full national operation by 1931. Originator of the bureau, and still its chief in 1940, was Jack Levin. Bicycling was indirectly the cause of the creation of CPB. It all began in 1915 when Levin worked for the Mutual studio in New York where one of his duties was to deliver movie prints to local exhibitors. "Bicycling was widespread then and duping was so common that producers used to stamp every foot of their films with a distinctive trademark," he recalled. When he delivered two-reel Chaplin comedies he only let the exhibitor hold one reel at a time. Later Levin became an investigator for one of the film companies and looked into bootlegging, cheating exhibitors, and so on. On one of his first tours of inspection in Albany, New York, he found a cinema owner who had been booking movies for three houses but had been playing them in 14. Two years later, in 1921, the New York Film Club put Levin in charge of an investigation bureau. In 1927, the group, with Levin as head, was expanded on a national basis and named CPB. By 1940 the bureau maintained branches throughout the country and maintained a staff of 1,500 to 3,000 investigators to check for improper practices in a system which involved the distribution of more than 50,000 prints daily to 18,000 theaters. Most complaints came from other exhibitors, and discharged and/or disgruntled cinema employees informing on their former bosses. Frequently the CPB worked "hand in hand" with government agencies such as the FBI. From this account it seemed clear that the bureau was concerned almost exclusively with domestic improper practices. Also, it seemed to focus more on exhibitor scams such as bicycling and percentage cheating than it did on ordinary piracy. Likely that indicated where the greatest problems were located.[9]

One example of the CPB in action occurred in 1936 when Mexican distributors and exhibitors complained to the bureau about bootleg items.

Upon receipt of the complaint the CPB sent investigator Harold Groves to check on the situation. He unearthed a smuggling ring based in San Diego, California, wherein a number of border exhibitors had banded together in booking movies for American houses and then snuck them into Mexico. Because Mexico received U.S.-made first-run features on a delayed basis the bootleg prints beat the legitimate Mexican release dates by four to eight months. Groves estimated the loss to legal exhibitors and distributors through these bootleg practices at $500,000. This marked one of the first times a specific dollar figure was attached to pirating activities. And, like almost all the numbers that would follow in its wake, this one was highly exaggerated.[10]

Exhibitors clashed with distributors over possible revisions to the 1909 Copyright Act. At a 1936 hearing before the House Committee on Patents Edward Kuykendall (appearing for the Association of Motion Picture Theater Owners and Exhibitors) vigorously denounced the existing statutory provisions of a minimum damage fee of $250 for infringement of copyright—this applied to exhibitors caught bicycling, for example.[11]

At the same hearing Edward Kilroe of Fox and Gabriel Hess representing the MPPDA argued in favour of retaining that provision. What all unauthorized exhibitors had in common, said Hess, was that "they not only destroy a portion of the only market available to distributors, but by their dishonest competition seriously injure the honest exhibitor." Elimination of minimum statutory damages was not in the interest of the consumer, declared Hess, and would encourage pirate screenings, resulting in "unfair competition to honest licensed users."[12]

With America continuing to not be a member of the International Copyright Convention (sometimes called the Berne Convention) things were difficult in terms of dealing with offshore piracy. When the Senate Foreign Relations subcommittee held hearings in 1937 on U.S. ratification of the international convention there was opposition from many quarters, including the film industry. John G. Paine, chairman of the Music Publishers' Protective Association, typified the opposition when he said the music industry favored bilateral agreements. Entering into multilateral pacts, he added, was not "the traditional American way of solving international problems." Bilateral treaties allowed the retention of some ability to retaliate. MPPDA counsel Edwin Kilroe agreed with Paine and added that foreign countries took views that were not in accord with U.S. views, pointing out that in Europe there was a tendency to give the author film rights that would "infringe on contractual relations." He particularly attacked the European idea that the principal scenario writers should be considered authors. The State Department urged entry into the copyright union. Thorvald Solberg, former U.S. Registrar of Copyright, and an internationally known authority on the subject, declared that every institute of higher learning in the U.S. approved of a move to join the international convention. Later, the Senate Foreign Relations Committee urged no further delay in the immediate ratification of the copyright union. But it did not happen.[13]

The idea of replacing separate copyright treaties between different European countries with a general International Copyright Convention resulted in the first Berne Convention (for the Swiss city) providing for reciprocal copyright, in 1886, in most of the 17 nations represented at that conference. Similar follow-up conventions took place in Paris in 1896, Berlin in 1908, Berne again in 1914, Rome in 1928, and Brussels in 1935. Over time more nations joined and the treaty was revised and amended in various ways.[14]

MPPDA's Kilroe traveled to Europe in the spring of 1939 to confer with foreign office officials about proposed changes in the international union that would come up for discussion at the convention to be held in Brussels in 1940. Although not a member, American officials planned to attend. Amongst the amendments Kilroe wanted to see, in any treaty America might sign, was the elimination of restrictions in the moral rights clause, involving film producers' rights to re-arrange, adapt and change films in accordance with American law. That law made the producing studio the sole author instead of accrediting authorship of a film to many participating in its production, including the writer of the screenplay as then happened in the copyright union. War caused the Brussels meeting to be cancelled.[15]

Bicycling continued to be a popular scam for exhibitors to pull in this period. One 1931 account observed that "For many years the distribs have had trouble with theaters which held pictures longer than contracted for, or bicycled them to another house, distrib not getting any rental for the added playing time. Now and then exhibitors get away with this in small towns." The CPB then had crews traveling in various parts of the country, policing the field with a view to uncovering accounts that screened movies for an added day or more without paying rental or that bicycled prints to another house. When such practices were discovered, lawsuits were started against the exhibitor or fines were levied.[16]

A "heavy percentage" of exhibitors were reported to be involved in bicycling in the southwest part of the country, especially in Texas. Overall it "Seems that the extra-day-or-two gag has been customary in this section for some years." Fines levied by the CPB were $250 for each infringement. That was all on a voluntary basis. If the exhibitor and the CPB reached an agreement and the exhibitor paid the amount assessed, the matter was ended. However, if the exhibitor refused to pay, then a court case against him was started. H. A. Cole, head of a Texas theater owners group, attacked the existing methods of film booking and high pressure film salesmen as all being conducive to considerable bicycling.[17]

The Court of Appeals for the First Circuit (Massachusetts) held in 1932 that the unlicensed exhibition of a movie constituted an infringement of copyright. That ruling was announced in a case in which the distributor of copyrighted films charged an exhibitor with copyright infringement by the showing of films one day later than the date fixed in the licensing agreement between the distributor and the exhibitor.[18]

Warner subsidiary Vitagraph sued the Portland, Maine, New Portland Theater for copyright infringement for exhibiting eight of its shorts without authorization. They had been booked to play only at the Casco House (owed by the same chain). Federal District Court assessed damages of $250 times eight against the cinema chain. In a separate case in U.S. District Court, New York, Fox and RKO successfully sued the Parkway for exhibiting films without permission—as in the first case these were items held over for screening on unauthorized days. In each instance the cinema was ordered to pay $250 per screening.[19]

Copyright infringement suits instituted by MGM and Universal against the owner of a chain of cinemas in Mount Vernon, New York, were won in 1945. MGM charged the chain had played two of its releases, *Tortilla Flat* and *San Francisco*, on days beyond the contract period. Universal levelled the same charge over its release *You're a Sweetheart.* By about this time bicycling disappeared, or at least accounts of it did. Likely, though, it did become a negligible problem. For one thing, the majors did a lot of checking and the practice of bicycling was far too easy to detect and to successfully prosecute. Secondly, exhibitors had found another scam to attempt, one that was much more popular with exhibitors as it had a greater change of being successful—cheating on percentage film rental contracts. First reports of the practice surfaced in 1930.[20]

Cheating on box office figures was tied to the huge increase in the volume of percentage film rental contracts, starting in the 1929-1930 period. Distributors complained that something drastic had to be done or the industry would have to return to the flat-rate rentals. Distributors did not want to do that as percentage booking had come to be described as "an economic and essential upshot of the invasion of sound." Film rental by exhibitors had been on a cents-per-foot basis until the early to mid part of the 1910s when the dominant method was flat rate—so many dollars per day, or week, and so forth. Renting movies on a percentage of the exhibitor's gross began in the late 1920s. Among the Hollywood major studios, more than half of the rentals were on a percentage basis by 1930. Paramount was the highest then with flat rates applied to only 30 to 35 percent of its releases while MGM's percentage-rate leases were in the 50 to 60 percent range. In explaining the sudden rise of percentage booking one account said that "The industry on the whole favors percentage, although it was forced into that form of selling when sound came in, and no one knew what rentals to charge, as a safety to both sides." With the talkies becoming quickly and firmly entrenched, the percentage play became widespread. Industry leaders felt all rentals would be on that basis within a year or two, if the proper safeguards against cheating could be found. Film studios employed checkers but it was not uncommon for the checkers themselves to be caught cheating. Over the previous 12 months one of the Hollywood majors had discharged 50 of its checkers for bribery and other offences. In some cases bribes ran into three figures, indicating the amount of money being stolen. Many other ways of cheating the percentage system were employed. Some exhibitors closed off their receipts at nine o'clock at night, so that everything taken in after that hour applied to the next day's business— when a different movie was being played on a flat rental. One cashier revealed that her exhibitor/employer told her to hold out 100 or more tickets daily from the checker. A checker in one case stationed himself in the exhibitor's box office to do his checking only to discover the owner had opened a spare box office for cheating purposes, unknown to the checker. Some exhibitors did not even keep books. Theoretically that meant a checker needed to be at the box office all the time. Percentage rentals then usually charged the exhibitor 25 percent of the gross up to a certain dollar amount, then 50 percent of each dollar beyond that.[21]

Two of the largest distributors— each with over 50 percent of their rentals on a percentage basis— were then trying out the William J. Burns detective agency to do their checking work, instead of using company employees. In this experiment, it was hoped the employment of detectives (many of whom were former police officers) to do the checking "will have the desired moral effect on the exhib." Not only were some checkers taking bribes. It was reported that some had taken the initiative and showed the exhibitor how he could cheat the distributor, with the pair splitting the amount cheated. Cinemas were then being secretly checked. That is, checkers were openly checking exhibitors in the usual fashion while other secret checkers were watching both the checkers and the cinemas.[22]

Still, in 1930, the industry fretted that percentage booking might have to be abandoned in view of the large number of accounts that could not "be trusted" and the difficulties of conducting checks in the more remote areas where written statements also could not be trusted. With the idea in mind that a requirement that cinema owners keep a full set of books would reduce the cheating, one Hollywood major refused to sell any of its percentage-based releases to anyone not keeping books. However, many exhibitors responded to that by keeping two sets of books. Checkers were paid $10 a day and expenses; they traveled a lot. When an exhibitor contracted a film for a week the checker left town immediately when the contract expired. In a bicycling move, the exhibitor then played the movie the next day and kept all the proceeds—a practice discovered from newspaper ads. That method worked best in rural areas, but cheating was a problem everywhere. One distributor caught an account in New York City playing one of its major releases on percentage, which had cheated it to the tune of 1,000 admissions.[23]

Action by the Copyright Protection Bureau, according to exhibitors in the southwest, resulted in fines to percentage accounts from $500 upwards each for alleged violations of contracts with exchanges. An estimate was also made that as many as 75 accounts in Arkansas had been assessed fines. Exhibitors blamed distributors for their plight, claiming it had been a custom to play features an extra day to make the percentage, with approval of the exchanges. Checking was being tightened then, in 1931, mainly through the use of a private company, the Federal Auditing Bureau. Federal was then doing the checking for all producers, except RKO. Men from Federal (none were former police officers) were thought to be better for checking than a producer's own employees because it was believed they were not likely to work in concert with cheating cinema managers if they were "not schooled in the tricks of the trade."[24]

Another aspect of the situation uncovered was that exhibitors themselves had been cheated many times by their own employees. In doing its investigative work, Federal Auditing had "dug up instance after instance where managers, assistants, cashiers, etc., have been gypping two ways—the distrib and the theater."[25]

Another exhibitor upset by the issue was H. A. Cole, the head of a Texas cinema owners group. He alleged that exhibitors signed percentage contracts with onerous terms "because the film salesman or branch mgr. assured them that the exchange wouldn't check the b.o. and a little gypping wouldn't be amiss."[26]

As time passed, a deep resentment by exhibitors toward checking took hold, leading to radical steps taken by some theater managers which had led to several checking company agents ending up at local jails, albeit briefly. Annoyed by accredited checkers sent to their venues to keep tabs on the gross, several managers not only forced the checkers to perform their duties from the outside but actually caused them to be arrested for loitering either in the theater lobby or in front of the house. Gross receipts was an important figure because it was used by the distributor in fixing the percentage figure for future contracts. A favorite method of cheating involved the resale of tickets taken in by the doorman. When a customer entered the house, the doorman tore the ticket in half and gave one half back to the customer and put the other half in the ticket box. In palming the doorman kept a half ticket and gave it to the next customer, keeping the second person's ticket intact to later be given to the box office for resale. Other theaters had varied ways of notifying the cashier when to start selling off a spare roll of tickets. Sales of passes at a reduced price was another device used by managers. Supposedly, passes represented free admissions but an excess of them was "readily detected by an efficient checker." One theater went to the trouble of selling passes cut-rate from a store across the street.[27]

For the 1941-1942 season, distributors checked many more theaters than in the past. They were said to be checking virtually all accounts "excepting those known to be reliable" and their collections increased accordingly. Many of those accounts were said to have kept two sets of books. When percentage selling first came into vogue, distributors checked virtually all accounts but the practice had been relaxed during the last half of the 1930s, due partly to the cost. Some distributors, in 1941, maintained their own checking crews throughout the country, while others contracted with outside firms to perform that function.[28]

More attention was focused on percentage cheating in 1944-1945. By then, outsiders not connected with the motion picture industry were selling a service to exhibitors showing them how rental payments could be reduced on percentage movies and were asking for, and getting, 50 percent of the amount that they showed the exhibitors how to "save." The worst areas of the U.S., in losses suffered through misrepresentation of box office receipts were, in order, Pittsburgh, Boston, Chicago, New York City, and Philadelphia. Distributors had been double-checking grosses in many cases, employing auditors not known to checkers or theater operators, and had found differences ranging from $500 to $1,000 weekly.[29]

Increasingly worried over the situation and their ability to control it, major distributor representatives had been in consultation with the U.S. Internal Revenue Service agents with a view to achieving stricter control in checking box office receipts. With the federal government collecting a newly imposed admission tax, Hollywood hoped it might somehow unite in establishing more certain means of checking box office receipts. Under the Revenue Act, the switching of ticket rolls in the box office was barred.

The majors hoped a tightening of the enforcement of such provisions would aid in the reduction of cheating.[30]

Losses on percentage rental films through unreported grosses were estimated by the industry in 1944 at over $20 million annually. Plans were then under consideration by the Hollywood majors for the establishment of a central checking bureau to service the entire industry. "It is proposed to remove checking from a haphazard, part-time form of employment and tighten checking nationally by employing checkers on a regular, fulltime basis," noted one account. Warner, which employed its own checkers, was in favor of any industry system; MGM, also with its own checkers, was cool with the idea. Double-checking was still undertaken and, in many instances, revealed "startling deficiencies." This despite the fact the checking cost to the industry was estimated at some $4 to $5 million annually.[31]

One of the reasons the checkers themselves seemed so open to corruption was perhaps captured in one account that said the pay to checkers was "so inadequate" that those inclined to cheat "can hardly be blamed for playing a little ball with the exhib, even if the gain is only a dinner or some drinks."[32]

Nor was life on the job easy for a checker. Ross Federal was a private company used sometimes by the majors as a checking agency. Ralph Browder, a checker for Ross and its distributor client, was awarded $10,000 in damages against Fulton Cook and his wife, owners of the Bunagle Theater in St. Maries, Idaho, because the Cooks called Browder "a stoolpigeon, a peeping Tom and Jekyll and Hyde." A federal court jury in Coeur D'Alene decided those words were defamatory.[33]

The formation of an industry-wide checking bureau to stem the losses from percentage deals and other evils was announced by the Hollywood majors in March 1945. Called Confidential Reports, the new agency had been organized by five majors—Paramount, RKO, UA, Columbia, and Universal—at a reported initial investment of $500,000 in total. The remaining majors—MGM, Warner, and Fox—refrained from joining the new agency. MGM and Warner employed their own checkers while Fox used Ross Federal, once used by most of the majors. Jack Levin resigned from the CPB to be appointed vice president and general manager of Confidential. He stated that about 5,000 men would be needed for the new checking service and that wages would be paid at a $5, $6, and $7 minimum daily rate. Thirty branch offices were to be established in key distribution centers. The position of president of Confidential was then vacant as a search was underway for a "big name" to fill it. Reportedly, J. Edgar Hoover, head of the Federal Bureau of Investigation, had turned down an offer to be president of the new agency.[34]

Less than a year after it was launched both distributors and exhibitors were expressing dissatisfaction with Confidential Reports and its services. A move was then afoot to re-establish Ross Federal Service as the principal checking agency. Main complaints levelled against Confidential were that it was too costly and that its checking, of necessity, was being done by comparatively inexperienced workers. Distributors had been getting bills for $8.50 and $9.50 per day for checking with some alleging the charge had gone as high as $12 daily. On the other hand, Ross Federal charged around $6 to $7.50 per day. A second complaint lodged against Confidential employees was that "some of them [were] femmes." Ross had 5,000 men in the field and had been in business as a checking agency (for other industries also) for 20 years. Its attitude "on femme checkers has been that the gals were more inclined to take it easy and take an exhibitor's word on ducats rather than actually clocking."[35]

In this period, Hollywood's own stealing extended to creative talent as the studios raided each other. So bad was the situation that the studios, after a conference in Hollywood in 1931, set up a tacit agreement against all forms of piracy within the industry. Those meetings were held in private. Particular emphasis was laid upon star stealing and other forms of "personality larceny." More formal rules were applied to that agreement at the end of 1931 when the major studios agreed the anti-stealing agreement would include a deadline of 30 days before the expiration of a contract as the time when rival producers could approach stars or other "expensive talent." Raiding producers agreed to notify the employing studio of intent to bargain with the individual and to state the best offer that would be made to the talent.[36]

Despite the anti-raiding pact a number of Hollywood majors were irate in 1933 at Fox's tactics charging it with indiscriminate raiding of other firms' personnel. Several of the studio heads planned to appeal to Will Hays to have him step in and insist that Darryl Zanuck (Fox chief) desist from the open raiding tactics. Warner and RKO were reportedly the worst hit, Warner declared Fox took Loretta Young before her contract expired. Executives from MGM and Paramount both said raiding of their personnel had only been stopped by loaning of actors to Fox — Wallace Beery from MGM for one film and George Raft from Paramount for one film. Warner also claimed that in Zanuck's zest for employees, he even took four stenographers, a number of script clerks, several assistant directors, and a man from their production department.[37]

By late 1934, many of the studios that had signed the anti-raiding pact in 1931 had pulled out. RKO, Universal, United Artists, Fox, and Samuel Goldwyn all withdrew, leaving only Warner, Paramount, and MGM still in the pact. Columbia, the only other major, had never been a party to it. Originally the agreement had been drawn to stop the inter-company talent raids following the pirating of Ruth Chatterton, Kay Francis, and William Powell from Paramount by Warner.[38]

Cutting of material continued to be an issue. It was something studios did even to newsreels whenever it suited them but never allowed to be done by those who created the film. All Fox house managers were ordered in 1931 to delete all propaganda, politics and controversial screen matter from their theaters in order to meet the Fox policy of operating on "100% entertainment." Cinemas were not to show clips of breadlines nor any economic discussion on which patron reaction could be divided. This directive was aimed at newsreels, which were part of virtually all movie programs. Clips of Mussolini had drawn both boos and cheers and Fox declared that "Demonstration for or against a subject is taken to mean the clip is not entertaining." Any material cinema managers cut was to be saved and returned to the film exchange with the reel.[39]

There were said to be many "under-cover" protests by name directors against the studios' practice of prohibiting a director from editing his own picture. Lewis Milestone had to battle over *Rain* just to get the right of first cut. There had also been a blow-up between Paramount and Josef von Sternberg over the editing of *Blonde Venus* with the director only having the right to the first cut. Mervyn LeRoy was said to have won a point from Warner whereby he was left alone until he had completed the first cut of his film. Then the movie was screened for studio executives and changes were made at the executives' discretion. Said LeRoy, "It should go further than this. The director should at least be allowed to edit his own stuff until the first preview." He felt that way because he believed that audiences should be the judge on all disputed points, "which should not be changed until cash customers have been allowed to give a verdict." Directors in this period had to battle hard just to get the right of first cut, and first cut was well removed from the right to final cut.[40]

In the area of legal action, the U.S. Circuit Court of Appeals, in 1936, reversed a decision handed down by Federal Judge John Woolsey in 1934. Judge Learned Hand wrote the opinion in which the court decided the film *Lettie Lynton* was based (plagiarized) on the play "Dishonored Lady" written by Margaret Ayer Barnes and Edward Sheldon. The defendant was MGM. Hand said a drama could be pirated without having its dialogue borrowed. If that were not so, there could be no piracy of pantomime—yet pantomime was drama. Woolsey had said both the movie and the play had been based on the story of Madeleine Smith, who was tried and acquitted in Edinburgh in 1857 for the murder of her lover. The story, Woolsey said, had been written many times and was in the public domain. Commenting on the case, the *New York Times* remarked, "The decision is one of the few handed down in this district in years favoring a plaintiff in a plagiarism action."[41]

The U.S. Supreme Court issued an order in 1936 in which it declined to hear an appeal from MGM in the *Lettie Lynton* case (damages of $21,000 were awarded to the plaintiffs). Some 17 producers had joined together to issue a petition as a friend of the court asking for an appeal. Those 17 studios argued that if the lower court was sustained, the motion picture industry was likely to be saddled with a "heavy burden" in the future. They were concerned with the interpretation of the law as it applied to public domain material, or what the industry deemed to be public domain.[42]

A verdict of $10,000 in damages was returned by a jury in Los Angeles in favor of Henry Barsha and David Weissman, writers in a $150,000 plagiarism suit against MGM over the movie *A Day at the Races*, starring the Marx Brothers. Charges against the actors were dismissed. In a different action, Charles Livingstone and his wife Harriet filed a $900,000 plagiarism suit against Paramount charging the studio's *Double or Nothing* had been stolen from a dramatic sketch written by the plaintiffs. Although the Livingstones failed to state how Paramount had gained cognizance of the sketch material, Paramount settled out of court for an undisclosed sum. Plaintiffs' lawyer Ralph Routier said the amount of the settlement was for a "nominal sum and not enough to mention."[43]

Anthony Richard Pinci filed suit against Fox, charging it had pirated his play "Woodrow Wilson" in producing its film *Wilson*. Pinci alleged that prior to filming *Wilson*, Fox, in 1936, had requested a script of his play which was delivered and held by Fox for one year before being returned to his agent. In February 1940, the play was again presented to the Fox office and remained there until April 1940. Both submissions were made by Pinci's agents. Fox denied plagiarism and said any similarities in the story and the film were due to the fact both had to draw from actual facts of Wilson's life. All such matters were items of public record, continued the studio, and it was upon the public record the movie was based. Pinci was not successful in his action.[44]

One landmark decision was handed down in 1930 in the case of Nichols v. Universal Pictures. Judge Learned Hand determined that the author of "Abie's Irish Rose," a generic play about Irish-Jewish intermarriage, had no claim against *The Cohens and the Kellys*, a generic movie about Irish-Jewish intermarriage. Small changes sufficed to make it new. What was reinforced was that ideas—and most characters—could not be copyrighted. Fifteen years later an unnamed federal judge admonished that most copyright suits were premised partly upon a "wholly erroneous understanding of the extent of copyright protection" and partly upon that "obsessive conviction, so common among authors and composers, that all similarities between their works and any others which appear later must inevitably be ascribed to plagiarism."[45]

Throughout this entire period the Hollywood studios were not leaving a deposit copy of each film on file with the Library of Congress, as required by law. The Library of Congress allowed the arrangement; decades later the nation was poorer since so much of its early film history had been lost as no prints then existed for many early films. Hollywood studios had decided it was more important to save the cost of a print—an average of $140 in the mid 1930s. An average print run of the time was about 250, with a range in the neighborhood of 180 to 300 prints. A print could be exhibited 90 to 180 times before it was worn out.[46]

This period was fairly inactive in terms of piracy. Most of the stealing revolved around exhibitors engaging in various schemes. It was becoming more difficult for outsiders, pirates who were not exhibitors, to use the stolen items domestically. They were 35m prints that required formal exhibition quarters, for the most part. A more sophisticated motion picture industry, constantly checking, made that a difficult undertaking. It was much easier, and more lucrative, to use the pirated material offshore. However, the coming of World War II closed off that option. Legitimate prints could not get to Europe and neither could pirated material. As rich as the cartel members were they could easily afford to bankroll the antipiracy units that sprang up in this period. Although Hollywood expected foreign nations to honor its copyrighted material that same cartel continued to lobby the federal government to not join the international copyright union, which would have given them reciprocity, at least on paper. The idea that the creative talent involved in producing a film might have some rights in the product—such as the moral rights mentioned in some European contexts—was indeed foreign to Hollywood. Only the studio could hold copyright.

4

Larceny in the Box Office, Butchery in TV's Grindhouse, 1945–1974

"It is the humiliating effect on the small exhibitor of having his patrons see a checker on the job."

— B. J. Berger, 1946

"The bald-faced piracy of Hollywood scripts by lazy or untalented Mexican scriptwriters..."

— *Variety*, 1959

"None but the true hack could fail to be upset by the gutting of features for tv..."

— Bill Greeley, 1966

Pirates from outside the film industry made a comeback in this period as the offshore market reopened. Also important, especially domestically, was the widespread arrival, and use, of 16m film. It meant a whole new set of individuals and organizations could be targeted by pirates. Major studios had always been ambivalent toward the use of the narrower gauge film even though 16m film offered many advantages over the standard 35m film — it was cheaper, smaller, more compact, and so on. At the very end of 1945, MGM's exhibition subsidiary Loew's International announced it was entering the 16m market, but offshore only. It was a move implemented to expand the possible markets in foreign nations especially those with financial limitations in the aftermath of World War II destruction. Hollywood's majors had always shied away from 16m (the size usually screened in America in schools, churches, and so on) because, observed a journalist, "they worried it would lead to more pirating."[1]

Two decades later, in 1966, United Artists announced it was forming a 16 millimeter department to distribute narrow gauge films non-theatrically in the U.S. An estimated 3,500 to 5,000 smaller-screen outlets were believed to exist, although no figures were available on 16m receipts because the majors did not like to talk about it as regular exhibitors got upset by that competition. Because of that, most major studios distributed their movies in 16m format through independent firms, partly to avoid irritating exhibitors. Columbia was the only other major directly in the 16m field. It operated a narrow gauge department through its art house subsidiary. Movies were not released in 16m format until at least two years after theatrical release.[2]

The degree to which the studios worried about 16m distribution antagonizing exhibitors could be seen in the response from Carl Nater, director of Walt Disney's 16m division, to requests from the National Association of Theater Owners' (NATO) non-theatrical competition committee. He assured it that "the basic business of the company is to produce films for motion picture theaters and it will not permit 16m prints to be shown where they are in conflict with, or competitive to any regular 35m commercial motion picture theater." Under its policy Disney did not even permit schools or PTAs to schedule 16m films on Saturdays—screenings on that day would be in direct conflict with regular cinemas. In a printed statement sent to 16m distributors and users, the Disney firm placed the following restrictions on the use of its 16m movies: showings had to be confined to members of a private group and not open to the general public; newspaper, radio and television advertising, newspaper stories or publicity and posters were all prohibited. Notice of a showing was to be given only by verbal announcements, bulletin board postings or memos mailed only to the membership. Use of Disney's 16m movies for profit or for fund-raising was not permitted. NATO president J. Corwin was full of praise for Disney's policy and remarked, "If all film companies would administer their 16m divisions and enforce their contracts as conscientiously as does Disney, financial loss and friction from un-fair non-theatrical competition would be minimal."[3]

Another group that made extensive use of 16m prints were the armed forces. The first pirating problems of this period involved the military. In the spring of 1946 it was reported that a nationwide black market in the sale of 16m films, which the major Hollywood studios furnished the Army and Navy for exhibition to servicemen overseas during the war, had been brought to light. According to the account, information had surfaced that servicemen had helped themselves to narrow gauge prints while overseas, and, due to the films' relatively small size, had been able to bring them back to the U.S. in their duffel bags. Once back home, those servicemen sold the movies for whatever the prints would bring. Buyers, in turn, sold them to fly-by-night 16m distributors who then proceeded to rent them out to regular film library customers such as churches, schools, civic groups, and so on. During the war those prints had been furnished free to the armed forces by the major studios. Pirating distributors, in booking out the items, passed them off as purchased from the government at alleged "surplus property sales." Among the movies that turned up pirated were some of the majors' top product, still in first-run in regular U.S. cinemas—having been screened in pre-release overseas. Films from all the major studios were involved. At this time neither MGM nor Warner permitted any 16m distribution of their movies in America. The other majors did not release domestically in 16m until two years after the films' original release date to protect the regular 35m distributors.[4]

Later that year Theodore Gilman, merchant seaman, was arrested by FBI agents near Los Angeles and charged with violating the federal copyright law through the sale of a 16m MGM release *Meet Me in St. Louis.* In his rooming house in San Pedro, FBI agents found the following movies: *Along Came Jones* (RKO); *Tonight and Every Night* (Columbia); *Affairs of Suzanne, Till We Meet Again* (both Paramount); *Of Human Bondage* (Warner); *The Merry Monohans* (Universal); and *Don Juan Quilligan* (Fox). All of those items had been made available by the studios for overseas showing to Navy men before they came into Gilman's possession.[5]

A few years later, in 1950, the "swarm of bootleg prints which cropped up in every corner of the country" at war's end was then said to be petering out as a result of the FBI's drive against the pirated films over the previous four years. In a report to FBI chief J. Edgar Hoover, Sargoy and Stein, film industry attorneys on copyright issues, advised Hoover that a total of 579 prints had been recaptured since the drive was first launched. Almost all those prints were originally donated to the armed forces for wartime use overseas. Every big picture released by the majors during the war showed up at least once in the prints recovered by the FBI. Since Hoover began working with Sargoy and Stein in 1946, prints had been recovered in 15 different states and the Hawaiian islands. Another reason for the decline in this type of piracy was that age was taking a toll—both the prints and the movies were getting old. Yet the percentage of movies pirated this way was tiny since a total of 43,000 complete prints of feature films in 16m had been handed over to the armed forces during the war. In all cases, those prints were to have been accounted for by either an affidavit of destruction or the actual return of the films to the distributors. Mainly those pirated films had been used in hotels, schools, and similar places.[6]

Sixteen millimeter movies continued to be a mainstay of the U.S. Armed Forces—films in that format were shown in bases around the world. After about 1950 they apparently posed no problem, until 1979. At that time it was reported that more than 700 U.S. Army and Air Force cinemas around the world would not be able to screen *Star Wars* because of the distributor's fear of piracy. Fox refused to release the movie in 16m format to the Army and Air Force Motion Picture Service due to the possibility of piracy. Fox officials wrote to the Army and Air Force Exchange Service (AAFES—responsible for films in military houses) outlining its position. A year earlier AAFES was offered the movie in 35m format only, which meant that only 436 of the 1,194 cinemas on the GI film circuit around the world had the technical ability to handle it. AAFES turned down the offer since 60 percent of its venues would not be receiving the film. That 60 percent represented just 15 percent of the military movie audience. In 1978 the Army and Air Force theaters had 33,945,520 patrons and only about five million of them were at the 16m sites. This episode marked the first time the AAFES had been unable to acquire film rights for its houses—16m sites screened the movies for free. Fox's increased fear of piracy was grounded in the arrival of a new technology: the videocassette recorder. It worried about how easy it might be to run off cassette copies of its blockbuster hit *Star Wars*.[7]

Most of the domestic pirating of movies in this period by the non-military connected operators also involved 16m prints. It was a simple procedure to take a 35m print and produce a 16m copy. One of the stranger cases, which involved 35m, came to light in 1952 when a U.S. Marshall in Lexington, Kentucky, seized and impounded three prints of *Uncle Tom's Cabin* after Universal obtained a court order alleging that an independent distributor was illegally selling the movie. Universal claimed Howard G. Underwood of Pine Grove, near Lexington, had duped the 1927 film from an old print, had added a narrator who read the titles from the silent feature, had removed all Universal credits and markings from the print, and added instead "Howard G. Underwood presents *Uncle Tom's Cabin*. Produced by Howard G. Underwood, Copyrighted 1950." Oddly, the film had been screened in hundreds of theaters and drive-ins over the previous two years during which it recorded tremendous business, often out grossing new releases. A couple of years later Underwood was found guilty of copyright infringement. Universal was granted the injunction it requested; all impounded prints of *Uncle Tom's Cabin* were ordered destroyed.[8]

An unidentified film industry executive complained in 1961 that the bootlegging of 16m prints of the majors' product had become a serious problem, representing a "substantial loss of revenue" to distributors. He estimated at least 150 to 200 such prints were making the rounds, being sold to unsuspecting church groups, YMCA's, fraternal orders, camps, schools, hotels, bars, and other renters of narrow gauge material. Pirates obtained their prints through thefts from regional exchanges and sometimes by theft from television stations that were then maintaining bigger and bigger feature film libraries. Occasionally, too, they were booked from a legitimate sub-distributor by a concern using a phony name and address, which then did not return the movie. This executive speculated that at least some of those bootleggers had to be legitimate cinema people supplementing their income.[9]

Legal action by Fox in the middle 1960s closed down the small, 25-seat Award Film Club Theater (AFC) located on Selma Avenue in Hollywood. A default judgment stripped the house of its seats, screen and equipment. It all came about as a result of a claim against Pat Rocco and Paul Forbes after the club exhibited three 16m prints of Fox movies—*Tobacco Road*, *How Green Was My Valley* and *All About Eve*. Operators Rocco and Forbes did not reply to the complaint and a default judgment was entered. Fox had sued for $871. AFC claimed it did not operate as a commercial house although it was open to the public, but on a membership only basis, and that in no way was it in competition with larger commercial houses. Also, AFC said Fox asked it to reveal the source of its film prints as a way of resolving the complaint, but AFC declined, believing that to reveal the private film collectors that fed films to clubs such as itself would give the studios the ability to invade their privacy. Fox admitted it had asked for names. Rocco and Forbes noted the club grossed $400 to $600 a week and did not respond to the complaint because it had no money. Sherrill C. Corwin, president of the National Association of Theater Owners (NATO) and chairman of its non-theatrical competition committee, said he was "delighted" that Fox was taking action against 16m bootlegging, as in the suit against AFC. NATO had solidified opposition to the alleged competition from film societies and others who screened 16m prints and charged admission.[10]

Eight major film studios filed copyright infringement suits in Miami in 1970 against Martin Abrams, Barnett Kaufman, and various associated firms. Each complaint charged the defendants, in a manner and from persons unknown to the plaintiffs, illegally obtained positive prints of copyrighted films, in 16m or 35m format. Listed in total by the plaintiffs were over 350 titles. It was further alleged that operating out of Dade County, Florida, the defendants made offerings of those movies to film library operators, film distribution services, dealers, exhibitors, collectors, traders, and other customers, both domestic and foreign, as well as renting prints to cruise operators coming and going in the busy port of Miami for exhibition aboard ship to cruise passengers. Only United Artists was missing from the list of plaintiffs that included Fox, Columbia, Paramount, Warner, Universal, MGM, Disney and American International Pictures.[11]

Not quite two years later what was described as the biggest pirate operation in the film business was broken up when Abrams, Kaufman, and a few others signed a consent order admitting to more than 1,000 violations of copyright law and agreed to refrain in the future from dealing in prints of U.S. distributors without their written consent. The Abrams's operation was understood to have been worldwide in scope, involving the sale or rental of prints to exhibitors in the U.S., Canada, Europe, the Caribbean and South Africa. Another aspect of the February 17, 1972, court order issued by the U.S. District Court for the Southern District of Florida required Abrams and the others to pay the plaintiffs $25,000 in damages, a figure that escalated to $1.25 million should any of the conditions of the agreement be violated. In addition, Abrams was required to list all the sources from which he obtained his pirated prints. To that date he had supplied the studios with 87 names. They were mainly considered to be firms long suspected, or accused, of engaging in piracy, but the list of names was also expected to lead to the discovery of prime suspects, including lab workers, shippers at local exchanges, and print handlers at army bases. Abrams also agreed to hand over a list of all the people who bought or leased his prints. Some 200 names in that category had been handed over to that point. To ensure the handed-over data was accurate the plaintiffs were given full access to all of Abrams's records. Pirated films he handled included *Born Free*, *Cactus Flower*, *The Carpetbaggers*, *Dr. No*, *Dr. Strangelove*, *El Dorado*, *Georgy Girl*, *Harper*, *Lillies of the Field*, and *A Man for All Seasons*.[12]

Later in 1972, Martin Abrams was in New York making the rounds of the film studios in an effort to obtain 16m prints for his "legitimate" operations in the Caribbean and elsewhere. All declined to do business with him, citing various reasons such as not wanting to have competition against regular exhibitors. An account described him as being "genuinely amazed" that any ill-feeling would exist toward him, calling his treatment at the hands of the Hollywood majors discriminatory and saying such discriminatory treatment "forces you to become a thief." Abrams started his pirating operation in 1949. He was of the opinion that anyone who wanted to be in the film distribution business should be allowed to do so, even if the films he wanted to handle were already owned.[13]

In a raid in Middlesex, New Jersey, in 1971 U.S. Marshal Ezra Nolan and three assistants seized approximately 80 suspected bootleg prints including *Taking Off*, *Ice Station Zebra*, *Son of Paleface* and *The Four-Poster*.

The raid resulted from an order obtained in connection with lawsuits filed by nine distributors in federal court in Newark against Eugene Edelman Film Entertainment Service and Film Service 16 alleging Edelman traded in unauthorized prints in violation of copyright. The plaintiffs were Columbia, Universal, Fox, United Artists, MGM, Warner, Paramount, Disney, and American International. Similar action was taken later that year by eight majors (all but Paramount) against Evan H. Foreman of Mobile, Alabama, and his firm, 16m Filmland. Seized in a raid by a U.S. Marshall were about 250 prints.[14]

At a 1972 meeting of the Authors Guild during discussion of copyright in general, the film piracy problem was described as a "persistent evil" and that college and film society buffs were "notorious" buyers of stolen prints and "that a whole sub-culture of copyright jumpers has grown up. These are the ones who encourage shipping clerks in film exchanges, boothmen in theaters and other intermediaries to steal prints."[15]

In another action, a U.S. Marshall raided the Los Angeles film lab of Thomas Dunnahoo after an order was issued based on a suit filed by the majors. Seized were 67 allegedly unauthorized movies including *Topaz*, *Anatomy of a Murder* and *Antony and Cleopatra*.[16]

Two years later, prints of some major studios' films such as *His Girl Friday*, *Meet John Doe* and *Rain* were openly being offered over-the-counter by a Los Angeles film distributor who said those movies, and other features, were then in the public domain. The Thunderbird Films catalog listed around 100 features including *Santa Fe Trail*, *Topper Returns*, *Stage Door Canteen* and Alfred Hitchcock's *Murder*. Columbia's 1940 *His Girl Friday* sold for $165; Warner's 1941 *Meet John Doe* went for $250; UA's 1932 *Rain* cost $137.50. Most titles were available in 16m; others were only in a Super 8m format. Company owner Tom Dunnahoo said features he handled were those whose copyrights had lapsed due to the failure of studios to file for renewal for a second 28-year period, after the initial 28-year copyright, and other oversights. Self-described as having been "the biggest bootlegger in the county" until about two years earlier, Dunnahoo said he switched to a strictly legal operation after the majors raided his offices and sued him for copyright infringement. That action was settled when he agreed to abide by a court order to stop handling copyrighted films. An attorney for the Hollywood majors who kept close watch on Dunnahoo's catalogs, Albert F. Smith, said, "I do not believe he is distributing any copyrighted pictures of our clients." Dunnahoo admitted he enjoyed finding such movies that had been overlooked by the majors and declared "I love to come up with something the majors screwed up on or forgot about. There isn't a goddam thing they can do about it."[17]

Three prints of the *Godfather* disappeared en route from Omaha to the Paramount office in New York in 1972. When the three prints were lost between Kennedy Airport and the Queens, New York, depot of Novo Freight, a licensed and bonded film carrier, the FBI was called in. Soon, an individual phoned Paramount's print man Albert Lopesti and offered to sell him the copies at $500 each. Lopesti agreed, then notified the FBI. After a sting operation involving marked bills and so forth, three men were arrested.[18]

Jim Buckley, publisher of *Screw* magazine, did a 1974 article about pirates who had muscled into the porn film distribution business. He also claimed the following legitimate movies were available and that pirated copies sold for the following prices: *Bonnie and Clyde*, $125; *Cool Hand Luke*, $125; *The Graduate*, $135; *Little Big Man*, $175; *Dracula*, $75; *Klute*, $125; *Plaza Suite*, $175; *Rosemary's Baby*, $125; *The Wizard of Oz*, $160; *Cactus Flower*, $125; *A Tale of Two Cities*, $125; *The Candidate*, $175; *Public Enemy*, $85; *The Conformist*, $175; *Exodus*, $175; and *Dumbo*, $150.[19]

At a 1975 meeting in New York the Educational Film Library Association asserted that copyright infringement was all too common in schools, and especially community colleges, around the U.S. The organization declared that "Students, with no faculty restraint, often illegally and unethically duplicate rented 16 millimeter films onto videotape for the schools internal use, and rather more unscrupulously, to rent or swap the pirated versions with other schools."[20]

Piracy of American movies was probably more pervasive offshore than it was domestically. According to Irving Maas, head of the Motion Picture Export Association (an arm of the majors' MPPDA), in 1946 Poland and Yugoslavia were screening U.S. movies but without any authorization from the studios that owned the features. Nor did they pay any rentals. Protests had been made through official channels, explained Maas, about the unauthorized and uncontrolled exhibition of U.S. films, but no satisfactory answer had been received.[21]

The U.S. officially asked the Soviet Union government to stop showing, and to return "to the rightful owner," two American movies put on view in Moscow in 1950. *Mr. Deeds Goes to Town* and *Mr. Smith Goes to Washington* were being presented to Russian audiences in "mutilated and distorted" versions to serve Soviet propaganda, said State Department spokesman Michael J. McDermott. Both were Columbia movies released in the 1930s; neither was authorized for exhibition in Russia. According to the State Department, Russia had been showing the pair as "trophies of war" captured in Germany and that both features were then being used to show Americans as "money-mad" and "corrupt." Officials said the State Department had acted at the request of the MPPDA.[22]

The *New York Times* felt strongly enough about the issue that it printed an editorial expressing full support for the State Department in asking that the films be returned.[23]

A few months later it was reported that three more American movies—Warner's *The Story of Louis Pasteur* (1935), MGM's *Romeo and Juliet* (1936), and UA's *The Man in the Iron Mask* (1939)—also acquired in Germany as war trophies, were being given unauthorized screenings in Russia. Additionally, *The Three Musketeers* (a comedy version starring the Ritz brothers) was also being illegally screened in Moscow. Fox leased it to Russia in 1941 but those rights expired in 1946.[24]

The State Department directed the U.S. Embassy in Moscow in 1952 to make another protest over pirated movies. That would follow four previous complaints. It was only recently that the Russians had even bothered to acknowledge the first four complaints. Since it seized the prints in Berlin, explained the Soviet government response, they were "booty" and no payment would be made to American owners. An official note later in 1952, from the Soviet Foreign Office, declared Russia would not return any of the American films.[25]

Four years later, in 1956, while on a visit to New York, Grigory Alexandrov, film director and member of Russia's Ministry of Culture, said at a press conference that the Soviet Union wanted to establish closer relations with the U.S. film industry. Asked by a reporter about the *Smith* and *Deeds* films, Alexandrov declared that "A law was passed in Russia a year ago forbidding exhibition of those films and they will be returned to the American companies." However, he admitted he had no idea when that would happen.[26]

Arthur Miller's play "Death of a Salesman" was filmed in 1960 in the Soviet Union without his knowledge or consent and with no payment to him. It was titled *The Bridge Cannot Be Crossed.* Although the Soviet Union was bound by the laws of the International Copyright Convention, in August 1959, the Supreme Court of the Russian Republic ruled that foreign writers were not entitled to royalties or other compensation.[27]

Author Garson Kanin complained in 1959 that the Mexican film *El Hambre Nuestra de Cada Día* (Our Hungry Days) was a straight steal of his *Born Yesterday.* Visiting authors who accidentally viewed Mexican versions of their work had complained about the practice with no success. "The bald-faced piracy of Hollywood scripts by lazy or untalented Mexican scriptwriters" was a practice, remarked one reporter, that had been going on for years. One of the most recent big picture steals was *Kermesse* (The Fair), an "obvious" steal from *Picnic.* The journalist concluded that "The open or thinly rewritten plagiarism of American films has been going on for too long, involving everything from super-productions to Hollywood quickies and oaters."[28]

A decade later it was reported that the native Mexican film industry was also a victim of piracy with the pirates traveling around the countryside and going into isolated regions that had no theaters. National Film Bank director Emilio Rabasa estimated the annual loss to the legitimate industry from illegal exhibitors was more than $3 million.[29]

During a period of anti–American activities in Indonesia in 1964, a number of U.S. films there were seized by the government when the U.S. Information Agency and film company offices were sacked. There were at the time around 1,200 films in Indonesia; most were quite old and none had entered the country in the previous two years. By 1966 those movies were being screened on weekends in the Hotel Indonesia auditorium before an elite audience, and in other spots. No permission to screen had been given and no payment was made. While Indonesia's Information Ministry had ordered the return of all American movies to its office, the purpose was not to return them. It was to censor them so they could be shown again. Information Ministry officials reminded exhibitors that U.S. film companies were entitled to one-third of the profits from any screenings but did not comment on those being distributed "for charity." Not surprisingly, most exhibitors said the proceeds from their screenings "are devoted to charity." A year later Robert Perkins, Far East director of the Motion Picture Export Association, announced he had recovered prints of 850 of those features stolen in Indonesia.[30]

Bootleg trade in 16m prints of U.S. movies from Saudi Arabia to Iran in the 1960s resulted in many of those films ending up on National Iranian Television (NITV), sometimes before the same movies were released in that area. However, by 1969 NITV was said to be cooperating, with the result the illegal circulation of prints was on the decline.[31]

India was another country with a piracy problem involving its own motion picture industry. Some 50 to 60 prints of Indian films were smuggled out of India every month to Dubai and other ports on the Persian Gulf. An estimated 300 prints of smuggled Indian movies were thought to be in the Persian Gulf in 1969, awaiting transport to final destinations. A few years later Sippy Films of Bombay, India, won an order from the Supreme Court of South Africa directing seizures of two prints of their Hindi film *Seeta Aur Geeta*, which had been smuggled out of India and were illegally playing in South African cinemas. Sippy had taken action under the Berne Copyright Convention — both countries were members.[32]

Sedat Pakay, a Turkish filmmaker returned to Istanbul in 1970 after receiving a master's degree in Fine Arts at Yale, said that of the approximately

250 features produced annually in Turkey (few of which left the country), about 90 percent were unauthorized re-doings of American properties. Some of those "borrowed," he said, were *Some Like It Hot*, *Of Mice and Men*, *Sabrina*, *Shane*, *Mr. Deeds Goes to Town*, *Born Yesterday*, *Roman Holiday*, and *Come September*.[33]

Reporter Jack Pitman declared in 1970 that print piracy, usually 16m, was a big problem, especially in the U.S., Britain, Continental Europe and the Middle East. London sources estimated bootleggers had a sales turnover of $2 million yearly in Great Britain while the annual loss to legitimate distributors there was put at $10 million. Pirated prints had a broad market that included a growing number of private collectors. Most ardent among the private buyers were said to be "oil-rich sheiks" willing to pay "any amount of money." On the British market, private collectors had paid as much as $1,000 for a single feature. Bootleg prints were peddled by middlemen with a dozen or more of them operating around the UK. The only deterrent to the trade was a fine of $500, which the industry believed was not severe enough. The biggest of the bootleggers was thought to be a man operating in Wales who did a large business supplying pirated prints to working class clubs in that area.[34]

South Africa was a country where piracy was said to be flourishing at the beginning of the 1970s, with one distributor executive estimating the amount of lost box office receipts at over $1 million annually. Pirated product included some of the very latest Hollywood releases, in some cases even before their theatrical release there. To try and minimize the problem some distributors were releasing product closer in time to U.S. release dates. For example, Paramount moved the South African release date for *Love Story* ahead to April from July. Industry observers there were convinced that the bootleg prints originated in the U.S. in a "lab in Miami."[35]

Around the same time, Charlie Chaplin won a major legal victory in Germany in his continuing battle against the distribution of pirated prints of his old films. He sued Atlas Distributors for releasing an unauthorized silent version of *Gold Rush* (1925). Atlas presented the movie in 1964 with considerable success, adding its own music to the film. Chaplin brought out a reissue himself through his regular distributor, UA, in 1942, adding music he composed himself along with his own commentary. That version was released in Germany after World War II. As a result of the court case Atlas was ordered to stop distributing the film, to destroy its prints, and to pay Chaplin the profits earned from its release. Other Chaplin films had been sold without his authorization and released in other nations. *Gold Rush* was also distributed illegally in Switzerland. Chaplin won a Swiss Supreme Court decision to halt those screenings.[36]

Italy's exhibitor trade organization reported a notable increase in print thefts around 1970. At the same time, Columbia delivered a legal warning to exhibitors in Sicily to avoid screening illegal prints of *Framed*, *Man from Colorado*, *H.M.S. Defiant*, and *The Night Holds Terror*, among others.[37]

Piracy in the UK had become prevalent enough by 1972 that the film industries of the two countries were discussing the formation of a united campaign against the practice. Leading the effort were the MPAA and the Kinema Renters Society (KRS), the distributing trade body in the UK, which consisted of the Hollywood majors and a few UK distributors. One idea was to employ former FBI and Scotland Yard operatives. Most of the illicit trafficking in Britain was believed to occur up north in the workingmen's social clubs that entertained their members with cards, bowling, bingo, and increasingly, 16m first-run movies. Little happened at this time with the idea of a joint effort except the MPAA and the KRS did agree to exchange information on the subject.[38]

A major ring in the UK was broken up in 1973 with 10 people arrested and charged with dealing in pirated films. One of the defendants, Arthur Whiting, was identified as a projectionist at a London cinema who allegedly made "standby" copies of films available to his confederates for illicit print duplication.[39]

Yet another country to suffer losses to its own industry was Egypt. Mohammed Lamely, marketing director of the Egyptian Cinema organization, complained in 1973 that Egyptian pictures were being smuggled to many parts of the world and that it had been going on for a couple of years. Movies were smuggled through Lebanon. Also, he had reports that Egyptian movies were shown in Israel a week after they first played in Cairo. Australia, Canada, the U.S., and South America were other areas screening those illegal prints. Lamely added that "the reputation of our films is jeopardized because the duplicate copies are poor and the sound is mutilated. It is damaging for us when we try to make deals to find the market saturated with our films and bad copies at that."[40]

Within the area of attempts at a solution was a try at another international copyright pact. The Universal Copyright Convention, sponsored by the United Nations Educational, Scientific and Cultural Organization (UNESCO), became effective in September 1955 with 15 nations (including the U.S.) then having ratified it. Thirty other nations had signed on but not yet ratified the agreement. Under the terms of the Convention (the culmination of eight years of work), every country that was a signatory extended the same protection to the works of foreign authors, artists, filmmakers, and so on, as to its own nationals. Each country, though, still had its own copyright rules. Reportedly, it was a simpler system than the Berne system, with less formalities. When President Eisenhower signed on for the U.S. in 1954, one of those at the signing ceremony was film executive Austin Keough, representing the Motion Picture Association of America (MPAA). Moral rights were not a factor in this convention. Until this agreement was implemented the world of international copyright was split into three main sections. One centered around the Berne Convention (all of Europe except Albania and the Soviet Union) while another was the Pan American Convention (most countries in North and South America). The third group consisted of the Soviet Union and certain countries in Africa and Asia which did not belong to either of the other groups.[41]

One step the industry took to limit internal fighting among the Hollywood majors was to set up a film title registration system. Titles themselves were not copyrightable but they did have some protection resting in common law, unfair business competition, and priority. That Title Registration Bureau had been set up by the MPAA so the Hollywood majors could register titles for motion pictures (and television series) even before filming started, or a script was written. No other major could then use it. Columbia's Academy Award winner *On the Waterfront* was so named because of television, and the bureau. The studio wanted to use only *Waterfront* as the full title but could not do so as there already was a series by that name on the air.[42]

In 1956, 4,977 different titles were filed with the MPAA. In case of conflicts the studios tried to work out an agreement among themselves, or they resorted to arbitration. A total of 18 percent of those 1956 titles (896) were protested — most were settled by negotiation, with just 27 of the disputes being resolved by arbitration. Some disputes that were then current included Disney having *Banner in the Sky* and not liking UA's *Tower in the Sky*. Columbia, with *Sirocco*, was annoyed with Warner's *Sorocco* while UA, with *Paths of Glory*, griped about MGM's *Awake in Glory*.[43]

Sometimes the studio infighting over titles and ideas got serious. Fox had announced, with great fanfare, that George Stevens was to produce and direct *The Greatest Story Ever Told*. After Fox spent quite a bit of money on the project MGM announced it had bought into Samuel Bronstein's movie about Jesus called *King of Kings* and would distribute it in the U.S. An infuriated Spyros Skouras, Fox president, demanded the MPAA restrain MGM from what he called unfair competition. It said it could do nothing and Fox withdrew from the MPAA in a huff for a brief period before it rejoined the group.[44]

With the James Bond craze in full swing in 1966, UA was carefully watching for imitators. The Bond protectors had made a pre-emptive title registration of not only 007, but 001 through 009. UA had persuaded Continental to change the name of its recent release from *Agent 008¾* to *Secret Agent 8¾*. Each company was then allowed to register only 100 titles per year; therefore, most of the majors took to registering titles under several different corporate names. A limitation was imposed because title registration had gotten out of hand. Hollywood studios registered titles when that was all they had—they were not even backed by a vague idea. At the beginning of 1970 the Title Registration Bureau's index of features and short subjects contained about 50,000 titles.[45]

Another thing the majors did to battle the problem was to increase the funding devoted to combating 16m piracy abroad when the Hollywood studios contributed a total of $175,000 to a Motion Picture Export Association fund.[46]

Additionally, a trade organization comprised of 18 major suppliers of feature films to the U.S. non-theatrical market, the Non-Theatrical Film Distributors Association (NFDA), was formed in 1973 to combat the "growing problem" of film piracy. Compounding the problem was said to be the growing installation and use of videotape equipment in high schools and universities, one of the prime markets for the 16m non-theatrical distributors. It was much easier for a student to videotape a feature off television and then show it to a high school film society that charged admission than to copy and peddle a 35m movie. Initially, the thrust of the NFDA's anti-pirate program was instructional—a letter was sent out to ensure that people understood the legality and illegality of taping activity. The NFDA would find itself irrelevant within a few short years as the VCR and the videocassette came to be the dominant format for film transmission, at least for individuals and small groups; the 16m format faded away as the piracy problem centered more and more on the cassettes.[47]

Exhibitors continued to engage in widespread cheating, especially in the early part of this period. Hollywood's majors complained in 1946 that in the previous "few years" they had lost $20 million from fraudulent returns on percentage pictures. In the Pittsburgh territory alone losses over that period were put at over $1 million. Auditing teams hired by local lawyers, who were retained in turn by the distributors, were then working the east and middle west parts of the country. With the right of auditing a standard clause in sales contracts, any refusal by an exhibitor to allow the audit invariably resulted in legal action. All eight majors filed suits (identical ones in separate actions) against the George Manos circuit of 12 Ohio houses, and against Fred W. Anderson, owner of 11 film houses in Illinois. All suits alleged the defendant falsified box office reports on percentage pictures in order to pay lesser amounts than were due.[48]

Rumors that year that MGM might join the common checking system, Confidential Reports, proved unfounded. With some ex–GIs returned to their old jobs as checkers, MGM planned to have about 1,000 of its own employees in the field as checkers within the coming few months. MGM also used agents from the private firm, the Willmark Agency, to do some of its checking.[49]

Those increasing numbers of lawsuits launched by the majors against exhibitors who were alleged to have cheated on percentage deals were said to have had at least one beneficial effect — that of cementing cooperation between the motion picture industry and the government. When suits were filed the IRS immediately became involved, checking to see if the exhibitor might also have filed falsified federal tax returns.[50]

In some cases "blind" checkers were still used — that is, they were theoretically unknown to the exhibitor. In other cases the checker identified himself before doing his work. They continued to evoke a harsh reaction from some cinema people. According to reporter Ira Wit, one common trick used once a blind checker was spotted was to trip him in front of the theater, simultaneously break a bottle of whiskey on the sidewalk, and then call the police. If the checker was inside a house, a young girl was planted beside him and would suddenly scream she was being molested. All sorts of inducements were offered to checkers on the road from distant points that keeping tabs on the venue for the 2nd and 3rd days of a run was unnecessary. When the offer of a free dinner successfully removed a checker, it was possible for the house to sell a couple of hundred tickets from a duplicate roll. Outright bribes were offered if more subtle inducements failed to work. If a checker got upset and threatened to report the bribe, the exhibitor might launch his own counter-attack by ejecting the checker from the house claiming the latter demanded a bribe. Other tricks included substituting lower-priced children's tickets for those actually sold to adults, producing a bunch of passes at the end of the day to make up the difference for a series of under-the-counter cash sales, and splicing of two ticket rolls together so that admissions were halved as far as the distributor was concerned. One ticket roll was sometimes substituted for another; tickets could be sold twice; cash sales could be made with no tickets involved. Double sets of books were standard in making the records conform with the activities in the front of the house. With accredited checkers "on the scene daily at almost every theater," observed Wit, absentee management was sometimes benefited in that those checkers "kept many an employee honest who might not have been otherwise."[51]

Still in 1946, many exhibitors who were targeted in lawsuits accusing them of cheating on percentage deals complained the distributors themselves were responsible for the situation because of overzealous sales employees who wanted to achieve as much playing time as possible during recurrent sales drives that put pressure on exchange employees. A story from many exhibitors was that frequently they were won over to signing licensing deals on the promise that no checkers would be posted when the films in question were screened. According to one account the "Claim is made that these promises were often given by exchange managers and salesmen to win over exhibs to inking the pacts after the deals were nixed by the theater men because the rentals were deemed exorbitant."[52]

Lawsuits continued to mount up and by the fall of 1946 the majors had a total of 140 actions filed against exhibitors in 11 states, mostly in the northeast and the middle west. At the same time, a legal battle in Pittsburgh featured 27 plaintiffs, who operated 41 cinemas and jointly sued the eight major studios in an action to restrain demands for audits. However, inspection of the theater records was granted to the majors and upheld on appeal. All 140 of the filed suits (ranging from 13 to 19 actions per major) alleged fraudulent reporting of box office returns.[53]

Adding to the total of pending lawsuits was one against a nine-theater circuit in Minneapolis owned by George Miner. Several Miner venues had recently banned checkers from Confidential Reports. Also, requests made by the majors for an audit of receipt records of the involved houses were ignored. As of late 1946, cinema record falsifying was said to be costing the Hollywood majors from $20 to $25 million yearly.[54]

Cinema owners continued to be angry. B. J. Berger, president of exhibitor organization North Central Allied and operator of 33 houses in Minnesota, advocated the end of all percentage rentals. "It is the humiliating effect on the small exhibitor of having his patrons see a checker on the job," he explained. In response, A. L. Adler, MGM exchange manager in Kansas City, Missouri, replied, "It's too bad there should be so much misunderstanding about checkers. They are essentially an aid to efficiency. This talk about humiliating the exhibitor by what he claims is suspicion of him is nonsense." Giving no specific details, he added that "from this checking system has come appalling revelations— even in our own houses. This admission should be quite enough to prove there is a justification for their use." His checkers were kept always on the move; one week they were in Maine, the next they were in Pennsylvania, and so on. Not only that, but they "put into operation methods copied from the FBI." Unconvincingly, he concluded, "Distrust of the exhibitor has nothing whatever to do with our using checkers." Home Strowig, owner of two houses in Abilene, Kansas, spoke of a town (which he would not name) where the city council imposed a five percent tax on gross theater admissions. As a result, all three cinemas in the town closed their doors rather than submit to the tax. "The point is it would never have happened if the local checker hadn't tipped off the City Hall crowd to the big takes those three houses were gathering in," said Strowig.[55]

Cheating had become so common by 1947 that the sales chief of one of the majors said his company found 3,000 customers out of a total of 12,000 to 14,000 were "habitually" turning in phony reports. Almost all of those violators were independent exhibitors with only a few discovered among the large cinema circuits. It was so bad, he said, that in many situations it would pay for a distributor to return to flat-rate rentals again. Annual estimates of a $20 million loss to the majors, were, he thought, too low. "We've found in very many instances, that the 40% rental boils down to an actual 20% of the real gross."[56]

Despite the seemingly high rates of exhibitor cheating, the majors were reported to be thinking, in 1947, about cutting back on checking as an economy move. Hollywood's majors figured it then cost each of them about $500,000 to $750,000 annually in checking expenses. In many situations it had been found that the cost of checking did not make up for the difference in earnings between selling a picture on percentage and letting the exhibitor have it on a flat rental basis. In this account the majors were said to put the annual loss from cheating theater reports at $15 million. Still, the studios emphasized they would not reduce checking if a reduction meant any sacrifice in the amount of rentals. On average the studios said it cost them $50 to check each engagement of a film and that they checked about 1,000 engagements for each movie. Releasing 10 to 15 pictures each year, as the majors then did, meant each spent $500,000 to $750,000 yearly. Confidential Reports still did the checking for all the majors, except MGM. Recently it had started to concentrate on using local checkers as one way to save costs by reducing a checker's travel expenses. MGM still used its own checkers, augmented sometimes by operatives from the Willmark Agency.[57]

Most of the lawsuits filed by the majors were believed, by industry observers, to be likely settled out of court in order to lessen "hard feelings." A 1947 suit by Fox against New York exhibitor Harry Brandt for $287,000 was settled out-of-court, by arbitration, for $237,000. Fox, not long after it filed charges and long before settlement, made a deal with Brandt to keep his Mayfair Theater on Broadway supplied with product. Paramount was also suing Brandt for $563,265. In that suit, Paramount showed that some of the checkers were bribed by Brandt representatives to turn in false reports; Brandt, in some instances, kept two daily box office records, one for his own use and one to be supplied to the distributor.

There was also evidence of sales of tickets of entirely different sequences of serial numbers than were currently being used and evidence of erasures and rewritings on Brandt's own records, showing a decrease in ticket sales and receipts on dates percentage pictures were screened.[58]

In a court case involving the Rivoli cinema in Buffalo, evidence was introduced that 18,000 duplicate tickets had been bought from three different suppliers. Distributors introduced evidence that additional bank deposits were made on days when percentage films were played. The Rivoli's booker admitted tickets were bought from more than one supplier and were unaccounted for either in box office statements or in the company's books.[59]

MGM was awarded a court judgment of $26,875 against Fred E. Lieberman of Boston (and his five houses there). Federal District Judge Sweeney ruled that a distributor could recover flat rental damages caused by phony returns on percentage pictures. In other words, if a distributor was misled by under-reporting on percentage movies to grant lower flat-rate rentals on other films, the difference was an element of damages that could be included in a suit. Distributors constantly monitored a cinema's receipts to set both flat-rate charges and the specific percentage to be charged on percentage bookings. Those charges against a specific house were subject to constant change.[60]

A survey of all majors using Confidential Reports (still all except MGM) in 1948 revealed a decline of 44 percent in the amount of checking being done, compared to the same time a year earlier. The main reason was said to be the slump in the box office itself—the dramatic decrease in film attendance, due mostly to the effects of television, was then just beginning. One company sales chief said his rental receipts on one film were $75, whereas his checking cost was $45. Under such circumstances the distributor would rather trust the cinema owner. Also, for most of the large houses and the big chains, the distributors could by then routinely ask for, and perform, an auditing of their books any time the rental returns looked false. Some chains, though, continued to refuse to open their books and in such cases the venues were still blind-checked periodically.[61]

By 1949 the number of exhibitors said to be cheating on percentage deals was showing a decline, following a three-year drive by the majors that combined a pile of lawsuits and nationwide auditing activities. The loss from such cheating was then put at $10 million to $15 million annually. Audits had by then been conducted in over 1,000 houses in America. Exhibitors suspected of cheating at the box office waged court battles over the right of distributors to examine their books. Once the court approved the audit most of the actions were quietly settled out-of-court. With few exceptions, those settlements were for the amount found owing in the books, after the audit was conducted. Agents of the IRS reportedly attended all the trials launched on alleged box office cheating charges. However, many of the cinema people who cheated the studios still reported the correct total income on their tax returns by shifting gross receipts made on percentage rentals to flat rental films.[62]

If cheating was on the decline it was not dropping fast enough to please some as MGM announced in October 1950 that thereafter the studio would refuse to do business with any exhibitor caught cheating. William F. Rodgers, MGM vice president, delivered that news to a Theater Owners of America convention. He emphasized that MGM would continue to prosecute all such offenders.[63]

During the course of a National Labor Relations Board hearing to determine bargaining representation for Sargoy and Stein, the New York law firm that represented the film distributors in matters relating to copyright issues and percentage licensing deals, it was revealed that Sargoy and Stein conducted 10,509 investigations of 1,500 theaters in 1949. Records revealed that 85 percent of those venues were located outside of New York. Sargoy and Stein collected in fees "in excess of $50,000" from each of five distributors, and "in excess of $20,000" from each of three distributors. Those were the eight majors then known in the trade as the Big Five and the Little Three, with the former involved in production, distribution and exhibition and the latter engaged in only one or two of those functions.[64]

When a few more lawsuits were filed against percentage cheating exhibitors in 1951, it brought the total number of such actions pending against exhibitors across the country to nearly 200. This account argued there had been no let up in the number of such cases since distributors first started suing over percentage cheating a few years earlier. From that period forward a total of 500 separate actions were instituted. About 300 of those were settled following the examination of the exhibitors' books. Most of the settlement sums remained undisclosed, by agreement of the parties. The total wasn't as bad as it seemed because the 500 suits named only a total of 100 exhibitors (an average of five majors sued each exhibitor).[65]

S. D. Kane, executive counsel for North Central Allied (a cinema owners' organization headquartered in Minneapolis), declared in 1953 that he was receiving an increasing number of complaints from exhibitors regarding percentage checking. While he acknowledged the exhibitors were to blame for signing deals that required payment of "unreasonable" percentages, he accused the distributors of "perpetuating a fraud by tricking exhibitors to sign such unfair percentage deals" by convincing cinema owners the "unconscionable" terms would not be enforced. Kane claimed that everyone in the motion picture industry knew that percentage deals by the thousands "have been made on the theory that we just have to put this figure in, but it doesn't mean a thing — we know you're paying enough film rental already—just make your own return and everything will be O.K."[66]

Distributors, particularly Paramount, were also accused by exhibitors of checking flat-rate rental movies, which the cinema owners felt the studios had no right to do. The Independent Theater Owners of Ohio reported receiving complaints from theater owners about that issue. That organization sent its members a bulletin advising them that they did not need to cooperate with checkers on flat rental pictures in any way. "If they act suspiciously, by all means put the police on their trail," advised the group.[67]

So annoyed did the exhibitors become over the business of checking that by the mid 1950s the Hollywood majors were briefly threatened with a new type of legislation. Bills introduced in the state legislatures of Texas, Oklahoma, and South Carolina would have outlawed the distributors' blind checking of theater admissions.[68]

On the other hand, New York State Senator Fred G. Morritt (Dem.) declared he would introduce a bill in the legislature at Albany making it a criminal offense for theaters to under-report their receipts to distributors on films being screened on a percentage basis. If an exhibitor cheated to a total of less than $100 it would be a misdemeanor; over $100 and it would be larceny. Under Morritt's proposal the keeping of two sets of books would also be declared a criminal offense. An estimate in this account put losses to Hollywood's majors from such cheating, over 20 years, at a total of $100 million.[69]

As an issue, cheating by exhibitors was much less prominent in the 1960s and 1970s than it was in the 1930s through the 1950s, although it was not absent. Hollywood received a favorable legal interpretation in 1966 when U.S. District Judge Dan Russell, Jr., ruled for MGM in a case involving the under-reporting of receipts by an exhibitor under a percentage rental contract. The defendant was Alexander Lloyd Royal and his three houses in Mississippi. MGM did not have to "prove" under-reporting by evidence but could prevail if it "reconstructed" its suspicions. Russell accepted the idea that a plaintiff could reasonably infer under-reporting of ticket sales by reference to available documents and records and the history of the seller/user relationship. MGM was awarded $4,274.[70]

At the end of 1969 one account of the problem remarked that box office cheating was often ascribed to larcenous managers, but some thought it came "closer to the truth to see owners as party to and architects of the practice, where it takes place." One major company executive used the rough ratio of two-to-five as the breakdown between what was spent in checking and what was taken; "for every $2 we spend checking they steal $5." Due to the expense involved, "comprehensive" checking was by this time said to be feasible only on the highest grossing films.[71]

Although distributors may have been cynical about the honesty of cinema owners when it came to reporting receipts, they faced a dilemma in that they did not want to disgrace or antagonize their customers too much. Rather, they wanted to keep them alert to the fact they were under scrutiny. Hollywood wanted to stop the exhibitors from cheating in the first place. They did not want to catch them at it and then be forced to take some sort of action. With the cost of checking increasing, it was only the Hollywood majors who could do it in any systematic fashion. It was the small, independent distributor who, relatively, was hurt the most by cheating exhibitors. Avco Embassy reportedly spent a six-figure sum checking theaters playing *The Graduate*.[72]

Even exhibitors began to turn against their larcenous brethren. The board members of theater owners' main national body, the National Association of Theater Owners (NATO), implemented measures in 1971 to deal with members who were found guilty of under-reporting their grosses to distributors. The directorate sought, in effect, to bar from membership for five years any exhibitor who cheated in his reports. That action was taken, said the board, because it wanted to emphasize "the serious concern with which NATO views this departure from legitimate business practices." It came in the wake of vigorous complaints by distributors to the NATO board. Non-cheating exhibitors were also highly opposed to the cheaters since they believed it hurt them in the long run. A reporter commented that the NATO action "amounts to the first formal acknowledgement that some exhibs are palming receipts."[73]

Fed up with the procedure for dealing with cheaters when they were caught, Universal studio came up with a proposal for a new procedure by which the distributor would be indemnified against under-reporting of box office receipts on percentage deals. When cheating was unearthed by the distributor or its hired checking service, the traditional method of resolution usually involved protracted haggling, which became tied up with negotiations on later play date terms. In effect, the film producer's sales staff was spending substantial amounts of time negotiating settlements while trying to continue selling newer releases to the same customer. Under Universal's proposal, the same preliminary investigative work would be undertaken up to a point, then the file would be turned over to the outside insurer, a disinterested third party. The distributor then had his money and could walk away. However, the insurer kept after the exhibitor in order to recover as much of the money as it could that it had paid out in claims.[74]

Hollywood began making more noise in 1971 about launching more litigation aimed at under-reporting cinemas. Several months had passed but NATO had not yet expelled any of its members. Jack Valenti, president of the Motion Picture Association of America (MPAA), asserted that "many millions of dollars" were lost to the "cheatin'-heart cinema operators" and it was time for strong action.[75]

A novel method of checking in the early 1970s involved the taking of aerial photographs of drive-ins at night with an infra-red camera to get a more precise car count. A frustrated Irving Cane, of Warner's checking department, grumbled, "You would think when a lawsuit was filed, other exhibitors who have a tendency to misrepresent grosses would be more careful about it. But they're not — it's the same thing over and over again." NATO's drastic measure had been on their books for some 17 months but they still had made no expulsions.[76]

A Long Island, New York, theater owner was indicted by a Nassau County grand jury in 1973 on charges stemming from the alleged under-reporting of rentals due Allied Artists for a run of *Cabaret*. It was a rare case of criminal prosecution involving charges of under-reporting. Studio 1 cinema owner Warren Wurtzberg, and manager Roger Donnelly, were charged in the indictment with three counts of grand larceny in the third degree, a felony, 13 counts of petty larceny, two counts of falsifying business records, and one count of commercial bribery. It was specifically alleged that during the run of *Cabaret* at Studio 1 in August 1972, the defendants falsified daily receipts by as much as $276.60 and withheld from Allied $2,130 on unreported ticket sales totaling $4,143.75 and bribed an Allied ticket checker with $30 to pass on incorrect attendance figures to Allied. According to the District Attorney, the age-old method of palming tickets was used. After tearing tickets in half, the Studio 1 doorman saved his halves instead of depositing them in the receptacle. Those saved halves were then given to subsequent customers which allowed the doorman to save a number of full tickets. When a set number of them had been accumulated they were returned to the box office for resale. Cases of under-reporting were almost invariably dealt with in the civil courts. Nobody in the industry could remember a previous instance in which criminal charges were brought against an exhibitor for under-reporting. Hollywood continued its practice of filing civil lawsuits against cheating exhibitors and those who refused to allow audits of their financial records.[77]

Although the old practice of bicycling had long disappeared, a variation of it had surfaced in the mid–1970s. Columbia announced it was going to clamp down on the exhibitor who moved a picture from one auditorium in a multiplex into another under the same roof, depending upon box office performance. The big chains and circuits were said to be the major practitioners of "a new form of the old bicycle." A multiplex exhibitor who used that method was at liberty to bid on a new release based upon an auditorium size he had no intention of using for the full run. A "no slide" clause in contracts prohibited the practice. For example, an exhibitor might bid for a 15-week run in a 700-seat auditorium but after two weeks move it permanently to a 300-seat auditorium. In that case, the owner of an independent, single-screen house with 500 seats would have been squeezed out with his bid and lost out to the "larger" venue.[78]

A new problem involving exhibitors emerged in the 1960s when the distributors complained that slow to stalling payments of rental percentages by cinema operators was a major grievance. Whereas the houses used to start paying the distributors their share within the first week of a movie's screening — with most paid off fully within 30 days — delinquency had reached the point where distributors sometimes waited as long as six months to receive full payment. That caused cash flow difficulties for them. In response to those charges the exhibitors brought up their usual grievances: that they were forced to pay terms that were exorbitant and distributors had them squeezed too tightly by forcing "unreasonable" percentages on them.[79]

Universal initiated a new policy in 1970, new to the entire industry, whereby it charged interest on monies owed by exhibitors for film rentals. A clause added to its rental contracts stated the exhibitor would be charged 1.5 percent per month interest on deferred payments (18 percent per year — the same as charged on department store credit card balances). This move marked the first time that a distributor tried to penalize slow-paying houses. One estimate had it that exhibitors were constantly in arrears on their rental payments to the extent of $10 million per month to the Hollywood majors.[80]

After Universal's announcement, several other major distributors said they were contemplating a similar move. Finally, after threatening to do so for some time, and four months after Universal had implemented the measure. Fox stated it would also charge delinquent exhibitors 1.5 percent a month.[81]

Going even further was Paramount, which announced a new policy effective in November 1975. Any exhibitor with unpaid film rental more than 30 days old would be contacted for immediate payment and, if not forthcoming, would be cut off from all film rental until the account was paid in full. An estimate given in this account was that a few years previous the seven major studios had $75 million constantly in arrears. Since then a decline in production volume had diminished the amount of constant late money to about $50 million in total for the majors in 1975. Commenting on the policy of Universal and other majors to penalize late-payers, a policy then five years old, a reporter remarked, "But there is no solid evidence that any company ever successfully collected the penalty."[82]

Yet another problem involving exhibitors was that some theater employees were cheating the owners and the studios. Mickey Gitlin, vice president of Dale Systems, a New York-based investigation company that serviced many of the large cinema chains across America, addressed a meeting of independent exhibitors and distributors in 1969. His firm had just completed a six-month investigation into all areas of amusement industry employee abuse. "Dollar for dollar, theaters are suffering greater losses from employee dishonesty than any other segment of American business," said Gitlin. While the timeless method of ticket takers and cashiers was palming (holding back) tickets to re-sell for themselves instead of tearing them was the favorite system used when exhibitors cheated Hollywood, it was also the favorite when employees cheated the exhibitors. In the area of concession sales Gitlin said that his survey found some employees brought in their own stock, sold it, and kept the proceeds. This left no missing items at inventory time.[83]

A year later Gitlin produced the results of another survey. This one was conducted by Continental Protective Service, a security organization headed by Gitlin. He said that theater stealing by employees amounted to $23 million annually—everything from palming tickets to cheating at the concession stand. One employee gave a written confession that during an eight week period she and other employees at the house palmed 50 tickets per week at $2 each, $80 in total. According to Gitlin, rings of dishonest employees were common in film houses. His organization reportedly broke up a gang in a New Jersey theater that involved every cashier and ticket taker employed. They were getting away with $500 per week. Gitlin's conclusions seemed highly exaggerated. Given that he was trying to sell security and protective services to the exhibitors he did have a vested interest in finding a lot of employee theft.[84]

The exhibitor practice that had ended, at least almost ended, by this period of time was that of the exhibitor cutting films. In 1957 it was reported there was an increase in the film studios plugging specific goods and services in their movies. Theater people had never liked the practice and had from time to time complained about the use of the screen to "sell" a product and, "in years past, there have been instances of theaters actually snipping such footage out of films.[85]

Hollywood's contempt for its own copyrights, and the contribution of its creative talent, was nowhere as evident as in the butchery of its movies for exhibition on television. Initially, the Hollywood majors refused to release any movies to television on the grounds it would help the spread of television and weaken its own box office receipts. That resolve quickly evaporated, though, as television still inflicted major losses on Hollywood's box office receipts. By 1957 there was an increasing release of the majors' libraries to television. Reporter Murray Horowitz commented that "Television station censor scissors are butchering our feature films, the degree depending on the locale of the station, the orientation of management and on the definition of 'good taste.'" Some pictures were totally rejected for television screening, due to race, sex, or politics. MGM's *Cabin in the Sky*, with a black cast, was rejected by Miami outlet WOKT. A British film, *Captain's Paradise*, was rejected by WCS-TV in New York as too racy. WOR-TV (New York) then picked it up but cut out some parts. All of these titles, and most of the others being released to television, had received MPAA code seals (the majors' voluntary system of certifying a movie as inoffensive to all) and never received a "Condemned" rating from the Roman Catholic Legion of Decency, a powerful group in its day.[86]

Anthony A. Wollner, editor of the American Cinema Editors' official publication, complained in that journal that the entire relationship of the Hollywood filmmaking community to the public that sustained it was at stake in the practice of films being "mutilated" to fit television time. Wollner wrote of the rights of viewers and the rights of artists. Three years earlier, in 1962, the American Cinema Editors protested to the Federal Communications Commission (FCC) that "most movies being shown on television today have been wantonly divested of their carefully created mood and pace," in a pitch to the FCC to take steps to eliminate the practice of wholesale re-editing of movies. Yet three years later, he said, "Not one effectual step, to our knowledge, had been take to correct the prevailing condition." He added that perhaps the most important aspect of the matter, though infrequently mentioned, "is the increasing degree of restiveness on the part of the rank and file television viewer. He is not so tasteless and insensitive as not to be alienated by the frequent brash intrusions of the commercials." This latter statement by Wollner seemed due more to wishful thinking than to reality.[87]

Two prominent legal cases in the mid–1960s involved well-known Hollywood directors attempting to stop the studios from allowing television stations to mutilate their works for small screen viewing. New York

Supreme Court Judge Arthur Klein ruled against Otto Preminger's action to block the telecasting of his *Anatomy of a Murder* (Columbia). Preminger had sued because he objected to cuts for telecasting (time limitations) and commercial interruptions, contending that such excisions would "cheapen" the film and "damage" his reputation. Preminger had asked for a permanent injunction against Columbia and its subsidiary Screen Gems. In making his ruling, Klein cited a portion of the director's contract that granted the distributor television rights without reference to cutting and editing. According to the original contract, Preminger had final editing rights only with regard to the theatrical print. Admitting he was aware of television's practice of cutting movies for time and for ads, Preminger argued he had signed his contract without stipulation as to editing. Although the court gave a negative answer to the director's attempt to stop minor cutting and interpolations in the absence of specific contractual provision, Klein said that wholesale cutting or "mutilation" that might occur would be interpreted as such and that in future, plaintiffs could apply for injunctive or other relief. However, such assurances from the judge were so vague that they would never be used.[88]

Around the same time, director George Stevens was in court trying to block a scheduled NBC telecast of his *A Place in the Sun.* His contract also gave him the right of final cut for the theatrical print only. However, the contract for the 1945 release made, naturally enough, no mention of television. One month before the scheduled broadcast of the movie, Los Angeles Superior Court Judge Ralph Nutter warned the network that commercials must not be inserted in such a way as to adversely affect or "emasculate" the artistic and pictorial quality or to destroy the mood (NBC had already said it would make no cuts to the film for content or for time considerations). Both sides were able to claim victory based on Nutter's ruling although it did not establish any criteria for preventing emasculation. One of the briefs filed by Stevens showed what happened to Billy Wilder's *Stalag 17* on its 1965 NBC telecast—nine breaks for commercials for 31 different products. Stevens said he was suing because he felt his contract gave him such control and that his professional reputation could be damaged by exhibition of the film in a way other than that originally conceived by him in the editing stages of production. Directors Guild of America president George Sidney reiterated his earlier position that any interruptions of a film constituted a "defrauding of the public," in the same manner as fraudulent labeling of packaged goods.[89]

After NBC broadcast Stevens's film, the director succeeded in getting the network hauled into court to defend itself against a citation for contempt Stevens felt it deserved. However, the court ruled NBC did not damage the film or the experience of watching it. Both the Preminger and the Stevens cases received much support from other film directors. The Directors Guild of America declared it would mount a campaign to give film directors greater control over the exhibition of their films on television.[90]

Director Ralph Nelson asked for and received permission to re-cut his *Lillies of the Field* for CBS telecasting in the spring of 1967. Journalist Bill Greeley remarked that "Nelson is smart, for the butchery that is called editing of features for tv is one of the negatives in the mixed bag of benefits and drawbacks since the networks have become an almost nightly feature grind." When that was written, a movie was on at least one of the three networks in prime time on six nights out of seven. Not much later it was all seven nights. "None but the true hack could fail to be upset by the gutting of features for tv..." lamented Greeley. CBS had just telecast Carl Forman's 1963 film *The Victors*. Although it ran for three hours in theatrical distribution it was cut by 70 minutes for ads and for time constraints on the small screen. That left much of the story incomprehensible as, said Greeley, the networks "gut the pictures and use every device but a crowbar to wrench another blurb in sideways..."[91]

Reporter Paul Jensen recalled the Stevens and Preminger cases in 1968, noting that nothing more had been heard of that type of complaint in the few years that had passed since they were launched. Jensen thought it was fruitless for a director to pursue a complaint on the ground the director should have control over when and where commercial breaks were placed. Rather, he thought a more promising route for protest (assuming a feature was left intact) lay in the difference between theatrical film and the television screen shapes. Until the 1950s film proportions (height to width aspect ratio) were close to those of the television image. Then, to offer something not found on television (as Hollywood desperately responded to a declining audience), films got wider and wider — Cinemascope, and so on. In time those movies began to show up on the small screen. Networks and local stations tried to solve this shape problem but their methods, said Jensen, distorted the movie "substantially" and "materially." If a Cinemascope picture was telecast with no attempt at adaptation, the television set showed the center portion of each frame and missed quite a bit of both edges and sometimes action and dialogue, depending on how the director had used the sides of each frame. One way around the problem was to have several television cameras cover overlapping sections of film then jump cut as a character moved from one area to another. In essence, that reduced one shot to several, with a jerky effect. Broadcast stations also panned from one section of a film frame to another. For example, in Roger Corman's *I, Mobster*, one gangster guns down another on the film screen. However, because of the different aspect ratios the television screen could not show that—so it showed first the shooter and then the victim. But that could change the director's intentions. Another solution lay in increasing the distance from the television camera to the film image, which allowed the edges to be seen "but creates distracting black stripes across the top and bottom of the ribbon-shaped image. It makes tiny tv characters even smaller." Jensen felt this method—which came to be called letterboxing—was the least likely method to be used.[92]

Theatrical film directors remained unhappy with the manner in which their films were cut for telecasting. They sought to protect themselves through a contractual demand in negotiations with the Association of Motion Picture and TV Producers. The Directors Guild of America was asking that the producers be obligated to contact a film director when a movie was sold to television and give him the chance to edit the feature so that it would fit within the specified time segment and to indicate spots for the insertion of commercials. It was proposed that the directors would perform this editing for no charge. If the director was unavailable the producer was to contact the DGA, which would supply a director to assist in editing.[93]

George Ferris III spent a year as a film editor at WMAL-TV in Washington, D.C., in 1974 where his job was to insert commercials and cut films' running times to fit the format of "Money Movie 7" each afternoon from four to six pm. He had 90 minutes of air time each day for the movie with the remainder given over to sponsors and station promotions. Ferris admitted he "hacked several hundred movies to pieces." One of those was *The Train* (1965, Burt Lancaster), which ran for 143 minutes in theatrical distribution and from which Ferris cut 53 minutes. Musicals were by far the easiest type of film for him to edit because songs rarely advanced the plot. His most challenging editing job was *Beast from 20,000 Fathoms*—an 87-minute feature. On the telecasting day "Money Movie 7" was pre-empted and he had to reduce the picture to 45 minutes. In his year on the job, Ferris said that on only two occasions did an editing job elicit phone calls from viewers. One was with *Exodus*, a 243-minute epic cut to 180 (telecast as a two-part movie) minutes. Ferris cut all the introductory scenes and jumped right to the ship. "But too many people remember that film by rote, so we got a lot of calls," recalled Ferris. The second instance involved *The Pink Panther*, which was said to be too popular for the cuts to pass unnoticed. "We editors were pretty well insulated, though," observed Ferris. "Someone would remark about it the next day and that would be it." Only once did he edit strictly for content. A single word was excised from *I Could Go On Singing* (1963) with Judy Garland and Jack Klugman. He had to keep Garland from saying the word "god" in "goddamnit."[94]

The length of a film was also an issue for the industry as both distributors and exhibitors were said to be complaining, in 1959, that movies were becoming too long. A top sales executive was quoted as saying that "Most pictures are too long. Films should be cut to play. If the picture is 'good' I've never known a man to come out and complain that it was too short." In what was described as a new era of independents, the studios were supposedly less able to exert control over directors, who were in a better position to defend their productions against editing. Still, the account noted that George Stevens did agree to a cutting job — even though it took a great deal of convincing — on his *Diary of Anne Frank*, which ran 170 minutes in the theatrical road show version. Fox was cutting 30 minutes partly because "the original length just doesn't fit in with ordinary exhibitor requirements." Apart from the "practical" aspects the studios added that the overly long film releases also "tend to be slower than they need be and tighter editing would improve them." Reporter Fred Hift listed a total of 17 examples of overly long movies yet 11 of them had a running time ranging from 111 to 125 minutes.[95]

Doug McClelland was a film cutter who published *The Unkindest Cuts* (1972), a book dealing with his experiences in the industry. He wrote about the pressures brought to bear on the editor by the producer, director, studio executives, influential stars, and even exhibitors. Also discussed was the arbitrary cutting of lengthy films between their road show and regular engagement, citing such examples as *Lawrence of Arabia*, *Cleopatra*, *Exodus*, and *The Greatest Story Every Told*.[96]

Anything along the lines of moral rights in American copyright legislation for the creative talent involved in films remained beyond the pale for the U.S. motion picture industry. In France in 1949, Marcel Carne and Jacques Prevert, director and screenwriter, respectively, for the Pathé release *Children of Paradise* sued Pathé on the ground their "moral right to the film was injured" when Pathé allegedly excised several sequences of the film without their permission in order to make it easier to release. A lower court decision granted the pair permission to seize the movie on the ground that all artistic collaborators in a movie had a "moral right." Appealing the ruling, Pathé won a decision in which a higher court held that no film could be seized under conditions described in the complaint. However, this court still recognized the plaintiffs' moral right.[97]

Director Robert Aldrich sued Titanus Film in Italy when the producer tried to cut his film *The Last Days of Sodom and Gomorrah* against his wishes. The Rome Civil Court reconfirmed the right of Aldrich to be a co-copyright holder in the movie. Rejected by the court was a Titanus claim that it alone was the copyright holder, and thus allowed to change the movie any way it liked because the contract had been signed in America under the laws of New York State, which granted all rights to the producer and none to the director. However, the court ruled that since the movie was shot in Italy, Italian law, which gave full authorship of a movie to director, screenwriter, and composer, applied. Therefore, Aldrich had every right to oppose any move designed to "deform, mutilate, or otherwise modify" his negative. Any such modification could damage the director's "moral rights."[98]

It was those moral rights, among other reasons, that kept the U.S. from ratifying the Berne Convention and would keep them from doing so for a century. Typifying the position of the American motion picture industry was attorney Herbert T. Silverberg in a 1957 address to the California Copyright Conference. Speaking of copyright ownership of a film he said that "only one man should own the copyright and that man is the producer." Silverberg added, "The U.S. goes along with this concept but in France, for example, directors, writers and sometimes performers get into the copyright ownership act."[99]

Producer Leland Hayward deplored the position of the writer in Hollywood, in the same year, observing that "he's not the master of his own work. Someone's always 'improving' it for him." Hayward noted that when a person wrote a book, the editor might suggest changes, but they were only made with the approval of the author. With regard to stage productions, for years the Dramatists Guild contract had specifically forbidden any changes without the author's consent.[100]

MGM had organized a committee in the 1950s for the purpose of selecting titles for motion pictures on a long-range basis. For example, if the studio purchased a novel in galley form it was decided before the book was published whether or not the title was suitable for subsequent promotion as a film name. That policy resulted in altering the title of Tom Chamales's novel, which MGM acquired, from its original *No Rent in His Hand* to *Go Naked in the World*. As a result, the book was to be issued under the new title when it was published, thus giving MGM what it believed was a better title for the film version.[101]

Reportedly, all the majors followed an anti-raiding policy, with respect to creative talent, in the late 1940s. It was a policy that lessened competition, kept salaries down and was also blamed by some for imposing stagnation on the industry by keeping out new faces. Those long, seven-year contracts, often signed by actors, were just one way of reducing any piracy of talent. However, as the industry contracted in the face of competition from television Hollywood production fell off drastically. The studio system and long contracts disappeared.[102]

Hollywood's record keeping and number generation was also criticized. Producer David O. Selznick declared in 1948 that recent financial statements by the major studios indicating their theater circuits were responsible for big profits while their studio production affiliates lost money were the results of "nothing but phony bookkeeping. The whole industry, as a matter of fact, is built on phony accounting." Specifically, he lashed out at arbitrary charges in film rental rates and at the studio rule of adding 50 percent overhead to each movie, regardless of the actual costs. It meant that $250,000 was added to a $500,000 film, while $500,000 was tacked on to a $1 million production when there was nothing like that in the real difference in overhead costs. If getting a big star for a film cost an extra $200,000, it added $100,000 to overhead yet really made no change.[103]

A 1968 account dealt with the inflated box office numbers issued by distributors for their releases playing on Broadway in New York. Presumably those inflated numbers, said a reporter, might con small town exhibitors and remote film buyers into paying higher rental terms than they would otherwise accept. Some of the New York distributors inflated the box office totals "by the traditional 10–20%," although several had been caught hiking figures on certain weak movies by as much as 50 percent. "Generally speaking, onus for inflated quotations falls on the distribs, not on the Manhattan houses. Rather than antagonize a major, most theater managers are willing to play along with the distribs and obligingly overquote boxoffice results," explained the journalist. For example, Paramount's *Half a Sixpence* claimed an opening week gross of $53,000 (actual was $41,000), a second week of $36,000 ($25,500), and a third week of $32,000 ($25,250). According to the account, the biggest "self-inflator" of the seven majors was MGM "and figures from that company are believed to be released only after lengthy management debate about the size of the added air." MGM's *Gone With the Wind* was then on Broadway, in reissue. For its twenty-first week MGM stated a gross of $36,000, when the actual was $27,500.[104]

Lawsuits by individuals against the Hollywood majors alleging plagiarism continued to be launched. Occasionally the plaintiff won. For example, the settlement of a $200,000 suit filed in 1949 in Los Angeles over the movie *Seven Sweethearts* was announced in 1954 by the attorney for Ferenc Herczeg, the Hungarian playwright who charged the studio based its 1942 film on his play "Seven Sisters," produced in 1903. While the amount was unreported the suit was said to have been settled for a "substantial amount."[105]

A bizarre lawsuit involved Warner Brothers, which had bought certain rights to author Dashiell Hammett's detective creation Sam Spade when it purchased rights to the *Maltese Falcon* in 1930. When Hammett continued to produce Sam Spade stories, Warner sued him for damages in a copyright infringement suit. In 1954 the Ninth U.S. Circuit Court of Appeals ruled Hammett could continue to feature Spade's adventures in novels and on the air, despite the sale to Warner, whose claim was rejected.[106]

Another issue that arose in this period was whether or not film ads had to feature scenes that were actually in the movies they advertised. That question of truthfulness came up in connection with the ads for Warner's *The Prince and the Showgirl*, which showed a scene between Laurence Olivier and Marilyn Monroe that was not in the picture. Critic Bosley Crowther pointed that out in his regular review of the film, an action that annoyed Warner. The same tactic had been used for other films such as *Lust for Life* and *Spirit of St. Louis* with the attitude that there was nothing wrong with "staging" special scenes for film ads described as something new. While advertising executives from the majors generally agreed that a promotion campaign should not falsify the meaning of a film, a reporter remarked that "this has been done at times out of desperation, when New York felt that a picture lacked sales appeal."[107]

The New York City Consumer Affairs Department, headed by Bess Myerson, introduced a regulation in 1971 that would bar "false and misleading" quote ads for films, plays and books. That was defined as quotes used in advertising in a way that distorted the conclusion or opinion of the review or comment considered as a whole. Myerson's example was a quote ad using only the word "beautiful" when the full sentence was "the scenery is beautiful." After some revision the Consumer Affairs Department adopted the regulation in 1972.[108]

While film piracy occurred throughout this period, it did not seem to be particularly prevalent, either domestically or offshore. It was an activity that could never be completely eliminated but the Hollywood majors appeared to have the problem in hand by the mid 1970s. Also, the issue of cheating exhibitors seemed to be on the decline, after some heavy larceny in the late 1940s and early 1950s. Hollywood continued to engage in its own shady practices although these received scant media attention, except for the butchery and mutilation inflicted on films to make them ready for television exhibition. By the mid 1970s, Hollywood was probably content with the efforts it had undertaken to limit piracy and larcenous exhibitors. Those efforts, if somewhat expensive, had been effective. Although this period saw the emergence of 16m as a popular format and, because of that, a resultant enlargement of the market for pirates looking to sell illicit dupes, the situation did not get out of hand. But Hollywood's worst period for piracy lay ahead of it. It was all due to the arrival of a new technology which started slowly in the mid 1970s and then took off. The videocassette recorder (VCR) would soon make almost everyone in the developed world a potential buyer of pirated films, knowingly or not.

5

Domestic Piracy, 1975–2001

"The illegal pirating of prints in this country and around the world is a cancer in the heart of the film industry and we aim to cut the cancer out."

Jack Valenti, 1975

"The video recorder is here. Its only mission is to record other people's copyrighted material."

Jack Valenti, 1982

"There is no ultimate victory [over piracy]. The best you can hope to do is eliminate the egregious violations."

Jack Valenti, 1987

"Online movie piracy is a cancer in the belly of our business."

Jack Valenti, 1999

Nothing revolutionized the home entertainment business and the film industry the way the videocassette recorder (VCR) did from the mid 1970s onward. It generated a huge financial windfall for the Hollywood majors, although they fought its arrival in the courts, were slow in entering the market and tried to sell their films to a public that only wanted to rent them. VCRs also expanded the potential market for pirates with anyone who owned one of the machines being a possible customer. Prior to the advent of VCRs, only individuals with 16m equipment were possible buyers, and before that only people with 35m facilities were possible buyers. In both cases it was a tiny fraction of the population.

Back in 1970, both RCA and CBS were talking about cassette systems then ready or about to be launched. CBS was touting its Electronic Video Recording (EVR) and saw the huge Hollywood backlist of movies as a prime item for its pre-recorded cartridges. Robert E. Brockway, CBS EVR division president, felt cinema lobbies would eventually be turned into depots for rentals of earlier films made by the stars whose first-run releases were then playing the theater.[1]

Even as early as 1970 some systems were operational, if only in a rudimentary way. A dozen movies had been playing over the previous year in a number of Spanish resort hotels where television sets with Vidicord teleplayers had been fitted in the guest rooms. Vidicord was a small British company whose machines were not then on sale to the public. Those films were all from the vaults of British Lion and Anglo EMI studios, six from each, on lease to Vidicord at a fixed royalty per copy (regardless of the number of plays) and in turn re-leased to the hotels. Movies ranged from five to 15 years old and included *Station Six Sahara* and *Carry On Sergeant*.[2]

By the end of the 1970s videodisks were touted as ready to go to market, with at least two different systems ready to launch. Videodisks were seen as a format that would drastically reduce piracy since the duplication of videodisks involved a relatively complex plant with a multimillion dollar investment. Videodisk systems did not, of course, catch on with videotape cassettes increasingly becoming a part of the American home from about the mid to late 1970s onward. Videotape would dominate the home video area until the end of the 1990s at which time the digital video disk (DVD) arrived on the scene to mount a challenge.[3]

According to Arthur Morowitz, owner of Video Shack, the first retail chain created to sell videocassettes, in 1977 there was not one store in America dedicated to videocassette retailing; in 1983 there were more than 6,000. Home video was expected to provide approximately $240 million in royalties that year to the majors, about seven percent of all the revenues studios would get from their films. In December 1977, as founder and chairman of a small company called Magnetic Video, Andre Blay was the first person to get a Hollywood major studio to license movies for cassettes. After being turned down by nearly every movie studio, he obtained rights from Fox to 50 movies, including *Patton* and *M*A*S*H* for $6,000 each. When people started to rent movies instead of buying them, the majors found they could not stop it because of a part of the copyright rules known as the First Sale doctrine. It meant the legal purchaser of a movie could sell his specific copy to a third party or rent it as often as he wanted for as much as he could get. Copyright-holding studios could do nothing about it. Seriously annoyed because they could not share in the rental income, some of the majors tried to set up programs wherein they only leased the cassettes to the video shop. All those attempts failed, however, because they were complicated, had a lot of paperwork connected with them, and met total resistance from retailers. Then the majors started to drastically reduce the price of cassettes in an attempt to achieve much higher sales figures.

For example, the majors were selling their movies on cassettes in the range of $80 or so at the start of the 1980s. Then Paramount introduced a new tactic by pricing *Star Trek II* at $39.95 each, an unheard of low price at the time.[4]

A year before Fox licensed some of its movies for cassettes, in 1976, the majors (led by Universal and Walt Disney) launched a suit against Sony and its VCR, contending that home taping was a violation of copyright and therefore not legal. Seven years would pass before a final resolution was reached. An appeals court sided with the majors in October 1981 declaring that the copying of television programs and the sale of VCRs was illegal. That court said the industry was entitled to a share of the profits from VCRs and videotape sales as compensation. On January 17, 1984, the U.S. Supreme Court ruled five to four that it was legal to tape television programs (including movies) for home viewing, rejecting the contention of the entertainment industry that viewers who taped programs were stealing copyrighted material. In reversing the appeals court's decision, the Supreme Court justices said the average viewer taped for "time shifting" purposes (to watch at home at a later date), not for commercial purposes or to build a library. Also, the court ruled this time shifting did not harm the entertainment industry financially and was thus a "legitimate fair use" of the copyrighted programs produced by the entertainment industry. The majors also failed in their attempts to get Congress to legislate taxes on VCRs and blank tapes, although they lobbied vigorously. Of course, by the time of the Supreme Court decision, the Hollywood majors were doing much better financially than hoped for in cassette sales. Ironically, the winner of the case, Sony, had by then lost the battle of VCR formats as its Beta format was then losing (and would soon disappear) against the rival VHS system.[5]

Addressing a group of campus film instructors in 1979, MPAA vice president James Bouras estimated there were then some three million VCRs in home use — 900,000 in the U.S. alone, "a market served almost entirely by film pirates." Bouras added, "We know that the demand by home users will be filled by pirates if the major motion picture companies don't fill the gap. Nine of the 10 largest companies in the MPAA already are making pics for home use."[6]

Some analysts who followed the industry said its delay in entering the videotape business created the vacuum that gave bootleggers their foothold. Valenti complained, "The video recorder is here. Its only mission is to record other people's copyrighted material. The new technology has outstripped copyright law all over the world." Robert M. Greenberg (purchaser for Tape City International) said that once a film was released on cassette by the majors "the black market pretty much disappears" because there was not much profit. Hollywood's majors did not release in cassette until six to eight months after a film debuted in cinemas. That, of course, gave pirates a great opportunity. In 1982 the studios estimated that about five percent of the stock in the nation's video stores was pirated.[7]

The changing nature of piracy operations could be seen in FBI statistics. In 1975 the agency confiscated 5,867 pirated films and 1,195 illicit tapes. In 1980 those numbers were vastly different; 312 films and 16,635 tapes were seized. Nine years later, in 1989, the FBI confiscated 659,615 illegal tapes. During 1980, 60 people were convicted of video piracy and 90 others were arrested and awaiting trial. By contrast, between 1975 and 1979, only 84 people were convicted on piracy charges— 37 of them in 1979. For 1989 the estimated videocassette revenues of the majors were: Warner, $481 million; Buena Vista (Disney), $439 million; Paramount, $310 million; CBS/Fox, $272 million; MCA (Universal), $246 million; MGM/UA, $223 million; and RCA/Columbia, $215 million.[8]

Although videotape dominated the piracy in this period, it began with a high profile 16m case that prominently featured actor Roddy McDowall. A sweeping investigation of film and television piracy, centered in Los Angeles, began in 1974 with a grand jury there studying the matter. Investigations were being conducted by the U.S. Attorney's office and the FBI. Assistant U.S. Attorney Chet Brown confirmed later in 1974 that there had been a number of raids with a number of copyrighted films and television programs being seized. Several prominent actors had been interviewed but none were identified.[9]

On December 18, 1974, a search warrant was executed on McDowall's North Hollywood home. Copies of more than 500 films and television shows were removed from the premises by the authorities. Some were movies the actor had personally starred in, including *My Friend Flicka*, *Lassie Come Home*, and *Planet of the Apes*. McDowall was said to have told the FBI he had bought a number of films from Ray Atherton, whom the FBI identified as a "large-scale dealer in the purchase and sale of illegally produced or stolen motion pictures." Also, the FBI said that McDowall, well-known in Hollywood for his extensive film collection, was suspected of attempting to sell a portion of his film collection through Atherton and an associate, Roy Henry Wagner. Possession of material that broke federal copyright laws was a civil violation, but willful infringement for profit was a misdemeanor with a penalty of up to one year in jail.[10]

In June 1975, the U.S. Attorney's Office cleared McDowall in connection with alleged film piracy. Brown said no charges would be filed against the actor because the government had no evidence McDowall ever made a profit on films he allegedly sold from his private collection. However, the government issued a warning at the same time to those people who collected movies as a hobby saying their activities could constitute "serious violations of both state and federal law." Specifically, the purchase of copyrighted films from unauthorized individuals could constitute "receiving stolen property in violation of state law. In addition, persons could be aiders or abettors or conspirators with a person from whom they purchase protected films."[11]

At the same time, the grand jury issued 16 indictments charging film piracy against a total of 20 individuals. In a few months some 27,000 cans of films had been seized from unauthorized owners. It was then estimated that 65,000 private collectors across the country might be in violation of federal laws that protected copyrighted movies. Reporter Jon Nordheimer noted that the mere possession of an unauthorized film could subject the owner to a civil damage suit for infringement. "This has created a secret society among private collectors, even within the Hollywood community itself, where for years the stars and production personnel have illegally accumulated and exchanged prints for reasons of personal amusement," he added. Although McDowall was not charged his seized collection of over 500 films remained in the hands of the government and Nordheimer said the presumption was that he would get back only those movies authorized by the motion picture studios to be in his hands.[12]

Following a four-week trial several people indicted by the Los Angeles grand jury, including Albert Drebin and Lawrence Fine, were convicted of conspiracy, the transportation into foreign commerce of stolen property, and of criminal copyright infringement. Most of the major studios, as well as a number of actors, assisted in the prosecution. Among those that made appearances were Gene Hackman, Rock Hudson, Robert Young, Ryan O'Neal, and McDowall. Commenting on the convictions, MPAA president Jack Valenti declared, "the film pirates may have had a run in the industry but they are now on the run, and will be put out of the filthy business of stealing and selling motion pictures."[13]

A year later in Los Angeles, U.S. Attorney Dominick Rubalcava said the operation and prosecutions in Southern California had made the pirates less brazen in their operations and had driven them underground. He added, though, that pirates were still out there and selling movies every day. "It's not open. It's not blatant. It's not the way it was a year ago. We feel we have been successful to a large extent, but there's still work to be done, and the FBI is working very hard in this area." Another one of those convicted was Ray Atherton, on five counts of copyright infringement and one count of interstate transportation of stolen property. Atherton was sentenced to six years in prison, reduced to six months in custody. Said Rubalcava, "He was a fulltime film dealer—or pirate. He didn't work at anything else."[14]

When McDowall's home was raided and the possibility that he might be charged existed, film collector magazines and the general media all denounced the actions as a case of harassment. It implied, they felt, that any actor might be criminally charged with possessing copies of his own work. McDowall may have been selected and singled out, they argued, because he was high profile and as a warning to film collectors. Atherton and McDowall had sold movies to each other. During Atherton's trial the defense called not only McDowall but also Gene Hackman and Rock Hudson in an attempt to show how the Hollywood circuit duplicated and sold prints. That caused Valenti, as industry czar, to implement a new rule that prohibited any private screenings of movies outside the studios themselves (many actors, executives, and others had screening equipment and facilities in their homes). When the rule was announced Bud Yorkin complained "Somebody spends $30,000 to put in projection equipment and then the high and mighties tell you you can't get a film." Even before the no outside screenings rule was imposed, the studios were said to have made their own actors sign strict loan agreements before they were allowed to borrow films for a private screening. Actor Robert Young testified in court that he had possession of prints of only two of the 125 movies he had made during a 40-year career.[15]

A major setback to efforts to curb film piracy occurred in 1977 when the Ninth Circuit Court of Appeals reversed a criminal conviction won by the government and laid down new standards of evidence that would make it more difficult to prove prints in the marketplace were illegal bootlegs. In a unanimous opinion, written by Judge Shirley M. Hufstedler, the three-judge panel reversed the conviction of Ray Atherton. Hufstedler said the conviction was wrong because the government had failed to negate the "first sale" copyright doctrine that might have sheltered Atherton's trades. Also, the government failed to show that *The Exorcist* (one of the titles Atherton was accused of pirating) was worth the $5,000 value needed to bring it under federal interstate transportation laws, no matter how successful the title had been theatrically. Under the first sale doctrine a copyright holder lost exclusive rights to a specific copy of a work he sold. For example, the purchaser of a book was free to sell that book to anybody else he wished, although he was forbidden to copy or reprint it. At the trial, the government tried to avoid the first sale issue with the argument that films were never sold but were just licensed, leased, or rented. If it could prove that no prints were subject to the first sale doctrine, then the government felt it followed that the prints Atherton sold could not have been subject to the first sale doctrine. However, the court held that first sales had taken place in the licensing to television, in some cases, whereby a station could, at its election and cost, retain a print in its library permanently. Also, the court said that first sale could be involved in the peddling of worn-out films to salvage firms. The government's case failed because it made no effort to prove the source of Atherton's prints, relying entirely on its theory that first sale was not relevant.[16]

The focus on private collectors seemed oddly out of place since a decade after the raid on McDowall, Robert Young or anybody else could have easily picked up a videotape cassette copy of all one hundred plus films he had appeared in. He also could have done it much more cheaply than McDowall could have at the time of the raid on his collection. By waiting a few more years the cost would have been cheaper still.

One of the first steps the industry took in this period to combat movie piracy was to revert to a strategy it had not used for some time: the setting up of a specific agency to deal just with piracy. At the beginning of 1975, Jack Valenti announced that a print security office was being established in Hollywood by the MPAA on behalf of its member companies—Columbia, Warner Brothers, United Artists, Paramount, Fox, Universal, Allied Artists, and Avco Embassy. Valenti fumed, "The illegal pirating of prints in this country and around the world is a cancer in the heart of the film industry and we aim to cut the cancer out." It was envisioned that this new unit would work in close liaison with the FBI, Scotland Yard, and other foreign police organizations.[17]

When he announced the new unit Valenti observed that although piracy was as old as the film industry, the illicit copying "has reached very high proportions in recent years. Of course, we've been dealing with the problem over the years but we've done so on a disorganized basis. Now, hopefully, it will be attacked on a coordinated constructive basis."[18]

The MPAA announced in the spring of 1975 that it had hired two retired FBI agents to head its newly formed Film Security Office (FSO). Named as director was William John Nolan (a 33-year FBI man) and named as assistant director was Ewing G. Layhew (24 years). Both men had been involved in West Coast film piracy cases when they were with the FBI.[19]

Three years later, in 1978, Richard Bloeser and Layhew were, respectively, director and executive director of the FSO, with its sole office located in Hollywood. The MPAA announced it would open a similar FSO office in New York City because of, said Valenti, "the seriousness" of the film and television program piracy problem. Since new technology made it easier to illicitly duplicate films the MPAA head felt piracy would remain a serious problem "for the foreseeable future."[20]

Many other solutions were tried in the remainder of the 1970s in an attempt to reduce piracy. One of those was the result of a collaboration between entertainment industry attorney Robert Mirisch and Assistant U.S. Attorney Chet Brown. It was a warning label that read "This motion picture photoplay is protected pursuant to the provisions of the laws of the United States of America, and any unauthorized duplication and/or distribution of this photoplay may result in criminal prosecution." It first appeared on the MGM film *The Sunshine Boys*. Today, of course, a similarly-worded warning can be found on any film, videocassette, or DVD. Mirisch and Brown had discussed the idea for the purpose of finding some way to cover a piracy defendant's possible defense that "he didn't know." It was an attempt to close off a possible escape hatch and brought to mind the strategy of the early motion picture industry of branding all films, and sometimes each individual film frame, with a studio logo.[21]

In 1976 the MPAA announced it was engaged in a research effort to find an economical method of coding each motion picture print with an identifying mark as a primary means of combating print piracy. "Identifying prints is the one elusive objective in trials against pirates," said Valenti. A few years later a Hollywood company, Video Duplication, working with both the FBI and the FSO, claimed to have come up with a system to electronically prevent the unauthorized duplication of cassettes. Nothing came of that announcement.[22]

Also, the MPAA instituted the previously mentioned "no outside screening" rule, with violators subject to $5,000 fines as determined by the MPAA. One reporter said that "Print security in the film industry has long been something of a joke, what with rather casual studio, laboratory, exchange and shipping facility practices, along with major ripoffs in the extensive 16m film libraries of tv stations." Thus, when the FSO opened in March 1975, the industry itself was guilty of a lot of in-house sloppiness. When Valenti issued the "no outside screening" memo, he did so citing the "urgent counsel" of the FSO acting on the "firm recommendations" of the FBI and the Department of Justice as the motivating forces. That policy declared there were to be no private film screenings outside the confines of the studio proper, the studio home office, or the MPAA "except" for senior executives of the member firms. It meant that only top senior executives of the Hollywood majors could continue to enjoy screenings in their homes where lavish projection facilities were paid for by companies which then took related income tax deductions. However, the rule lasted only a few months before Valenti backed down. No one was ever fined and the Beverly Hills/Bel Air circuit returned to normal.[23]

Another solution tried was one of the oldest around — rewards. Warner Brothers, in a 1977 letter circulated to all its employees, announced it was offering a $5,000 reward to any employee furnishing information leading to the arrest and conviction of movie pirates. Employees were also asked to submit suggestions for ways to improve security procedures in order to prevent further piracy.[24]

National Film Service (NFS, a lab) announced around the same time that it was offering a $1,000 reward to any of its employees who supplied information leading to the indictment and conviction of anyone who illegally obtained, duplicated or sold prints that were in the custody and control of NFS. Arnold Brown, NFS vice president, wrote to FSO head William Nolan to suggest the MPAA create a fund consisting of contributions made by all interested companies to reward individuals who were not employees of the motion picture industry for providing information that led to the conviction of individuals involved in piracy.[25]

Apparently taking up that suggestion, the MPAA announced in 1977 that it was offering a reward of as much as $5,000 to anyone providing information leading to piracy arrests and convictions. The MPAA would determine the specific amount of the reward in each case, up to a maximum of $5,000. All nine MPAA members— Columbia, MGM, Universal, Paramount, United Artists, Fox, Warner, Allied Artists, Avco Embassy — plus two non-MPAA members— American International and Walt Disney — supported and contributed financially to the bounty idea.[26]

American copyright law was also strengthened in the late 1970s with the old protection period of 28 years plus one renewal for another 28 years replaced by a single protected period of 75 years, for works for hire. Those who violated copyright could be brought to court in either civil or criminal proceedings. In civil cases the copyright owner could sue for an injunction to stop the distribution or sale of the pirated work, the destruction of the illicit material, and the recovery of actual damages and estimated lost profits. Also, plaintiffs in civil cases could ask for up to $50,000 in statutory damages. Conviction in a criminal case meant a penalty of a fine up to $25,000, up to one year in jail, or both, for a first offense, and double that for subsequent offenses. The old law provided only for a fine of up to $1,000 and less than a year in jail. A criminal case of infringement, unlike a civil case, had to show that the defendant infringed on the copyright both willfully and for profit. Under the old law, two copies of the film had to be filed with the Copyright Office at the Library of Congress. However, by convention only one print had ever been deposited. And for much of the time that print had been immediately "borrowed" back by the depositing studio. The new copyright law of the late 1970s required only one print of a film had to be filed. However, 83 days after the law was passed, wrote James Monaco, the Copyright Office bowed to industry pressure and reinstated the "motion picture agreement" permitting the studios to "borrow" back those deposit prints so as not to lose even a penny in extra costs.[27]

Many other domestic piracy operations took place in the last half of the 1970s. One saw a Manhattan man described as a major distributor of pirated pictures arrested at his Broadway office in 1975. A police raid seized illegal master copies of over 500 movies, including *The Godfather*, *Planet of the Apes* and *Deep Throat*. Sol Winker grossed an estimated $500,000 a year selling cassette tapes of the pirated movies for an average of about $175 a copy to resort hotels in Florida and the Caribbean. The raid came after a four-month investigation by the police, FBI, and investigators from the MPAA law firm of Sargoy, Stein and Hanft. According to one of the raiders, Sgt. James Robert, Winker used 16m prints stolen from television stations, airlines and film libraries to make master tapes for illegal reproduction. He sold cassettes of individual films for prices ranging from $75 to $350 for *Gone with the Wind*, the most expensive. Winker's major market was resort hotels offering a variety of popular movies played over television sets in guests' rooms. Most of his sales were made to Florida, California, the Caribbean and at least one Middle East nation which went unidentified by Robert except to be described as a "member of OPEC." Robert added the investigation included several undercover purchases from Winker by police agents with the last one having taken place on the morning of the raid when an undercover cop paid $100 for a cassette of *Claudine*. Winker had been arrested on a similar federal charge in 1973. At that time he pled guilty to a charge of theft from an interstate shipment after he was caught with a print of *The Godfather*. Sentenced to a year's probation, which had only recently expired, Winker had continued and expanded his operation since 1973, according to police. Winker reportedly told undercover agents that his cost was $17 for each cassette film he sold and that he sold at least 10 movies a day at an average of $175 each. One source was said to be "unscrupulous" employees of television stations. Customers included some social organizations such as volunteer fire departments but few private individuals as not many people owned VCRs in 1975.[28]

Commenting on the Winker case an unnamed attorney who followed the pirate field closely remarked that "Up until now most of the big pirates simply sold the 16m prints outright. Now we see a large-scale operation using videotape. The trend in that direction is likely to increase in coming years."[29]

Commenting on the situation in general, *Time* magazine said that in

1974 while *The Towering Inferno* was still in production, a San Diego cinema was screening a 90-minute pirated version put together from prints of individual scenes (the completed film ran 165 minutes). Some prints were even advertised openly for sale in publications such as *The Big Reel* (North Carolina) and *The Film Collector* (Houston). In this account, *Time* also came up with the estimate that "up to $500 million annually that should have gone to major studios in legitimate film rentals" went to bootleggers. It was a very exaggerated figure.[30]

A 1978 raid by the FBI on a Houston, Texas, firm, Television Systems, resulted in the seizure of about 400 illegally copied film cassettes including *Star Wars*, *Jaws*, and *Rocky*. After a representative of Fox viewed a closed circuit showing of *Star Wars* at a Huntsville, Texas, motel, he alerted studio security, which led to the federal raid. According to the FBI, the pirated movies had been distributed from Houston to California, New Mexico and Louisiana. Some 20 titles were listed as seized by the FBI, ranging from *Ben Hur* and *The Ten Commandments* to pornography. Langston Boatman, owner of the Sam Houston Inn in Huntsville, said he was not aware that the 10 cassettes used at the motel were in criminal violation of the copyright laws. He said his system that screened movies via closed circuit television in individual motel rooms was installed by Television Systems.[31]

Seven men were charged in the Sam Houston motel case, with some 40 counts related to piracy. Valenti announced, "This should be a warning to other pirates that the easy days are over." The defendants were alleged to have engaged in an elaborate bootleg scheme in which pirated material was shipped from Los Angeles to Dallas and then to the Houston area. A Houston post office box was set up to receive orders for cassette copies of hundreds of pirated titles described in a brochure called "The Greatest Shows on Earth." Also alleged was that the defendants tried to induce apartment house owners to rent videocassettes of pirated movies for viewing by apartment tenants.[32]

Taped copies of pirated films seized in Wichita were being advertised and offered for sale nationwide. Several hundred of those illicit tapes were seized in 1978 by the FBI in a raid on the home of Robert L. Lindsey, 1453 Park Place. The raid followed an investigation that began a year earlier with a letter to FBI director Clarence Kelley from FSO head William Nolan. In the letter, Nolan complained that an ad in the current issue of *Film Collectors World* offered Betamax format videotapes of copyrighted movies such as *King Kong*, *Dracula*, and *Giant* at prices ranging from $75 to $150. Prospective buyers were directed to write to 1453 Park Place in Wichita or to call Robert L. Lindsey. Two FBI agents in California posing as customers phoned Lindsey. Then they mailed $120 to Lindsey and in return got videocassettes of *Star Wars* and *Semi-Tough*.[33]

A 14-month FBI probe that began in 1978 and covered nine states, centered in Tulsa, Oklahoma, started after an agent in Tulsa first encountered evidence of a piracy ring that sold cassettes, 16m and 35m films both domestically and offshore. According to the FBI, prices for the pirated tapes ranged from $50 to $150 for the videotapes, and between $125 and $1,000 for films sold in the U.S. For offshore sales prices were much higher. Sales had been made to companies, individuals, and some theaters. Sources for the prints were people inside and outside the motion picture industry. Said an FBI agent, "A theater projectionist can duplicate a film in two hours and no one would know the difference." One of the pirates told an undercover agent who made purchases of illicit films and tapes that he could get pirated films out of the country with no problem from customs. He also offered the agent a partnership in the operation. Five arrests for copyright infringement followed the investigation in Tulsa.[34]

An investigation lasting several months in 1979, conducted by the FBI in conjunction with the FSO and the U.S. Attorney's Office in Portland, Oregon, resulted in raids in Portland and Vancouver, Washington, and the seizure of $100,000 worth of unauthorized masters and videocassette copies of dozens of films. It had been verified, said the FBI, that copies of the pirated films had been sold recently in the northwestern United States.[35]

Theater projectionists were fingered as the most probable "connection" in piracy by Richard Bloeser, director of the MPAA's FSO. He called them "the weakest link right now during the first few weeks of exhibition" despite his acknowledgement that there had been to that date, mid 1979, no FBI prosecution of projectionists. Bloeser added that authorities had "indications" of such complicity and it was "common knowledge" that pirates had been tempting projectionists with a standing offer of $500 for any feature they delivered.[36]

Jack Valenti told Harry Reasoner on CBS-TV's "60 Minutes" that film piracy "is a cancer in the belly of the film business." It was part of a segment the weekly newsmagazine did in 1979 entitled "Who Stole Superman?" Using a hidden camera, the show visited Adwar Video in Manhattan (in response to an ad in the *New York Times*) and bought videocassette copies of *Grease* and *Star Wars* for $50 each. The store clerk did not try to hide the fact that the business being conducted was illegal. Also interviewed on the program was convicted pirate Tom Dunnahoo (then legitimate) who told of being offered prints by "thieves that work at different laboratories, projectionists, film collectors...." According to Valenti, one change over the previous six months or so was that convicted pirates were then going to jail for as long as three years as well as being slapped with heavy fines where they used to be let off with a slap on the wrist and a $250 fine. Reasoner, though, commented that less than one pirate in 20 was caught. On the program Valenti estimated losses to the Hollywood majors at $100 million and up annually.[37]

Late in 1979, the FBI was hoping Fox's latest blockbuster release, *Alien*, would continue to not be pirated, unlike *Star Wars* and *Superman. Alien* was released on May 25 that year with hundreds of prints in circulation by the end of June, but no pirate copies then on the go. Tom Rupprath, acting supervisor of the FBI copyright squad in Los Angeles, remarked, "Why it hasn't shown up in videocassette form is, to me, absolutely amazing." Rupprath said the first pirate to get hold of a 35m print and change it into a master videocassette print "could easily make himself about $35,000 or $40,000 in a week." He was critical of the motion picture industry for not coding prints, for dragging its feet on a major weapon. As to why *Alien* had not yet been pirated the agent said, "I think basically the leaks that could be plugged have been by the industry because they've been cutting their own throat and they're now more careful." The release was protected by tightened print security with a stepped up policy of accountability and limited accessibility.[38]

Throughout the 1980s the motion picture industry continued to work on solutions to the piracy problem. One was to strengthen and enlarge the FSO, which acted as a liaison between the movie industry and law enforcement agencies and carried out the initial investigative work. By around 1985 the FSO had 12 offices located throughout the world. Their work was supplemented by the Regional Anti-Piracy Counsel and investigators who worked closely with local organizations in more than 40 countries. According to MPAA vice president William Nix, those operations coordinated raids against violators of copyright in order to enforce existing laws, educated enforcement authorities and the public, worked to enhance present legislation, and helped to tighten industry preventive security practices. In addition, the MPAA was affiliated with national and international film industry federations in 14 countries, and participated in anti-piracy campaigns in 19 other nations. Also maintained was an ongoing relationship with the office of the U.S. Trade Representative. Partly through those efforts the MPAA seizures of pirated videocassettes in 1985 amounted to 529,000 items.[39]

Nix noted that the MPAA's anti-piracy work included the preparation of a comprehensive Prosecutor's Manual and an Investigator's Manual. Those guides were shipped to every U.S. Attorney and FBI office in America in order to aid their offices in the investigation and prosecution of piracy. Similar guides had also been prepared, or were in preparation, for Germany, the Netherlands, Belgium, Spain, Brazil, Canada, Australia, South Africa, and several other countries. FAP, the Spanish Anti-Piracy Federation in Madrid, and GVU, the German Anti-Piracy Federation, set up "with close MPAA participation" were examples of groups that operated in foreign countries to try and reduce piracy — groups that appeared local but were largely controlled by the MPAA. In its continuing expansion the FSO was then in the process of setting up a new office in Japan.[40]

The FSO employed several hundred investigators, informants, attorneys and lobbyists, many on a part-time or retainer basis. Virtually every FSO investigator in the U.S. was a former FBI agent, which provided useful access to the exclusive fraternity of bureau agents. Despite all the resources arrayed against piracy, FSO head Richard Bloeser said, pessimistically, "As far as we're concerned, just about every new picture of any importance is going to be pirated before it is legitimately released to the home video market. It's just a fact of life." Jack Valenti said in 1988 that the MPAA's anti-piracy budget was $20 million a year.[41]

That represented a substantial increase as back in 1980 Valenti reported the MPAA's global anti-piracy budget was $1.5 million annually.[42]

Among the many technical solutions that were attempted in the 1980s to limit piracy was a new print identification system that debuted around 1981. Developed under the auspices of the MPAA, the system photographically built an otherwise invisible and unique latent image into theatrical prints that could later be optically retrieved from pirated dupes, even after several generations of video copying. By itself it did nothing to limit piracy. However, it allowed investigators to trace illicit copies back to the cinema to which the original print had been assigned. Thus, certain "problem" theaters could be identified, stakeouts mounted, and so on. This system of uniquely identifying each 35m print with a latent image continues to be in use today.[43]

A much more low-tech approach was used that same year when Paramount sent a policy letter to some 1,200 exhibitors prior to the shipment of its *Raiders of the Lost Ark*. It put the onus of any piracy venture traced to a theater directly on the venue's manager and furnished a hotline telephone number specifically for employees to call in tips. According to Paramount film and videotape security vice president Joseph Moscaret, the letter (written by him) outlined various measures to insure managers used personally supervised checks and procedures to guard the print within their cinema. "If a piracy case develops on this picture and the FBI through investigation identifies your theater with the case, the full legal remedies available to Paramount will be taken against all concerned with the theft of our prints," the letter warned. As a result of that letter an employee phoned in a tip that led to FBI agents seizing a stolen print of *Raiders* and breaking up a piracy operation near Chicago. A follow-up letter to those same exhibitors (with an attached copy of the FBI press release on the *Raiders* seizure) restated Paramount's position that "You, as the theater manager, are being held fully responsible for the security of the print that is assigned to your theater." Paramount then shredded and destroyed its junk prints on its own premises. Traditionally distributors used middlemen salvage companies to junk large print runs—a careless procedure. Also, there was a legal question as to whether such transactions constituted sales under the First Sale doctrine in copyright law.[44]

Jack Valenti had a well earned reputation as one of the premier lobbyists in Washington. Through the 1980s he labored long and hard—and unsuccessfully in this case—to have royalty payments levied on home taping, in the form of, say, a $50 royalty tax on each VCR purchase and $1 on each blank tape sale, with the proceeds going to the motion picture industry.[45]

An outraged article by Valenti in the *New York Times* in 1985 urged the adoption of a "modest" copyright royalty fee on VCRs and blank tapes. Motivation for the piece was to express his dismay at the development and marketing of the world's first double-cassette VCR—put a pre-recorded tape in deck 1, a blank in deck 2, press the play/rec button and you've got a copy. A nightmare scenario for Valenti was one in which a person rented three tapes for $2 each, took them home and called his friends who arrived with their blank tapes. At the end of the night each friend had several movies permanently inscribed on tape. "Thus, for something like $6 in total rental costs and from $8 to $10 per blank tape, the group now owns movies costing a collective $50 million!" wailed Valenti. Multiply that by several million such taping parties a week, he fretted. Pity the Hollywood majors, he argued, because they received no compensation from VCR makers, nothing from the sale of blank tapes, and no payment from the rental of movies—their sole income came from the sale to video stores of pre-recorded tapes. Yet he then turned around to point out that the sale of films and television programs offshore returned over $1 billion annually to the U.S. in a surplus balance of trade with the rest of the world.[46]

Tighter regulations governing those film festivals approved by the International Federation of Film Producers' Associations were issued in 1982 from the organization's Paris office. Mainly those regulations were concerned with tightening print control with a strict limit put on the number of screenings allowed, a limit on television's use of working prints, and a strict demand that excerpts of films used for broadcast had to be destroyed immediately following the telecast. Federation general secretary Alphonse Brisson said it was part of a general anti-piracy policy: "We are not saying that any festival print has been pirated. But we know that there can be as many as 15 television networks present at a festival like Cannes, and a dozen at Berlin, and we want to ensure that no working copies of motion pictures are left lying around at tv stations."[47]

Paramount's Joseph Moscaret explained that his company had tightened security in several ways. As a courtesy, the studios always made screening prints of new movies available to industry VIPs. In the past their drivers had picked up a print one night and returned it the next day. Under the new system a Paramount driver escorted the print to the VIP, waited while the movie was screened, and then brought it back to the studio the same night. Also, Paramount used a sign-in, sign-out system so the studio knew where the print was at all times. Paramount also placed lead seals on every film can that went out to theaters for the first time. Parcel handlers could then not "borrow" and copy a film without breaking the seals.[48]

When cassettes of *The Cotton Club* went on sale in April 1985, they were coded with a new anti-piracy device to prevent home taping of a copy for friends and to stop dealers from buying one copy and duping a few more. Aimed at the casual copier, the industry agreed that a professional pirate could easily defeat the process. Robert Mann, an FSO staff investigator, said that in the U.S. copying by dealers was a "tremendous problem" and that "most store owners are not professional enough to defeat" this new device.[49]

One of the more offbeat attempts at reducing piracy came in 1986 when Warner Brothers placed an unusual full-page ad in *Variety* that said "Warning: Warner Bros. and *Cobra* declare war on video piracy." Molly Kellogg, anti-piracy director for Warner, said the studio placed the ad for the Sylvester Stallone film because "the more pirates who know we're after them, the better. That's one of the reasons police forces have black and white cars and wear uniforms." Some months later Kellogg declared that ad had apparently slowed the pirating process as the first illicit copies made from a theatrical print took 29 days to reach Bahrain, 45 to get to Japan, and 117 to surface in France. All of those times were relatively slow.[50]

And then there was the constant lobbying of the U.S. government by the Hollywood majors, through Valenti and the MPAA, to step in and assist the industry. Nowhere was that more evident in the 1980s and 1990s than in the office of the U.S. Trade Representative (USTR), which placed countries on "watch lists" after complaints were lodged with the USTR by the studios. If after investigating the complaint the USTR agreed with

Hollywood that the country in question was not doing enough to fight piracy, then the country could be placed on a watch list. This was a first step in further investigations and the possible imposition of economic sanctions if the complaint was not resolved. For example, in 1989, USTR Carla Hills removed South Korea, Taiwan and Saudi Arabia from the priority watch list because they had started to crack down on pirated versions of U.S. films and other products. Washington left five other countries—Brazil, India, Mexico, China, and Thailand—on the priority watch list. The U.S. also warned Malaysia and Turkey that they must provide better protection. Those two nations were on a separate list of 17 countries whose trading practices Washington was dissatisfied with, although not to the same degree as with those in the first category, the priority watch list.[51]

Offshore lobbying and complaints by the industry often targeted the laws of other countries when the MPAA decided they were not adequate to the task of protecting American films. Due to the lobbying of the MPAA, the MPEA, native film industry groups (often set up and controlled by the MPAA), and "along with the vigorous support of the Dept. of Commerce and U.S. Trade Representative," said reporter Lorin Brennan, "the problem of inadequate laws in many territories has turned around." In the last half of the 1980s, Australia, Singapore, Taiwan, France, Turkey, and South Korea were all reported to have enacted new copyright laws, at the urging and behest of the United States.[52]

Within the area of copyright law, the United States finally, after a century, became the 78th nation to join the Berne Convention, in 1989. One reason America signed on after a hundred years of stalling was to bolster the fight against international piracy by obtaining copyright protection for U.S. films in other Berne Convention nations. However, as reporter Thomas McCarroll commented, "the U.S. did not sign on to controversial provisions concerning 'moral rights,' which allow artists and authors to maintain control over revision of their works."[53]

The Berne Convention for the Protection of Literary Works, which was first signed in 1886, and revised periodically thereafter, remained the primary copyright treaty in the world. Its membership had increased from 10 nations to more than 80 by 1990, including the entire European community and, as of March 1, 1989, the United States. It was then administered by the Geneva-based World Intellectual Property Organization (WIPO). America joined because it was assumed Berne would be established as the basis of a new section of the GATT. A lack of enforcement of the Berne Convention in the past was one of the reasons why the U.S. was then pushing to place intellectual property under the auspices of GATT. A suggestion to place the international protection of intellectual property under

GATT originated in the 1970s and such an initiative was introduced at the Tokyo Round of GATT negotiations (1973–1979), which mainly addressed trademarks. However, the proposal met with opposition from less developed countries and was never passed. A second attempt was made during the Uruguay Round of GATT talks (1986–1994). Advantages of placing intellectual property protection under GATT included the ability to bring together high-level government officials who could put the issue in a "trade" context, tie it to other related trade and investment issues, and take action that would be binding. A key reason why the wealthy countries preferred a GATT solution was that it contained an effective dispute resolution mechanism that could be employed when disputes went unresolved — sanctions. The loss of trade benefits under GATT provisions, such as most-favored status or the General System of Preferences, could mean extreme hardship for the less developed countries. It made it easier for a private business area such as the U.S. motion picture industry to call in its government and have that government take effective action against another country in response to the film industry's complaints. America was already unilaterally doing something like that with its "priority watch list" under Section 301 of the Omnibus Trade bill.[54]

President Reagan signed the Omnibus Trade bill into law in August 1988. It put the weight of the government behind the fight against piracy (of all products, not just movies) and restricted market access. Required under the act was that the USTR had to negotiate on an expedited basis with countries violating U.S. intellectual property rights. When the USTR could not induce violators to respect intellectual property rights, the USTR was mandated to recommend remedial action. That could include retaliation, but there were also less-stringent options. U.S. Senator Pete Wilson (R. Calif.) wrote the anti-piracy and market access provisions of the new law. "This bill provides tough new negotiating leverage that would lead to millions of dollars of increased international sales for the U.S. movie and music industry," Wilson declared.[55]

An example of the Omnibus Trade bill in action could be seen in the USTR's response to a complaint filed with it in 1989 by the International Intellectual Property Alliance (IIPA), which represented 1,600 American companies with combined 1988 revenue of $270 billion. In a report to USTR Carla Hills, the IIPA said 12 countries, headed by China, were depriving the U.S. of more than $1.2 billion a year of foreign earnings through the piracy of copyrighted material. Other countries named were: South Korea, India, the Philippines, Taiwan, Indonesia, Brazil, Egypt, Thailand, Nigeria, Malaysia, and Saudi Arabia. Most of the named countries were said to then be in some form of negotiation with the trade office in order to prevent their designation as a priority watch nation under the Omnibus Trade and Competitiveness Act of 1988. The USTR was required to inform Congress by May 30 of each year of which countries it had designated as priorities. After the designation her office had to enter intensified talks with those countries. If no improvement was achieved in a period of 18 months, the President could curb imports from those nations. On January 19, 1989, the last day of the Reagan Administration, the President denied duty-free entry to $165 million worth of Thai imports because of what he said was Thailand's failure to protect copyrighted works.[56]

As in the last half of the 1970s, domestic piracy was active in the 1980s. Speaking at an industry forum in 1980 Sid Sheinberg, president of MCA (Universal), said that everything else in the entertainment business "pales by comparison" with the problem of piracy. At the same forum Jack Valenti moaned that "we're never going to stamp out piracy anymore than you're going to stamp out narcotics dealers or homicidal maniacs or anything else." Valenti also slammed what he described as "the casual neglect of property rights."[57]

Culmination of a 2½-year investigation came in 1980 when some 400 FBI agents in 10 states raided dozens of addresses and made piracy arrests in eight cities. The film piracy and pornography operation was centered in Miami, Florida, where the FBI began the probe by establishing a front business to give the appearance of being involved with the distribution of obscene material. As the pornography operation grew, it began to embrace film piracy. A $400,000 fund was used by the FBI to set up its front business and to purchase material from pirates and pornographers.[58]

A similar FBI sting the following year, reminiscent of the one in Miami, resulted in the indictment by a federal grand jury in Baltimore of nine men said to be involved in both film piracy and pornography-prostitution activities based in the Washington D.C.-Baltimore areas. The FBI operated a front company in Baltimore from summer 1978 through April 1981. Pirated films included *Animal House*, *Star Wars*, *Jaws II*, *Grease*, *Saturday Night Fever*, and *Popeye*.[59]

Donald F. Ewald of Tarzana, California, was arrested on June 4, 1982, for mail fraud and copyright infringement. More than 700 illegally duped videocassettes were seized, along with hardware. Out on bail and awaiting trial, he was arrested again on October 5 on new charges of illegally duping and selling films—more seizures were made.[60]

Late in 1982 MPAA vice president James Bouras declared that "The inescapable fact is that for the past year and a half, Chicago has been the worst city in the country. It's the nation's major video piracy area." Independently, around the same time, the same conclusion was reached by

Warner Home Video when the firm held a press conference about several piracy arrests in the Chicago area. Warner told the press the industry consensus held that Chicago was a big piracy area. Bouras stated that the FBI had always done a "superb" job in the area with their raids and arrests. The problem was that once the raids were completed the federal prosecutor did nothing to pursue them. "There's no question that under the previous U.S. Attorney, the FBI did conduct certain raids and there was no prosecution," said Bouras. "Everyone knew it, and they ran amok."[61]

Dan K. Webb was named U.S. Attorney for the Northern District of Illinois (Chicago was included) in July 1981. Late in 1982 he responded in a long interview with *Variety* to charges leveled by the motion picture industry that Chicago was the movie piracy capital of America. Admitting it had been a serious problem when he took over his post, he felt that due to concerted efforts by his office the situation had improved. When he started his job sales of pirated tapes, he said, "were so blatant and open, and were being done almost publicly — even to the extent that sometimes we were seeing advertisements to where retail outlets were advertising the availability of a tape, which had not yet been released by the copyright holder." Honest retailers told him they could not afford not to get involved in the bootlegging and the pirating of tapes, because their competitors were. "It was so blatant and so open," added Webb, "that the entire retail industry here in Chicago had become one cesspool of illegality." Asked about the public perception of the problem, Webb responded by saying; "I don't think the public is terribly concerned about the video piracy problem and, like other types of criminal activity, the public really is not the victim." Webb saw three victims: honest retail outlets; motion picture studios (the copyright holders); and the licensee who eventually released the film in videocassette format for the general public.[62]

During a two-week period in the summer of 1983, the season's blockbuster hit, *Return of the Jedi*, was stolen five times from cinemas in three states and in Britain to be turned into illegal videocassettes. The last occurrence was when two thieves in clown masks stole a print of the movie at gunpoint from a theater in Santa Maria, California. Earlier, thieves had broken down theater doors in Hastings, England, and Sherman Oaks, California, to get a print. In South Carolina the film was inexplicably missing while in Overland Park, Kansas, a projectionist was confronted in his theater's parking lot at midnight by an armed robber who forced him to return to the venue and surrender the print. FSO head Richard Bloeser said the price for a pirated *Jedi* ranged from $85 to $150. After the theft of the print in Hastings, England, distributor Fox took out an ad in the large-circulation British daily paper *The Sun* to advertise a $7,700 reward for information about the theft. James Bouras thought that tighter print security by the industry in general may have been partly responsible for a perceived increase in the actual thefts of prints. Bloeser added that his FSO had achieved 300 convictions since its start in 1975 to mid 1983, and had paid out well over $100,000 in rewards. Regarding piracy figures Bloeser said, "A low estimate of the film industry's loss from piracy is $100 million a year. It could be as high as $500 million a year."[63]

By 1985 the FSO was estimating the worldwide loss to the majors from film piracy at $1 billion. Keeping piracy at that level were several factors: the rapid increase in the number of video stores domestically; the explosive growth of VCR penetration in new markets where copyrighted product was often not then available; and the rapid spread of unauthorized exhibitions of cassettes and satellite-delivered signals in bars, motels, and restaurants, said Bloeser. An FSO estimate declared that five to 10 percent of the stock in U.S. video stores was illegally duplicated tapes stores had created themselves. Bloeser observed that in the first 10 months of 1985 about 1,200 illegal tapes had been purchased from video outlets and about 30,000 had been collected in a total of 40 to 50 raids. In all of 1984 about 14,000 illegal tapes were seized in 52 raids. In its $1 billion loss estimate the FSO assumed at least a $500 million loss was sustained by the motion picture industry and $200 to $400 million was lost by cable and pay-tv outlets. The total passed $1 billion when lost tax and customs revenue sustained by governments was added in.[64]

A couple of years later the MPAA still estimated that five to 10 percent of tapes found in American video stores were pirated. Ed Murphy, an MPAA investigator, remarked that one of the prime sources of information about the dishonest retailers were the honest dealers. "They're in the same locality, and they become aware of piracy either through mutual customers who complain about the quality of competitors' videocassettes or customers who say the other guys' rental prices are lower."[65]

MPAA agents caught a Brooklyn video store owner with 6,000 pirated tapes on his premises. A judge ordered him to pay the studios $100,00 in restitution. With the film industry then estimating that up to 15 percent of the tapes on the shelves of U.S. video stores were illegal, Jack Valenti exclaimed "There is no ultimate victory. The best you can hope to do is eliminate the egregious violations."[66]

A 1988 FBI raid on the residence of Lewis T. Phillips, Jr., in Red Bank, Tennessee, and nearby storage facilities, netted what the MPAA called the "largest haul" in the history of America's fight on film piracy. A total of 1,573 35m prints of a wide range of movies were seized. According to the FBI those prints were being exported overseas, sold to film collectors in the U.S. and dealt out to pirates who used them to produce videocassettes. The operation was said to have contacts in countries as diverse as Australia, South Africa, Sweden, the UK, and Zimbabwe. An MPAA spokesman said the actual value of the seized prints was $200,000 to $400,000 while the FBI put their street value at $10 million to $15 million. That meant each print was worth about $200 and had a street value of approximately $10,000. Regarding this operation, Valenti wailed "It's malignant. It can kill you if you don't—every hour of every day in every country—try to stay on top of it and deter it."[67]

Eight video stores in three states were raided by the FBI and the MPAA in 1988 in the space of four days. At three California stores 700 tapes were seized; at two outlets in Louisiana 800 cassettes were taken; and at three stores in Illinois 1,700 tapes were seized. In hopes of generating more similar investigations and raids, the MPAA had instituted a 24-hour toll-free number to which businesses and consumers could report suspected piracy. The new number was 1-800-NO-COPYS.[68]

When it came to estimating the amount of the losses the motion picture industry sustained from piracy, there was no consistency as the numbers were all over the place. Never was an estimate presented in which it was explained in detail how the figure was arrived at or what assumptions were used in generating the figure. Over time, the estimates, which were artificially high to begin with, tended to soar to even higher, and to more ludicrous levels. Estimates in the 1970s were still on the modest side. One from the MPAA in 1977 said the various forms of movie piracy cost the Hollywood majors nearly $40 million a year.[69]

Officials of the World Intellectual Property Organization, a United Nations agency, estimated in 1981 that worldwide at least $1 billion worth of unauthorized films and books were produced every year, with the same amount involved in pirated records and cassettes. A year later FSO executive director Ewing Layhew said the sales of pirated tapes cost the industry up to $700 million a year in lost revenues. A 1983 article in *Business Week* declared that pirates stole more than $1 billion worth of movies a year. That figure was sourced back to the MPAA. Around the same time a *Time* magazine account had it that the film industry was losing as much as $700 million a year in ticket and cassette sales.[70]

Late in 1983, William Nix, MPAA director of worldwide anti-piracy efforts, put the illicit take at $1 billion in that year. That came, he said, when the estimated $700 million take from cassette piracy was combined with that from the theft of satellite and cable signals. Nix thought his figure might be on the low side. Paramount vice president of film and videotape security, Joe Moscarat, declared worldwide video piracy amounted to $800 to $900 million yearly while Bill Riker, National Cable Television Association director of engineering, added that U.S.-only losses from cable television and satellite signal theft meant the cable industry was losing $400 million a year.[71]

Also in 1983, the UK-based International Federation of Phonogram and Videogram Producers (IFPI) estimated the worldwide gross of video piracy at $1 billion—a figure said to be based on the selling price of pirated product. Putting some perspective on piracy estimates were the revenues of the industry. In 1986 foreign film rentals and tape sales represented an income of about $1.2 billion for the nine MPAA members, about 38 percent of their total revenue of some $3.5 billion.[72]

A 1985 estimate, again by the IFPI, put the cost of global piracy at a total of $2 billion, although a year later the MPAA was cited as saying piracy cost the industry $750 million worldwide. In a 1989 report to USTR Carla Hills, the MPEA declared that foreign pirates and trade barriers cost the Hollywood majors more than $1 billion a year, with piracy accounting for $740 million. Yet just a couple of weeks later the MPAA was cited as putting the annual worldwide piracy total at $1.2 billion.[73]

In other statistics, the MPAA revealed that for 1985 a total of 102 establishments were raided or served civil writs of seizure; 45,528 tapes were seized (up from 14,276 in 1984); 137 illegal prints were seized; 48 convictions and guilty pleas were registered; 37 injunctions or awards of damages resulting from civil cases were registered; and 400 warnings to cease illegal duplication or giving public performances were issued. Valenti reported that complaints alleging various acts of piracy being received at the FSO were then approaching 1,000 a year.[74]

For 1986, investigations totaled 1,202; raids in criminal investigations numbered 62; tapes seized in those raids totaled 29,904; establishments searched in civil cases, 30; tapes seized in those searches, 8,867; convictions and guilty pleas, 44; warnings to cease and desist illegal duplication or unauthorized performances, 229; and illegal prints, 96.[75]

Figures for 1988 released by the MPAA revealed the MPAA assisted on 211 raids that year that included 134 civil-case searches, 62 criminal-case raids, and 15 searches conducted by local officials under state and county mislabeling and theft-of-service statutes. Tapes seized numbered 65,512 while 29 convictions and guilty pleas were registered. Fines collected amounted to $87,866 while restitution paid was $48,490. Civil fines in 1988 totaled $823,622.[76]

The total number of piracy investigations initiated worldwide in 1988 was 10,500. Some 3,799 raids resulted in the seizure of 612,738 tapes. Countries in which the greatest number of illicit tapes were confiscated were:

Japan (160,808 tapes seized), Italy (82,400), the U.S. (65,512), West Germany (48,286), Brazil (37,410), Taiwan (22,000), and the Philippines (21,322).[77]

A move to increase the number of actions initiated by the FBI occurred in 1988 when the bureau altered the guidelines that helped determine when it would pursue piracy cases. The guidelines reduced from $500,000 to $250,000 the "threshold loss level" that determined priorities for piracy investigations. It was a change which the MPAA had been pushing for. Early that year Valenti, FSO head Richard Bloeser, and MPAA North American anti-piracy director Mark Kalmonsohn met with FBI director William Sessions and executive assistant director Oliver Revell to discuss anti-piracy enforcement.[78]

One of the most exaggerated estimates came in 1988 when USTR Clayton Yeutter released a report stating that U.S. companies could be losing upwards of $23.8 billion in worldwide sales due to piracy. That figure included lost market shares from bootlegged goods and lost license fees. At the press conference Yeutter was accompanied by Valenti and Jay Berman, head of the Recording Industry Association of America. Each of them claimed their industry lost $1 billion annually. Valenti called piracy the "toxic waste" of the U.S. motion picture industry.[79]

That study released by Yeutter was done by the International Trade Commission (ITC). U.S. companies that responded to the ITC questionnaire numbered 193, with the $23.8 billion figure representing 2.7 percent of all sales in which intellectual property figured. Included in the figure were losses of $6.2 billion in the export of goods and services, $2 billion in royalties, and $9.5 billion of sales of goods and services imported into the U.S. Officials said that if the unsurveyed U.S. companies were factored in, and their loss rate was assumed to be one-quarter of that of the surveyed firms, total U.S. losses could be $41 billion. Assuming the unsurveyed loss rate to be one half would put the total at $61 billion annually, as the number grew more and more bizarre. So exaggerated were the numbers that some participants at a panel on international piracy questioned the report's methodology and expressed concern the ITC numbers were "unsubstantiated estimates by companies that have an incentive to claim serious damage by piracy."[80]

Into the 1990s and the new century, the industry was much less active in generating new solutions to the problem, relying instead on existing tactics. One novel strategy came in 1998 when the MPAA announced it was enlisting the public in its anti-piracy fight. Through December 31 that year, in 33 cinemas in New York City messages appeared on the screens before the films were shown asking audiences to watch for people using camcorders to record the films while they were on the big screen and to report them to the theater management. Tapes from camcorders were duplicated to make usually very poor—but occasionally quite good—copies of movies, which were then sold on street corners, in flea markets, and at similar places. New York City was described as a "hotbed of such activity." Thanks to improvements in technology camcorders were smaller and better than in the past. With regard to the use of camcorders, Valenti said, "They've always been a problem because you don't have to steal something or bribe somebody."[81]

As of 2001, the vast majority of commercial recordings contained coded signals that prevented VCRs from making a clean copy. Those copy protection schemes were different for videotapes and DVDs. An MPAA estimate then was that about 10 percent of the stock in the country's 3,000 video rental outlets was pirated. As in the past, those copy protections systems worked only against the home copyist who joined two VCRs together. They had no effect on commercial pirates who could easily defeat those systems.[82]

Helping out in the anti-piracy effort were many of the state governments. New York Governor Mario Cuomo signed a bill in 1990 that increased the state's penalties for unlawful copying from a misdemeanor to a felony. And in Louisiana Governor Buddy Roemer signed a law that made the unauthorized copying of video and sound recordings a felony. Still, the MPAA sometimes remained critical of government efforts, especially at the federal level. The trade group believed that federal investigators and prosecutors were often too reluctant to take up cases that many of the latter perceived as victimless. Chief MPAA East Coast investigator Ed Murphy declared, "It's a foregone conclusion that the FBI in New York City is not going to get involved in a case against a videostore." But he said they would go after labs where dupes were churned out on sophisticated equipment. The motion picture industry preferred to see pirates pursued under criminal laws "and not only for their greater deterrence factor; in civil cases, the plaintiffs have to foot the bill," noted reporter Max Alexander. Because state laws could not address copyright per se (a federal matter), suits generally fell under the heading of "true name and address" statutes, which required the duplicator of copyrighted product to place his name and address on each cassette. As of 1990, 34 states had such laws—18 of those states treated violations as felonies and the others treated violations as misdemeanors.[83]

A major technological change in the 1990s saw the arrival of the digital video disk (DVD) and the start of its attempt do away with the videotape. Hollywood's attempt to prevent pirates from copying films from

DVDs could be quite elaborate. One effort ran into problems due to America's legal restrictions on the export of encryption technology. Originally the DVDs were to have been launched around the middle of 1996 after a consortium of 10 electronics and entertainment giants, led by Toshiba, Matsushita and Time Warner, had developed the DVD. That consortium promised the Hollywood studios that they would use digital encryption to stop people from pirating copies onto blank disks or videotapes. But the U.S. government classified secure encryption as munitions. So without special dispensation, the export of both DVDs and DVD players would be banned. Encryption in the system was not just designed to prevent piracy; it was also intended to prevent people in one country watching the movie on disk while it was still being shown at the cinema. Films were released first in the U.S. and the tape and DVD often went on sale before the film had finished its run in theaters in, say, Europe. Encryption in the system was designed to prevent the use of disks exported from America to Europe (and elsewhere), even if the copies had been produced legitimately. The encryption split the world into five regions with the disks intended for one region being unplayable on equipment sold in the other four. Digital codes on the disk were scrambled and the player could only unscramble it when two halves of a digital key came together. One half of the key was recorded on the disk along with the movie. The user provided the other half of the key, either entering an authorization code or by inserting a smart card that stored the code. Each of the five regions was to have its own key. An extension of the system blocked analog copying so that people could not successfully connect the analog output of the DVD player to the input on an ordinary VCR.[84]

Philip E. Ross started a 1996 article in the business magazine *Forbes* by saying that film piracy totaled $2 billion a year but that it was "nothing compared with what is in store when movies go digital." Ross acknowledged that reissuing old movies in the new DVD format could generate billions of dollars for Hollywood but that the studios had till then refused to use the new medium because "Hollywood is terrified by the potential for digital piracy." Studio representatives had holed up that summer with people from the consortium previously mentioned to reach a copy protection standard that could thwart casual DVD copying. However, they had not come up with a workable plan. Although the article by Ross was full of pessimism and dire scenarios for Hollywood because of the new DVD technology, he concluded that methods would be found to limit piracy and "that the good guys are going to have the upper hand in the battle over digital property."[85]

Although the five-region plan failed to work, the search for ways to prevent casual copying of DVDs continued. Circuit City Stores (in partnership with other firms) reached licensing pacts in 1997 with the Hollywood majors and makers of DVD players for a technology that would create disposable rental films. Dubbed DIVX, these disks would not play on standard DVD players, only on DIVX players. DIVX-format films were to be sold for $5 each and were coded to allow a 48-hour viewing period from the time the disk was inserted into a player and the machine was turned on. Needless to say, nothing came of this plan.[86]

Five computer and electronics companies—Intel, Hitachi, Toshiba, Sony, and Matsushita—announced in 1998 that they had joined forces to develop and deploy proposed encryption technology to protect digital movies and music from being illegally copied by consumers.[87]

Domestic piracy in the 1990s continued much as it had in the 1980s. In its zeal to stamp out piracy, Hollywood sometimes attacked what seemed to be inappropriate targets. It was a violation of copyright to show a movie outside a private home even if no admission was charged. A person violated federal law if he rented a videotape for a Boy Scout meeting or to cheer up a sick friend in the hospital. Prison wardens had gotten into trouble for renting tapes to show inmates and nursing homes came under fire from Hollywood in 1990 for running videotapes for shut-in seniors. Sparked by complaints from constituents, a couple of U.S. Senators introduced similar bills that would have created a special exemption from the copyright law for nursing homes. Then Representative Bob Kastenmeier (D. Wis.) came up with what he called an "out-of-Congress" solution. He put together an agreement that was signed by all nine member studios of the MPAA and two nursing home associations. Preserving the principle of copyright, each of the associations (acting on behalf of all nursing homes) would make a token payment of $10 to each studio, which the majors would donate to charity. In return the MPAA agreed to allow nursing homes to screen an unlimited number of rental movies over the 10-year life of the pact.[88]

A series of FBI raids in New York and New Jersey in 1990, including private homes and video stores, netted hardware and 2,084 pirated tapes. As many as 30 MPAA investigators assisted the FBI and U.S. marshals with the 12-month probe that led to the raids. Pirated tapes were believed to have been sold to video stores in six states in the northeast. Some 1,500 videocassettes a week were produced in the pirate lab located in Queens.[89]

Over 50,000 tapes of Hollywood movies, along with 348 cassette-duplicating machines, were seized in 1993 in raids on three Fairfax County (Virginia) businesses. Raiders were members of the Asian Organized Crime Task Force, a regional law enforcement group composed of federal and local agents. Pirate tapes were fed to a region-wide network of Asian-owned stores. Losses to the industry from this operation alone were put at $50 million a year by the MPAA. Many of the cassettes seized were in jackets with titles printed in Chinese and Korean. Legitimate videotape copies of movies then cost $60 to $90 each; the bootleg copies were sold to store owners and customers for $20 to $40. An investigation began a year before the raids after police received an anonymous tip about one lab location. That led to months of surveillance, the identification of the other spots, and then the raids.[90]

Westchester County (New York) officials announced in 1994 they had broken up a ring of video pirates who took camcorders into movie theaters, taped such popular summer hits as *The Lion King*, *Speed*, and *The Shadow*, and distributed thousands of what appeared to be professionally packaged videotapes throughout the New York metro area. Although the packaging was slick, the quality of tape was poor, at times containing the sound of audience laughter and at other times showing the on-screen shadows of patrons coming and going. Because the tapes seemed to have been shot from a stable base like a tripod and, perhaps, shot from the angle of a cinema projection room, the police were exploring whether theater employees were involved. Based in Yonkers, the operation was capable of producing 2,200 videocassettes per day, which were sold for $10 each. Vans distributed the tapes to a network of street vendors and video stores throughout the region. Also, the operation made illicit copies of films already released on videotape — these being of high quality. In the Yonkers raid 4,600 cassettes, 200 VCRs, scores of televisions, computers, video casings, a laser printer, a plastic shrink-wrap packaging machine, three vans, and $104,000 in cash were seized. Officials said the $5.50 profit on each tape would yield $4 million a year if the pirates made 2,200 tapes per day. Douglas J. Corrigan, an MPAA spokesman, claimed an operation of that size would cost the Hollywood majors $40 million a year, based on the assumption they would make $55 on each tape.[91]

Federal agents seized a truckload of allegedly counterfeit tapes in Maryland in 1994 and then went after vendors selling them on Washington, D.C., streets. Six people were arrested, one of whom was a street vendor who had previously been issued with a cease and desist order. A total of 26 other street vendors were contacted by federal authorities but were not arrested because a new policy gave vendors of illegal items only a warning at the first violation. If they were found selling illegal items a second time, the vendors were arrested. About 100 tapes were seized from each of the 27 street sellers. Officials were alerted to the problem by Washington merchants who sold and rented legitimate videotapes.[92]

Apparently little changed on the streets of Washington because seven months later law student Ashley Merryman wrote an op-ed piece in the *Washington Post* that was full of righteous indignation. In a single block she saw six street vendors all selling bootleg tapes of movies still running in the cinemas, including *Crimson Tide*, *Apollo 13*, and *Die Hard With a Vengeance*. She first approached a federal cop, but he told her he could not do anything and advised her to call a D.C. Metro cop. Merryman approached one she came across but he also told her he could not do anything about it. "Even though D.C. has one of the worst piracy problems in the nation, according to industry officials, it seems the city has done relatively little to actually address the issue," concluded Merryman.[93]

A police raid on a Brooklyn address and 11 other spots in New York City in June 1996 yielded 100,000 illicit tapes of the latest Hollywood hits such as *The Nutty Professor*, *The Rock*, and *Twister*. Officials alleged the operation was grossing around $500,000 a week. For the first time ever in a piracy case, a New York grand jury indicted this gang on organized crime charges. According to police and MPAA agents, foreign nationals dominated the piracy business in New York with Israelis, Arabs and Dominicans vying for ascendancy in the trade. In addition to the seized tapes, police took 800 VCRs and various other pieces of hardware. Police arrested 35 people, including 30 or so who allegedly duplicated videos around the clock in shifts. This operation charged wholesalers $5 to $6 for each bootleg tape; retailers paid $7 apiece, and customers $10. An anonymous tip to the FBI started the investigation.[94]

Eventually the number of defendants in the 1996 Brooklyn case was six. Two of them fled to Israel. Another also fled but later returned and pled guilty to two felonies but got no jail time. The trial for the remaining three ended in acquittals for two low-level workers and a hung jury for a middle manager. Officials said they would like to see pirates get stiffer punishment but said they doubted that the courts would ever view piracy as a major crime.[95]

In a lengthy article, reporter Linda Lee summarized film piracy in the New York City area in the summer of 1997. *Men in Black* had just opened nationwide, about six weeks after bootleg tapes of the film went on sale on the streets of New York. *Batman and Robin* opened June 20; it was available the same day at a Harlem market for $5. A week before Disney's animated release *Hercules* opened, a bootleg version was on sale. Making it worse was that it had been camcorded from the balcony of the Disney-owned New Amsterdam Theater in New York. "Video piracy is thriving in America, and nowhere more so than in New York," said Lee. Many bootleg videos were surreptitiously copied because camcorders were smuggled into advance screenings. But some came from inside the industry: work copies of films from editing houses, special effects houses, and early test screenings. Said Tom Sherak, chairman of the Fox Domestic Film Group, "Work prints get stolen all the time. Now that we edit on AVID [a computer editing technology widely used in film and television], you can pull it right off. We try to watch it as closely as we can, but you can't watch everything." Using a $500 video camera and a tripod and occasionally making use of the theater's audio jacks for the hearing impaired, a bootlegger "can go to the movies once a week and make $1,000 or more," declared Bill Shannon, head of the MPAA's New York anti-piracy office. "If he makes 30 copies, and sells them for $100 apiece, that's $3,000." Commenting on the MPAA's estimate that the bootlegging of films cost the Hollywood majors over $250 million annually in potential domestic revenue, Lee argued that figure presumed a person buying illicit tapes would have spent $4 to $8 to see the movie in a cinema, "a risky assumption in neighborhoods where there are no first-run theaters." But Lee also stated that no one quarreled with the MPAA's assertion "that New York is the capital of American bootlegging."[96]

When Spike Lee's *Malcolm X* came out in New York in 1992, he took some of his friends, "muscle," he called them, to 125th Street with baseball bats to clean the bootleg copies off the street. "I don't know what's wrong with the African-American consumer in some urban areas," said Spike Lee. "They want to buy an inferior product and get something for a bargain." Bootleg vendors did not set up shop in highly visible areas of Manhattan, wrote Linda Lee. Instead, they sold along Hudson, Canal, and Duane streets in lower Manhattan and out of vans parked on the Upper West Side. They were also found around Fordham Road, at the Grand Concourse Plaza in the Bronx, and on Fulton Street in Brooklyn. The sale of bootleg tapes used to be widespread on 125th Street in Harlem, but by 1997 it was endemic at the Malcolm Shabazz Harlem Market at 116th Street and Lenox. With regard to enforcement, Daniel J. Castleman, chief of the investigation division of the Manhattan District Attorney's Office, complained that the MPAA "would like the police department to do nothing but pick up people for bootleg films. But there are murders and rapes." He added that his office was aware of the economic impact of bootlegging and "We have a terrific relationship with the MPAA. But they want us to solve their problem." When Linda Lee visited the Harlem Market she said the main business seemed to be videotapes. Booths, which vendors, many of them recent immigrants from West Africa, rented for $42 a week, were stocked with the latest Hollywood films. Several of the booths even had video players so customers could check the quality of tapes before making a purchase.

So popular was the site that it became a tourist attraction. Hayim Grant, president of New York Apple Tours, said, "It's not our concern what the vendors sell."[97]

Nine people were arrested and 30,000 illicit cassettes were seized in a 1997 Brooklyn raid. Also confiscated were 500 VCRs and various other pieces of hardware. Bootleg material was turned out at the rate of about two million tapes a year by the lab involved in this operation.[98]

Several months later detectives raided a Manhattan counterfeiting factory where pirates were producing 8,000 tapes a week of current movies and them shipping their product to video stores as far away as West Palm Beach, Florida, Houston, Dallas, and Chicago. Seized were 200 VCRs and over 4,000 videocassettes. Tapes that cost the pirates $2 to produce were sold to stores for $5, and then retailed for $10.[99]

Reporter David Halbfinger declared in 1998 that the counterfeiting of videotapes, "always a low priority for police and prosecutors more concerned with violent crime," was then so rampant in New York City that the MPAA had hired an entire squad of retired city detectives, set them up in the Bronx, bankrolled them with tens of thousands of dollars for paying informers, and sent them out to catch pirates. Philip Castellano, who owned the oldest video rental shop in Brooklyn, said he decided to close his business in January 1998 when he felt he had no choice but to start buying pirated tapes. Steven Scavelli of Flash Distributors, the only video wholesaler based in New York, said his customer list had declined to 800 video stores from 1,500. "Half the stores in New York City are illegitimate, easily," he explained. Desperate to reduce the problem, the MPAA hired William Shannon in January 1997. Top priority for Shannon, a retired New York police lieutenant, was to eliminate the black-market laboratories. Shannon first went out and hired seven retired, veteran detectives from the police department along with five graduates of the John Jay College of Criminal Justice as junior investigators.[100]

They did a lot of surveillance work, built profiles of the video-camera carrying moviegoers who supplied raw material to the pirates, and staked out New York theaters identified as frequent sources of pirated videos. Also, they trained 1,000 New York police officers to spot the telltale signs of a bootleg—blurry fine print, missing bar codes, and so on. Routinely they handed out as much as $2,500 for a good piece of information, a large sum to be paid to informants. "We've got the best-paid informants in town," said Shannon. One operation by this special unit led to a raid by Nassau County Police that seized 30,000 pirated tapes and resulted in the arrest of 39 shopkeepers at 35 video stores. MPAA detective Peter English said of that operation, "All these people are making a killing. They tell us the money's better than selling crack, and it's not dangerous at all." To avoid overloading prosecutors with routine cases the MPAA investigators first tried to use civil measures to eliminate bootleg dealers. In the first two months of 1998 they had sought 'voluntary surrender' of counterfeit tapes from 31 retailers, according to Andy Brogan, another of the MPAA's retired police detectives. "They allow us to cleanse their stock, and in return, we promise not to use it against them as long as they stay straight," Brogan explained. To that point 17 of the 31 had accepted the deal; the others faced civil lawsuits. Video retailers then paid around $75 for a legitimate copy of a movie and rented it for about $3 per time. Dealers buying bootleg tapes paid from $5 to $10 for each one, and rented them for $3 per time. Street peddlers paid about $3 per illicit tape and sold them on the street for about $10 apiece.[101]

Fifteen search warrants executed by the police in 1998 in Brooklyn, the Bronx, and Manhattan netted over 35,000 illicit tapes and resulted in the arrest of 43 people. The investigation, dubbed "Operation Copycat," started four months earlier after MPAA investigators received a tip that a man was selling master tapes of newly released movies. Then the MPAA contacted the police department, which sent out an undercover officer to infiltrate the operation.[102]

Estimates in the 1990s of how much piracy cost the Hollywood majors, like those in the 1980s, were all over the place, but at a higher level. An estimate from the MPAA at the start of 1990 put the worldwide piracy loss at $750 million while a year later journalist Faye Rice cited the MPAA as putting the figure at $1.2 billion annually. Just two months later reporter Thomas McCarroll declared that piracy of movies, books and recordings cost the entertainment industry at least $4 billion yearly.[103]

Writing in 1994, reporter Rex Weiner said the MPEA estimated its member companies, annual losses due to theft of film prints, unauthorized duplication of videocassettes, illegal cable-television taps, and hijacked satellite signals were $2 billion worldwide. In March 1998, Jack Valenti put the worldwide loss at as much as $4 billion a year while in August 2001 the *Wall Street Journal* reported that the MPAA estimated that Hollywood lost about $2.5 billion a year to piracy of all kinds.[104]

Worldwide statistics released by the MPEA revealed that in 1989, 5,726 raids were held in 37 countries and resulted in 659,615 tapes being seized. First time raids were held that year in South Korea, Malaysia, Thailand, and Ecuador. In Europe, 3,755 raids took place and 374,675 tapes seized while the Far East region saw 1,040 raids and 101,010 seized tapes. Latin America was the scene of 353 raids and 66,850 confiscated cassettes while in the Middle East 282 raids were held and 20,633 tapes were seized. Raids in the U.S. and Canada that year numbered 296 and led to the seizure of 96,447 tapes.[105]

During 1990 the MPAA participated in 394 raids in the U.S. and Canada and 180,062 tapes were seized. Of those cases, 241 resulted in civil suits filed by MPAA members while criminal charges were brought against pirates in the other 153 cases. MPAA communications director Mark Harrad reported that his group spent a total of $20 million to fight film piracy in 59 nations. Cities where the most raids occurred in 1990 were: Los Angeles (107 raids), New York City (54), Miami (37), and Chicago (24).[106]

In 1991 a total of 252,184 illicit tapes were seized from raids conducted in the U.S. Three years later, in 1994, the MPAA reported that a record number of pirated tapes had been seized — 425,896 — in American raids. Valenti estimated that in the U.S. market about five to 10 percent of the total videotape stock was pirated.[107]

The industry's worries over DVD piracy seemed to fade away after the disks were finally introduced. Replacing that worry was a fear of what might happen to copyrighted material on the Internet. After Philip Ross pointed out the possible increase in piracy that could result from widespread DVD usage he asked why shouldn't the movie industry be able to survive the DVD. Answering his own question he replied, in 1996, "Because the next stage in this evolution of piracy is the Internet." He was not referring to the slow system then generally available, such as through America Online, but a fast Internet through cable or over fiber optics. Christopher Wolf, intellectual property lawyer in Washington, D.C., commented, "Now, to download *Jurassic Park* with a normal modem would take days and days. But with cable modems it might be possible to do it in as little as an hour."[108]

By early in 1999 reporter Anita Hamilton noted that some 200 websites offered illegal copies of popular movies such as *Saving Private Ryan* and *Shakespeare in Love*, according to the MPAA. Images were often blurred and jerky. While downloading those movies onto your computer was a federal offense, violators were hard to catch. "Online movie piracy is a cancer in the belly of our business," complained Jack Valenti. "It's not a big problem today but it could plant the seeds for the garden of evil." Stealing and posting filmed images online was relatively easy. A pirate could simply take a digital camcorder into a cinema, tape the movie, and then upload the file to his personal computer and website back home. Or he could hook a standard VCR up to his computer and use a video capture card to convert the film to a digital format. DVD movies were more difficult to pirate because the files were encrypted. Several websites then posted legitimate copies of mostly independent films that could be viewed for free. All that was needed was a Web browser and a program such as RealPlayer which was available at each of those film sites.[109]

As 1999 rolled on the fear intensified. Journalist Marc Graser observed that several major movies, such as *The Matrix*, had been downloaded to the Internet but they were on a "Web-based system most Internet users don't recognize or know how to navigate." Those video-quality films could take from 20 minutes to download using a high-speed cable modem to several days with conventional Internet connections. And the files were very large; one movie could take up more than one gigabyte of space. Most PC hard drives held only four gigabytes. Nevertheless, David Anderman, Lucasfilm executive, said the availability of first-run movies on the Internet showed that the threat to the motion picture industry posed by digital piracy was real. In cooperation with the U.S. Department of Justice, the MPAA and Fox, he added, "we are addressing this serious matter head-on, by identifying and pursuing the sources of the infringement much in the same way that the owners of computer viruses are tracked down."[110]

Reporter Steve Wilson declared that digital piracy was made possible by MPEG (Motion Picture Experts Group, the developers of the system), a digital file format for compressing and playing video and audio and which also made it possible to swap video files, including illegally copied versions of current films, over the Internet. Then the digitized files could be played on a computer with MPEG-player software such as Quicktime or Windows Media Player and burned on a recordable disk called a VCD, which could be played on a DVD player. Movies like *Summer of Sam*, *Eyes Wide Shut* and *American Pie* had been made available online within days of their theatrical release. For the most part MPEG pirates were not making money from making movies available on the Internet. Wilson said they did it mainly for "ownership and bragging rights." Video pirates converted their camcorder-made tapes, or "borrowed" preview prints, into MPEG-1 files of 500 to 600 megabytes apiece, which were then compressed and broken up into 15- to 20-megabyte pieces. Still, downloading reportedly could take from two hours to two days, depending on the file size and bandwidth limitations on either end. The MPAA's Internet piracy division had asked Internet service providers to shut down a handful of pirates and was working with the FBI to take further action against others. Richard Taylor, MPAA vice president of public affairs, said that by pursuing those Internet copyright violators his organization intended to "change forever the perception that piracy is a low-risk and high-reward proposition."[111]

By the end of 1999, predictions were that by the following year some 30 million PCs in America were expected to be equipped with DVD-ROM drives, which could play any disk, and 10 million U.S. households were expected to have high-speed Internet access. Thus, said Valenti, the MPAA was bracing for an "avalanche" of Net piracy. Some Hollywood film executives were predicting that DVD and other emerging forms of digital delivery would soon force the majors to schedule global day-and-date openings of a film to combat piracy. In an effort to combat growing worries over digital piracy potential, the MPAA named Bill Hunt to the newly created post of chief technology officer, responsible for coordinating the group's Internet and optical media anti-piracy efforts. But Valenti did admit, "Bear in mind that we don't have broadband access today, so we don't have many movies on the Internet today. Of those that were available, the quality was often poor. Also, just finding them on the Internet could be difficult."[112]

Writing in *Forbes* magazine, also in 1999, John Dvorak vigorously attacked Hollywood and its "crusade" against underground movie fans who traded movies over the Internet. He called it "depressingly stupid" and likened it to the time music publishers tried to go after all the college kids who were using MP3s to trade copies of their favorite songs over the Net, "and lost an opportunity to make more money by failing to capitalize on emerging trends." For Dvorak, that "paranoia-cum-idiocy" went back as far as 1976 when the majors sued Sony over the VCR, convinced it would ruin their business. Instead, of course, it turned into a huge new source of revenue for Hollywood. Why, wondered Dvorak, did anyone bother to download a movie? It saved no money; the cost of disks and time online moved the transaction's total cost well past the price of a rental. He thought it was because people wanted to watch first-run movies and Hollywood did a poor job meeting that demand. First, it created demand by "promoting the hell out of new releases." But then Hollywood failed to deliver the product, in this case DVDs, in a timely fashion. "Hollywood's controlled system of distribution—theater, Pay-Per-View, HBO, rental, TV, syndication—does not cut it anymore," he explained. Dvorak went on to wonder "When was the last time you were threatened with prosecution by a company for trying to get the product it was promoting?" In conclusion he argued, "I guarantee the VHS tape you can pick up for $5 on the corner of Canal and Broadway in Manhattan isn't a bootlegged version of *Birth of a Nation* or *Gone with the Wind*. It's something playing right now in a theater near you."[113]

Jack Valenti authored an op-ed piece in the *New York Times* in June 2000 in which he issued a plea for copyright to be respected. Until then the slow transmission of graphic images had kept the problem confined mainly to audio but "movies are next in line, and their turn won't be long in coming," he worried.[114]

That piece provoked two letters to the editor. Dean Baker, co-director of the Center for Economic and Policy Research, argued there were many ways other than through copyrights to support creative and artistic work. One example he gave was through the use of an individual tax credit. Shari Steele, executive director of the Electronic Frontier Foundation (a digital civil liberties group), attacked Valenti and the MPAA's lawsuits to block the use of software that helped play legally purchased DVDs on PCs. Steele's group saw it as a violation of First Amendment rights.[115]

"Hollywood, your nightmare is here," wrote Lee Gomes in July 2000 in the *Wall Street Journal*. He based his statement on the fact that two new pieces of software allowed digital movies to be stored in much less space than that required just six months earlier. One of the pieces of software was a program called DeCSS, which broke the encryption that was supposed to prevent DVD files from being copied onto a PC in the first place. Several Hollywood majors had started court action to block the spread of DeCSS. The second piece of software was MPEG-4. Nevertheless, Gomes pointed out that most PC owners lacked both of those pieces of software. Both had to be downloaded and then tutorials had to be run in order for users to understand them. Creating a movie on a PC was still a complex and error-prone process that took many hours, at least compared to making a music CD, a relatively simple matter that took only a few minutes.[116]

Motion picture and music companies (totaling over 30) jointed together in July 2000 to sue and shut down the Los Angeles-based web site scour.com. Started by several UCLA students, the site pointed users to multimedia content on the Internet, including films and music, serving like a specific search engine. But the site also included a feature called Scour Exchange, which allowed users to trade movie and music files they kept on their computers. "This lawsuit is about stealing," explained Valenti. "It's a harsh word, but it's the only one that fits the definition." Some of the material traded over this site included first-run movies like *Gladiator*. Up to 25,000 people could be using the site at any given time.[117]

Earlier in 2000, the eight Hollywood majors filed suit under the Digital Millennium Copyright Act (DMCA) against Eric Corley, publisher of the online hacker magazine *2600.com*, for making available on his Web site a computer code that enabled someone to break the encryption system on DVDs. Studios also requested that Corley be forbidden from posting links to other Web sites where the code in question, DeCSS, was available. It was the first test of a 1998 federal law that made it a crime to manufacture or "offer to the public" a way to gain unauthorized access to any copyright-protected work that had been secured by a technology like encryption. That so-called anti-circumvention provision was part of the DMCA.[118]

Federal Judge Lewis A. Kaplan ruled in August 2000 that a web site operator could not distribute a computer program designed to crack codes that prevented the piracy of movies. Kaplan prohibited Corley from posting the program DeCSS then or in the future on his web site and from establishing Internet links with other sites that provided copies of the code.[119]

Under that new law, civil statutory damages for gaining access to a piece of copyrighted material secured by computer code ranged from $200 to $2,500. Criminal penalties included fines of as much as $1 million or 10 years in jail for repeat offenders. Groups like the Association of American Universities and the American Library Association maintained that broad exemptions were necessary to preserve the copyright concept of "fair use." After several hearings and receiving comments from proponents of various kinds of exemptions, however, the U.S. Copyright Office decided none had demonstrated evidence that there would be "substantial harm" if an exemption were not granted. No exemptions were granted.[120]

Within hours of its release to cinemas in the summer of 2001, Fox's *Planet of the Apes* was available on the Web. Internet providers were legally obligated to remove pirated material from web sites they hosted once a copyright holder asked them to do so. When the studios made such requests they usually complied quickly. Sometimes, though, the movie was on an individual's home PC and he used file-sharing programs to make it available. As a result, the movie industry had been asking Internet service providers to terminate the accounts of those found to be offering pirated movies. Fox's legal department sent an e-mail to service providers that said, "We trust that we will be able to count on your prompt action to disable such infringing postings and/or downloads and stop the infringement of our rights." Some service providers felt cutting off individual accounts was going too far, but, reportedly, some Internet service providers had started to suspend accounts of users who had been identified by film studios or recording companies to be trading copyrighted material. The MPAA regularly monitored file-sharing networks and compiled lists of Internet addresses and web sites where infringing material was found. Then the group asked service providers to match the addresses with individual accounts.[121]

Belatedly, some of the Hollywood majors made what they viewed as their own positive response to the Internet demand and problem. Five of the Hollywood majors unveiled plans in August 2001 for a joint venture that would allow computer users to download rental copies of movies over the Internet. Said Yair Landau, president of Sony Pictures Digital Entertainment, "We want to give honest people an honest alternative." Some saw the venture as a first step toward true video-on-demand. Initially, films would be available for downloading only onto PCs or television monitors linked to an Internet connection, but eventually video-on-demand service was expected to include cable television and other delivery systems. Studios involved were MGM, Paramount, Warner, Universal, and Sony (Columbia). Notably absent were Walt Disney and Fox. Each of those said they would announce their own independent video-on-demand service shortly. The first 100 or so films to be made available by the five for their venture were expected to be a mix of recent releases and older features from studio libraries. An average film was here said to be 500 megabytes in digitized form and would take 20 to 40 minutes to download. Only households with high-speed broadband Internet connections would be able to use the system, expected to be ready to launch within a year or two. A film would remain on a computer's hard drive for 30 days at most but would erase itself 24 hours after it was first run. A person could watch the movie as often as he wanted in those 24 hours but could not copy it. The majors used the following order for the release of a new movie: cinema, videocassette/DVD, pay-per-view, pay-cable networks, broadcast networks, and syndication. This order would be maintained with those movies released on the Internet, at least at first, made available when they entered their pay-per-view window, usually months after theatrical release. Landau remarked, "We are not looking to undermine DVD, which is a great business." Valenti added that the announcement confirmed that the Hollywood majors were eager for the Internet to enlarge and flourish. For the first time, he said, "in the very near future, a broad selection of motion pictures will be available online, protected by encryption, and delivered directly to consumers at a reasonable price."[122]

Hollywood's cavalier treatment of the copyrights of others, and its own films, continued in this period although it seemed to draw less mention in the media than in the past. Problems with exhibitors also faded away, perhaps no longer large enough issues to warrant any attention or supplanted by other issues deemed more important. The majors sometimes used bits of music soundtracks from their old films in their new movies without consultation with, or payment to, the American Federation of Musicians (AFM). Cecil F. Read, administrator with the AFM national contracts division, said Hollywood was "on notice" that they could not use any music from a previous source without paying for it because it was a violation of an AFM agreement. Read explained the rule had always been in effect but "the last few years producers interested in nostalgia, have been using lots of old clips. Now we're catching up with them. They got the feeling they could do whatever they want." MGM had to pay the AFM $75,000 for using an old music clip in *That's Entertainment* without consultation or permission while Disney paid $12,000 for a similar violation.[123]

When movies were sold to television, they almost always went to the small screen in packages of varying sizes. United Artists sold one such package to CBS containing 30 films for a total of $16,770,000 with one of the movies, *West Side Story*, having its share of the total set at $365,000 by UA. That caused three people with a financial stake in the movie to bring proceedings against the studio. Leonard Bernstein (who wrote the music), Jerome Robbins (credited with "conceiving" the production), and Stephen Sondheim (the lyricist) complained that UA undervalued the film when making television package sales. Following an 18-month audit and 2½ years of arbitration under the auspices of the American Arbitration Association (AAA), a three-man AAA commercial tribunal held in 1979 that UA's original assessment of the film's share of the 1971 package sale to CBS and a number of foreign licensing deals "was not the fair and reasonable value of the picture in each of those transactions." They valued *West* at $1,250,000 in the CBS package. Overall they put the total amount of the under valuation at $3,859,360. As per the original deal, the three plaintiffs were entitled to 10 percent of the movies post-recoupment distribution gross—$385,936 in this case. UA's method of valuing movies tended to allocate high to low grossing, non-recoupment movies. According to testimony submitted on UA's behalf during arbitration, its allocation methods were used by several other major distributors, including Columbia and Warner Brothers. A lawsuit in 1967 by James Mulvey against Samuel Goldwyn alleged that his five percent interest in a number of Goldwyn movies sold to television was diluted as a result of package sales allocation. After five years of litigation, in 1972, a jury verdict upheld Mulvey's claim, awarding him $348,000. Triple damages brought the final award to $1,044,000. In March 1973, however, by the stipulation of lawyers for both sides (the case was then under appeal), the case was dismissed and an out-of-court settlement was reached, the details of which were not disclosed.[124]

A 1998 article by Tad Friend wrote about the Hollywood studios being then "awash" in copyright suits and why they were so hard to win—for the plaintiffs, that is. Most of those suits were lost, thought Friend, because most copyright plaintiffs overestimated how much protection they had under the law. They also misunderstood how the Hollywood blockbuster got created. Studios, he added, did not make something so original that they'd have to steal it from some genius; "they want to recast familiar stories and have them endlessly rewritten until every star feels his part is juicy enough." Many studios had a philosophy that if something was totally new they would not want to see it. Under federal law, ideas— and most characters—could not be copyrighted. In 1994 Curt Wilson and his partner Donna Douglas sued Walt Disney Pictures because *Sister Act* resembled a script they had earlier submitted to the studio; both stories were about a woman who hid from the mob by disguising herself as a nun. The plaintiffs rejected a $1 million settlement offer from Disney only to have the jury rule against their claim. Said Wilson disgustedly, "They would have had to copy our stuff verbatim for us to prevail."[125]

The highest court obstacle to clear for plaintiffs was that most scripts contained a lot of boilerplate that had no particular author; it consisted of segments that were known legally as "scenes a faire"— defined by the courts in 1978 as "incidents, characters or settings which are as a practical manner indispensable, or at least standard, in the treatment of a given topic." For example, in a script about slavery one might expect to find attempted escapes, chases through the woods with pursuit by dogs, or the sorrowful or happy singing of slaves, among other things. A realistic portrait of a police officer in the South Bronx would of necessity contain drunks, prostitutes, and derelict cars. Copyright lawyer Martin Garbus commented that the people who filed these suits could not afford the $250,000 to $500,000 fight against the Hollywood studios and their insurance companies. The studio' theory was, said Garbus, "that if you spend the money and fight, you'll wear your opponent down and discourage others from suing. It's a successful tactic." Friend added the thought that "The giddiest aspect of copyright suits is how often the studios try to prove that their story was so derivative that they couldn't have stolen it from any one source." Garbus observed, "It's an industry that tries so hard to copy success. You know there are a lot of people out there writing *Wag the Dog II*, and when *Wag the Dog II* comes out everyone's going to sue, saying, 'Hey! That was my idea!'"[126]

Another instance involving film profits concerned well-known humorist Art Buchwald. He and his partner, producer Alain Bernheim, sued Paramount contending the studio's hit *Coming to America* was based on an idea they had sold Paramount in 1983. Paramount insisted the movie was developed from an idea of the film's main star, Eddie Murphy. Los Angeles Superior Court ruled in favor of Buchwald, which meant the pair was entitled, as per the original contract, to 19 percent of the film's net profit. However, Paramount argued the movie had not made any profit despite the fact it had grossed $350 million worldwide. In fact, *Coming to America* had lost $18 million, said the studio. Buchwald challenged that idea in court, arguing the studio's profits were concealed in Paramount's 35 percent distribution fee and 15 percent overhead charge.[127]

Superior Court Judge Harvey Schneider ruled in 1990 that Buchwald and his partner were entitled to compensation as the film had indeed made a profit. Among items in the original contract Schneider found to be "unconscionable" were a 10 percent advertising overhead and a 15 percent overall overhead. He said the advertising expense "bore no relationship to actual costs" while the overall overhead charges "do not even remotely correspond to the actual costs incurred by Paramount." In response to the decision, Paramount's public relations arm released a statement that called the decision "a threat to the free-market system."[128]

A new method of altering films was discovered in this period. The Library of Congress (which had jurisdiction over copyright) ruled in June 1987 that colored versions of black and white movies were eligible for copyright protection as "derivative work" under many circumstances. That decision, issued by Register of Copyrights Ralph Oman, was a victory for companies such as Turner Broadcasting, which was making a large investment in coloring old films for television broadcasting. Although the decision did not address the moral or artistic arguments about the procedure, it was a setback for actors, directors and producers who had opposed coloring on those grounds. Congress had been asked to deal with the question of whether coloring films might be blocked on moral or artistic grounds. An example was Frank Capra's *It's a Wonderful Life*. Hal Roach Studios had made a colored version of that movie, much to the dismay of Capra who wrote, produced and directed it and who regarded the coloring as tampering with a work of art. Representative Richard Gephardt (D. Missouri) had introduced a "moral right" bill that would allow directors and screenwriters to forbid the coloring of their films even if they did not hold copyrights to them. Roach said their cassette of *Life* had sold 25,000 copies at $39.95 although the black and white version was widely available at $9.95. Many prominent filmmakers had been outspoken in their opposition to coloring and saw the ruling as a blow. "Naturally, I think it's a bad decision, and I think it's something the motion picture guilds will fight," said Woody Allen. "It's yet another obstacle to overcome in the battle to protect American movies from mutilation." A brief opposing the granting of new copyright had been filed by the Directors Guild of America. "There is no protection for the motion picture artist, and with the new electronic aids that are becoming available, there is no end to the alterations that can be done," said director Sydney Pollack. "So every time there's a decision that permits material alteration, it's a great disappointment. We're just going to have to keep fighting it."[129]

Testifying at a 1987 Senate subcommittee about colorization, actress Ginger Rogers remarked, "I've learned the hard way that actors have few—if any—rights over the use of our work. And that is why I am here today.

This computerized cartoon coloring is the final indignity. It is the destruction of all I have worked for."[130]

More hearings about colorization were held in Washington in 1990, conducted by the U.S. Copyright Office of the Library of Congress at the request of a subcommittee of the house Judiciary Committee. Roger L. Mayer, president of Turner Entertainment (which had plans to colorize at least 100 black and white movies), said if a director or screenwriter should have any say about whether their pictures could be altered it should be left to individual or collective bargaining, not legislative action. Directors Guild of America counsel Arnold Lutzker conveyed the directors' denunciation of "technological assaults on our film heritage." Although the creative talent lost the battle over coloring films, the public displayed a studied indifference to this "new" product. As a result, colorization faded into obscurity.[131]

The controversial issue of coloring old movies brought the wider concept of moral rights for creative artist back into view again. Among others who testified at hearings about colorization were filmmakers Steven Spielberg and George Lucas, who addressed the wider issue. Both asked Congress to give artists final rights over their works. Spielberg said, "I've seen my first film, *Sugarland Express,* cut down to 76 minutes to fit a television time slot. Right now, I have no right to protest this." Lucas observed that "American law does not protect our painters, sculptors, recording artists, authors or filmmakers from having their life work distorted, and their reputation distorted." He also said, at the end of the 1980s, "The agonies filmmakers have suffered as their work is chopped, tinted and compressed are nothing compared to what technology has in store."[132]

Those creative or moral rights over who was the true author of a film, who had the right to alter it, and so on, became the main concern of a group formed in 1993, Artists Rights Foundation, made up of filmmakers such as Steven Spielberg and Roger Zemeckis. Among other activities, the group spent time lobbying Congress and working for better contracts. An example was the 1995 agreement between the Writers Guild of America and the Association of Motion Picture and Television Producers, which broke some new ground. Under that pact, writers had the right to view and comment on the director's cut of a film before it was screened for the producing company. Still, it was far removed from any true moral rights. Something as basic as the right to "final cut" still eluded almost all Hollywood directors. It was granted to very few, only a tiny handful of the most powerful.[133]

Foreign piracy of American movies intensified and moved to higher levels in the 1975 to 2001 period just as had happened domestically. Fueled by similar factors, the UK was the bad nation for piracy early in the period with China holding that spot at the end.

6

Foreign Piracy, 1975 to 2001

"Cuba never buys U.S. films. It simply copies them, in defiance of U.S. copyright laws, or buys someone else's illicit copies."

David Pauly, 1977

"Not a day goes by that some local [Italian] tv indie [station] fails to air feature-length films illegitimately from a legitimate distributor."

Variety, 1982

"Every video tape being sold in those two parts of the world [Far East and Middle East], with the exception of Japan and Israel, is a bootleg tape."

William Nix, 1986

"The Americans are anxious to protect their own interests, but they don't seem to care a damn about anybody else's."

Yossi Ashmawi, 1995

The increase in domestic piracy from 1975 onwards was matched or exceeded by offshore piracy during the same years. In South Africa, the Budget Film Hire, owned by Isak Vallie, paid Kinekor Films $20,249 in an out-of-court settlement after being charged in the Supreme Court with distributing films for which Kinekor had the exclusive license. Another distributor, Variety Film Hire, was barred by court order from hiring out certain films for which Kinekor had exclusive rights. Included in the list of titles were *Butch Cassidy and the Sundance Kid*, *Hello Dolly*, and *St. Valentine's Day Massacre*.[1]

A U.S. grand jury sitting in New York indicted two men for film piracy, allegedly for illegally shipping 16m prints of major theatrical releases to South Africa between May 1977 and January 1978 (the date of the indictment). One of the accused, David Barnes, pled guilty in New York Federal

Court to some 75 counts of unlawfully shipping films to Johannesburg. During the investigation, authorities said they unearthed several hundred reels of multiple copies of such titles as *Two Minute Warning*, *A Man Called Horse*, *The Island of Dr. Moreau*, *The Other Side of Midnight*, *The Spy Who Loved Me*, *Live and Let Die*, *King Kong*, and *Midnight Cowboy*.[2]

During the middle 1990s, private video-hire clubs flourished in African towns and cities with "no legal control over them whatsoever," according to author Oliver Barlet. In some cases they competed with film distributors in importing U.S. movies. For example, *Jurassic Park* (1993) was widely viewed in Ivory Coast on video before it was released there in the cinemas. It reached only a reported one-third of its potential audience, due to the availability of the pirated item. However, in Nigeria, use of the Nigeria Copyright Council label and substantial policing had restrained piracy appreciably. Back in the 1970s, video cassettes of American films such as *Rocky* and *Towering Inferno* went on sale in Nigeria before the films had been released there theatrically. Policing efforts in South Africa by private operators were reported to have been successful in reducing piracy in that country from 93 percent of the market in 1981 to 17 percent in 1994.[3]

In another part of the world, federal police in Australia seized more than 1,000 pirate videocassettes in a 1982 raid on a business in Newcastle, 100 miles north of Sydney. The raid followed several months of investigation, in response to complaints by the Motion Picture Industry Association of Australia (members included all the U.S. majors plus a few Australian firms. It was essentially a front for the MPAA and was typical of the way the MPAA operated in foreign nations). Operating out of a Newcastle storefront, this operation rented out cassettes to club members for a little less than $10 per time; there was a joining fee of $10. The club had hundreds of members who, on joining, were given a list of legally available cassettes, then later were given a list of pirated cassettes.[4]

A year later Michael Williams-Jones, vice president for UIP (a consortium of four U.S. majors that operated offshore), complained that piracy was the number one problem facing the film industry in Australia. He felt the international media still did not give enough attention to video piracy and that the word "piracy" itself was a misnomer since it had positive and romantic connotations with swashbucklers and Errol Flynn on the high seas. One specific problem he mentioned was that there was often a long delay between the time of a film's U.S. release and its opening in Australia, which provided much opportunity for pirates. For example, *Octopussy* opened in Australia on November 24, 1983, months after the U.S. release. Pirated videocassettes of the film had been widely available for some time. However, Williams-Jones declared it was not possible to overcome that situation by a simultaneous release, although he did not explain why it was not possible. Another problem he mentioned was that very often the Australian media depicted the video pirates as tough local battlers fighting against the multinational American giant.[5]

A series of raids in various Australian cities in 1985 led to arrests and the seizure of pirated cassettes. Ray Stevenson, director of the MPAA-funded Australasian Film and Video Security Office said the police action followed protracted investigations and surveillance by his team. Melbourne resident Victor Luciano was found guilty of unlawful possession of various goods, including 44 cassettes of movies such as *Jaws* and *Rocky II*, sentenced to seven days in jail, fined $A350, and ordered to forfeit the goods. Luciano was not charged with offenses under the copyright act because it contained no provision to jail anyone found in possession of pirated tapes. Instead he was dealt with under the state law of Victoria that did allow judges to jail offenders caught with stolen goods.[6]

Near the end of the 1980s, Steve Howes, regional director of the Australasian Film and Video Security Office, said that video piracy in Australia had declined around five percent to about 15 percent of the market. Howes attributed that decline to increased police activities and to stiffer criminal penalties.[7]

Not surprisingly, Europe was a major area of pirate activity. Major film piracy involving organized crime in Europe was, said reporter Ted Clark, the target of a sweeping security operation by the Motion Picture Export Association (MPEA—an arm of the MPAA) in 1977. An unnamed MPEA executive said the piracy had reached "very serious proportions" and that the newly discovered involvement of organized crime was "scary." Laboratories capable of processing 35, 16, and 8m film and videotape were shipping illegal material into some African and Middle Eastern countries. Also involved in the security operation was the Paris-based International Federation of Film Producers' Association (IFFPA), which had noted that protective legislation in the nations involved varied "from totally useless to severely limited. It is impossible to institute criminal proceedings for film piracy in many areas, and civil court action can only lead to small fines in many cases." Both the IFFPA and the MPEA intended to pressure UNESCO, the European Economic Commission, and other international bodies to press member states to provide legal recourse against film pirates. IFFPA general secretary Alphonse Brisson said the involvement of organized crime had led to courts and police forces taking an active interest in piracy suppression, whereas before there had been little interest in aiding the film business. According to the MPEA, prints used by pirates came from dishonest projectionists, from thefts of films in transit, and from some small laboratories. Traffic in illicit material was especially heavy between European nations and their former colonies. As well, there were television stations "shamelessly" shopping on the black market for movies and "flagrantly" telecasting them.[8]

Interpol, the international police liaison organization, was also reported to be ready to move in on the pirate gangs then "pillaging" the motion picture industry. The planning of action against film piracy had been formally put on the agenda of the next Interpol general assembly. Meanwhile, the security offensive launched by the MPEA in conjunction with the IFFPA was boasting of its first success. One gang of pirates who had engaged in systematic thievery in Europe for some time, and who had "solid links" with mob elements had been put "on the run," although no specific details were provided.[9]

Italy's Minister of the Interior, Francesco Cossiga, ordered the Italian head of Interpol, Romeo Iola, to help coordinate the international campaign against film piracy in close association with the Italian motion picture industry. At a prior point in time Iola had met with Maurice Pequignot, an ex-senior officer of the French police in charge of the MPEA's European office in Paris for international film security. One example of what was happening in Italy was the illegal sale of a videotape of a recent Italian feature to a Yugoslavian border television station. After the telecast, which was beamed to Italy, the producer took his complaint to the authorities and also brought suit. The worst offenders in Italian film piracy were said to be the private television station operators who were surviving almost entirely on film programs. They were big customers for bootleg pictures.[10]

At its meeting in September 1977, Interpol unanimously adopted a resolution designed to combat motion picture and sound recording piracy. That resolution called on police forces around the world — the police agency had more than 125 member nations— to cooperate fully in the fight to stamp out piracy. It also called for increased government awareness of the seriousness of piracy, adoption and enforcement of appropriate national legislation against piracy, and adherence to international copyright convention. MPAA head Jack Valenti hailed the Interpol action as "a tremendous step forward in preventing piracy and prosecuting pirates wherever they may be found." However, the agency's statements proved to be little more than vague generalities as nothing more was reported about Interpol's active involvement in film piracy.[11]

The hottest films on the black market in France were the illegal video versions of *Star Wars* and *Rocky*, selling in black and white for home viewing with prints of the illegal copies costing from $300 to $600. In Italy, some of the private television stations were showing movies so new that they had not yet reached Italian cinemas.[12]

Maurice Pequignot's MPEA office, working in conjunction with the UK distributors' group, the Kinematograph Renters' Society, had some success by 1978 in a crackdown on piracy, according to reporter Ted Clark. A seizure of pirated film in Holland resulted from MPEA investigations while the UK organization took successful legal moves to stop the showing of a video copy of *Saturday Night Fever* in northern Ireland before the movie opened in the territory. Highly publicized films opened later in Europe than they did in the U.S., thus provoking, wrote Clark, "unsatisfied demand" in Europe.[13]

By the end of the 1970s, Clark reported substantial progress had been made in Europe in reducing the problem. Police action had taken place in France, Holland, Sweden, Switzerland, West Germany, Italy, and Belgium. One successful action in Turkey shut down an illicit operation that had posters out for the theatrical release of *Grease*. Major obstacles included that in some countries the authorities sometimes showed little enthusiasm for pressing charges. The MPAA, through the International Federation of Film Producers' Association, was pushing justice ministers in different nations to be more vigorous in their piracy prosecutions.[14]

In one of those actions, 15 people were indicted for film piracy after a seven-month investigation across Italy. Raids took place in both Rome and Milan. Those indicted were accused of reproducing 35m film onto super 8 tracks for sale on the black market. Private television stations, which mushroomed throughout Italy after a 1976 high court ruling sanctioning local broadcasting, had been, and remained, the primary market for pirated pictures. Those stations programmed a combined total of over 400 movies each week. Titles associated with the 15 accused included *Close Encounters of the Third Kind*, *Saturday Night Fever*, *Jaws 2*, *Star Wars*, and all of Walt Disney's full-length features.[15]

Another action saw two men arrested in Stockholm with the police believing they had broken up a major ring. An illicit catalog with 534 features listed was also confiscated by the police. One retailer alone was alleged to have sold at least 1,000 pirate copies in the previous year, due to the introduction of video recorders to the domestic market. About 20,000 VCR units were sold in the first few months. One of the hottest pirate titles in Sweden was *Up in Smoke*, which began circulating about a month before its theatrical premier in Stockholm. *Superman* was being sold in at least three different illegal versions: with an uncensored English soundtrack, uncensored with Swedish subtitles, and censored with Swedish subtitles.[16]

Yet, just six months later as 1980 began, journalist Hazel Guild wrote a panic-type article about the huge amount of pirating in Europe. America's latest hit films were available on cassette in Germany for about $110—some were so recent they had not yet had their theatrical releases in Europe. Pictures like *Rocky II*, *Alien* and the James Bond films sold briskly in pirated cassettes. Many were already in dubbed German renditions. James Bouras and Marc Spiegel, vice presidents of the MPAA and MPEA, respectively, had just made a trip through Europe, "to survey the shocking situation." As Bouras saw it, three conditions were usually involved in film pirating: 1) the practice often occurred in a nation that either had no television or minimal television; 2) it happened in countries with considerable wealth; 3) there were relatively few recreational alternatives. Using those guidelines, Bouras felt there was heavy piracy in the Middle East, South Africa, the China Sea area, the Caribbean, Venezuela, and Europe. In Germany, reported Guild, in having conversations with record shop sales people, one was regularly offered under-the-counter deals on pirated videocassettes. Ads in video publications and in mass circulation newspapers offered lists of movie titles, which included pirated material. One print list that was widely circulated in Germany had 60 current film titles, all illicit. Former police officers were then working for the MPAA and/or MPEA in their offices in Hong Kong, Rome, and Paris.[17]

Throughout the 1980s much of the attention devoted to piracy focused on the UK. A 1982 article detailed how pervasive the problem was. Nik Powell, owner of one of London's largest retail outlets, pointed out that only 10 percent of the UK population went to the cinema and observed that "The trouble is that film men control homevid product and are reluctant to release titles simultaneously [with theatrical release]. But if they won't meet the demand for new films on cassette, the pirates most certainly will." Reporter Bert Baker estimated that pirates reduced the take from legitimate distributors' revenue by $200 million and also took an amount four times as large as that from the revenue of the legal export of tapes from London. The Society of Film Distributors estimated 50 percent of legitimate cassette dealers were handling pirated titles as well. Prints for duping were usually obtained by means of payment ranging from $900 to as much as $9,000 to projectionists and others in the film industry for the loan of a print for a short period of time. In the UK the motion picture industry was said to initiate around 20 civil court actions per week against dealers caught with illegal items.[18]

E. T. The Extra-Terrestrial opened in London theaters on December 9, 1982, yet by the end of August 1982, bootleg videocassettes of the Universal hit movie were readily available throughout Britain. Illicit tapes of *E. T.* rented for as little as 80 cents per night. Some legitimate videocassette retail rental outlets had shut down, complaining they had been driven out of business by competition from pirates. In just one year the number of those outlets increased from 5,000 to 25,000. Copyright infringement could only be prosecuted as a civil offense under British law until a recent amendment in the case of cassettes. But even so, criminal prosecution of tape pirates provided a maximum penalty of an $88 fine for a first offense, with a maximum of two months imprisonment for the second offense.[19]

After a nine-month investigation in 1982, raids on 14 premises between London and the north of England resulted in the seizure of 16,000 allegedly illegal videocassettes. Britain's home video industry then had over $1.7 million in civil prosecutions pending against copyright violators. So widespread was the problem that the MPAA, the British Videogram Association and the Society of Film Distributors cooperated to the extent that a joint investigative body was formed—FACT (Federation Against Copyright Theft).[20]

FACT was based in London and was led by former Scotland Yard official Robert Birch. Jack Valenti had traveled to London to assist in setting up the organization. Thanks to the low penalties and big rewards involved in piracy, declared an account, "nowhere is piracy more virulent at the moment than in Britain." Some estimates put the pirate take at more than $150 million in retail, or around 40 to 50 percent of the home video market, while their take from exporting the illegal tapes was put as high as $170 million annually. Financing for FACT was started with a fund of $1 million, half from the MPAA and the remainder from major UK theatrical and cassette distributors. While he was in England, Valenti met with Home Secretary William Whitelaw and trade under-secretary Iain Sproat who, he said, both gave FACT their full support and promised to use their influence with fellow lawmakers in Parliament in an effort to get stiffer penalties for piracy.[21]

As 1983 began, Britain was described in one source as the "world center of homevideo piracy." Mat Mullern, of the Swedish law firm Adolf Ohmans Advokatbyra, claimed that over 50 percent of the illegal cassettes seized by his country's police came from the UK. The British Videogram Association declared that 70 percent of the pre-recorded cassette market in the UK was illegal while Steve Barnard, head of RCA/Columbia Video (UK), said the latest industry estimate put piracy at 80 percent of the total cassette market.[22]

As an example of the startling growth in the industry, FACT head Robert Birch observed that expenditures on videocassettes in 1982 were approximately $320 million whereas the expenditure in 1979 was virtually zero. According to Birch, estimates of the share of that market going to pirates ranged from a low of 30 percent to a high of 75 percent "but I think it is reasonable to take 40% as an appropriate figure as related to piracy within Great Britain." He added, "Unfortunately, Britain at the moment has the justified reputation of being the major world exporter of pirated cassettes. These have been found on a large scale in Sweden, Denmark, Norway, the Netherlands, Israel, Middle East, Australia, South Africa, Hong Kong and Singapore." As to why Britain had become such a major center of pirate activity Birch believed several factors were involved: the country had extensive and sophisticated duping equipment; Britain was the first country that used the PAL format in which 35m theatrical prints were available and the first PAL country in which videocassettes were released; it was an English-speaking nation; and criminal penalties were ridiculously light. Because of that, and other factors, police, especially in London, devoted very little of their resources to the campaign against video piracy, said Birch. Formed to take over from the trade organizations all investigative activities involving copyright infringement, FACT also campaigned for amendments to the Copyright Act and for the education of the public and retailers. Birch felt the best way to try and eliminate a pirate then was through the use of a civil action.[23]

By early 1983 British film and television producers claimed that bootlegging accounted for at least half of the country's $400 million pre-recorded video market. Scotland Yard was reported to have acknowledged privately that the crime was not worth policing.[24]

Later that same year FACT set a task force of former Scotland Yard detectives led by Peter Duffy, who once headed the Yard's fraud and anti-terrorist squads, on the trail of pirates. Norman Abbot, general secretary of the British Videogram Association, declared that 70 percent of the 6.7 million pre-recorded cassettes then circulating in Britain were illegal copies— the comparable America figure was put at 10 percent. FACT was trying then to develop a "spoiler mechanism" that would not interfere with viewing, but would prevent taping. Thorn-EMI, a major UK distributor that lost an estimated $30 million in business to pirates in the previous year, said that bootleggers had neutralized its anti-duplication device within a month of its introduction.[25]

All the lobbying by the industry paid off because in 1983 the UK Copyright Act was revised and the "ludicrously" small penalties were replaced by hefty fines and prison sentences of up to two years. By early in 1985 those changes had produced dramatic results, according to Peter Duffy, who estimated the level of UK piracy had been cut back from 60 percent of the total in 1983 to 35 percent and then down to 20 percent. He thought retailers had too much to lose under the new copyright law. When FACT visited 19 videocassette rental outlets in East London, considered a prime area for piracy, in 1984, the organization found just 72 pirate copies. One year earlier the figure would have been 10 times that amount, Duffy explained. For 1985 the member companies provided FACT with a budget of $922,000, which was then increased to around $1.23 million by cash recovered from pirates through the courts. What was then happening was that the British home video market was hit by pirate tapes of movies such as *Scarface* and *Ghostbusters* coming in from the U.S. and the Far East, many with Thai or Chinese subtitles. Duffy said the last film to be pirated from a UK theatrical print was *Superman III* in August 1983, some 17 months earlier.[26]

The coding of theatrical prints with an unseen unique identification number (a technology that was widely used by the producers by the 1980s) allowed FACT to isolate three key cinemas as sources of pirated copies. A stakeout led to a clandestine laboratory and the cracking of a network of projectionists and cinema managers in league with the pirates.[27]

In the first prosecution of its type in the UK, a video pirate who used his satellite dish to tape movies for sale and rent was found guilty of contravening the Copyright Act and the Video Recording Act in 1987 in the town of Huddersfield. Raymond Starkey pled guilty to all 10 counts. He was fined $3,200 and had his four VCRs, 623 cassettes and satellite dish confiscated. Duffy said he was delighted the court had taken such a serious view of the case. By this time the UK was no longer much of a pirating problem, certainly not as a producer of illicit tapes.[28]

A full decade later it was reported that Glasgow, Scotland, customs officials arrested two men in possession of *Men In Black*, which was still a few days away from its American cinema opening, and a month more before the picture was due to open in Scotland. The pair had gotten off a flight from New York, where they had bought the copies from a street vender. Soon thereafter the seller was arrested and 520 cassettes seized. MPAA spokeswoman Marisa Pickar said the anti-piracy unit in Scotland had been tailing the two men for several months after noticing a higher than normal number of pirated cassettes circulating in Scotland. According to Pickar, the pair traveled back and forth to New York all the time. Working with customs officials, the MPAA helped capture the suspects who were believed to be couriers for a Glasgow video pirate.[29]

Piracy was said to be still flourishing in Italy in 1982 with not a day passing that some local television station failed to broadcast an illicit movie. Nor was it easy, said a journalist, to find a film rental store that did not keep at least a drawer of pirated videocassettes for sale to clients "on special requests." When a distributor's legal representative and a police squad paid an unexpected visit to Rome television station GBR, the outlet was caught in the act of telecasting a film for which they had no authorization. Also, the station's library contained "hundreds" of illegal videocassettes. According to Enrico De Santis, a lawyer involved in prosecuting all forms of film piracy, almost all Italian commercial television stations had violated the legal codes during the previous year by airing illicit features. Although habitual offenders were more likely to be small stations in the provinces, the larger ones and the commercial networks were not blameless. Of a list of 42 television distributors then active, De Santis maintained "at least half pass unauthorized films." Damage suits for piracy, before civil magistrates, were so backed up they could take up to five years to resolve.[30]

Umberto Virri, managing director of Italy's Crezioni Walt Disney, said that the total revenue for the Italian videocassette industry in 1986 was $61 million, and the pirates did at least that well. Other industry observers also said the market was divided about 50/50 between legal and illegal parts of the business. As in other areas, one reason given for the high rate of piracy was the slow release policy. One home video executive said major Hollywood movies such as *Platoon* and *Out of Africa* routinely showed up in Italy on pirate cassettes months before they were released there theatrically. In Rome a videocassette retailer noted piracy was widespread and that many dealers felt they had to have a supply of pirated first run movies to keep their customers happy. "If you don't, the customer just goes somewhere else." Although Italian law provided up to a three-year prison term and a maximum $4,600 fine for piracy, those who got caught often got off with a suspended sentence or no more than a few months in prison. Authorities seized about 65,000 pirate tapes in Italy in the first half of 1987, compared to a total of 79,000 in all of 1986. The video window (the amount of time between a movie's theatrical release and its video release in a specific country) dropped from 12 months to nine months in 1986 but was still felt to be too long. However, exhibitors were adamant it not be lowered any more.[31]

When Walid Nasser, MPAA's anti-piracy counsel, was posted to Italy in late 1985 he estimated pirates had a 60–70 percent share of the videotape market. When new legislation setting the above mentioned stiffer penalties was enacted not long after Nasser's posting, the pirates' share was said to have fallen to about 40 percent of 1987's $250 million gross revenue for the industry. Italy's new Federation Against Audiovisual Piracy, made up of various groups, including the MPAA, was formed early in 1988.[32]

Reporter Heidi Klaimitz argued in 1995 that little had changed, that piracy was still the Italian film industry's major enemy. Her estimate was that illegal sales accounted for 40 percent of the market, costing the industry $312 million and the government $75 million in lost tax revenue. Some 80 percent of videocassette outlets were thought to be involved in some form of illicit activity. This was in spite of the fact that FAPAV (the Italian anti-piracy federation) had been in the forefront in the battle against piracy since 1988. "Operation Hollywood" in northern Italy nabbed 17,000 cassettes and brought charges against 78 individuals. Raids during one week netted over 1,400 VCRs, 15,000 cassettes, and 571 masters. In 1994 alone, law enforcement agencies confiscated almost 700,000 illegal cassettes and preferred charges against 6,400 individuals.[33]

A tremendous market for pirated goods was said to exist in Italy in 1997, rivaling those in countries such as Taiwan and Thailand. Estimates put the size of the illegal market there at $6 billion a year (including products like watches, designer clothes, accessories, and so on). The U.S. Trade Representative's office kept Italy on its watch list at that time—a formal notification of Washington's displeasure that could lead to economic sanctions if trade offenses were not addressed. Deputy U.S. Trade Representative Charlene Barshefsky urged Italy to stiffen its copyright infringement penalties, which she said were "among the lowest in Europe." Italy's maximum penalty was three years in prison and/or a fine of $4,000, compared with five years and an unlimited fine in Germany and six years and $77,000 in Spain. According to the European Brands Association the worst industrial pirates in 1995 (rankings were based on weak laws, inadequate enforcement and the degree to which well organized piracy networks existed) were: 1) Turkey, 2) China, 3) Thailand, 4) Italy, and 5) Colombia. MPAA figures put the lost revenue from piracy to the Hollywood motion picture industry in 1995 at: Russia $312 million; Italy $294 million; China $124 million; Britain $112 million; and Japan $108 million.[34]

When reporter Hazel Guild surveyed the situation in West Germany in 1983 she painted it as exceptionally bleak for Hollywood. Pirated cassettes of *E. T.* (in English with German subtitles) were available there before the movie opened in German cinemas. While distributors supposedly kept tight control over the 250 prints dubbed in German, it took just five weeks after the premier before it was possible to buy illicit German-language tapes of the picture. "Right now, insiders estimate, pirated cassettes in this country are capturing twice as much income as the legally-made copies," said Guild. Statistics compiled by Manfred Goeller, general manager of the Association of Film Distributors (AFD—Germany) indicated that in the period between 1979, when a crackdown on pirated tapes first started, and the end of 1982, 93,258 illegal cassettes were seized by the authorities.

Some 927 legal processes against alleged pirates were started by the state attorneys— many at the urging of the AFD — during that period. Yet only 32 had been found guilty, with prison sentences ranging from six months to 10 months and total fines of over $100,000 handed out. Also, in 1982, eight lawsuits were brought against operators of discos or restaurants for illegally showing the pirated cassettes in public. When a U.S. or German hit film appeared in cinemas there it was often only a matter of days until the illegal cassettes were on the market, reported Guild. And for a successful movie, pirates could sell as many as 7,000 tapes. So serious was the situation reported to be that a recent German television program dealt with the problem, addressing the two million VCR owners there and urging them to be sure they were buying only legal videocassettes.[35]

The biggest crackdown against pirated tapes in European history took place in Germany in 1985. It netted the four ringleaders in the $20 million-a-year operation, with simultaneous police action in 45 German cities seizing 15 truckloads of illegal material, including 1,500 35m films, thousands of pre-recorded and blank cassettes, and copying equipment. Prints were "borrowed" from theaters in Europe to make dupes by paying off personnel. Participating in the raids were eight representatives from the GVU, the organization that discovered the ring after many months of investigation. Set up in December 1984, the GVU was founded by the MPAA, the German Association of Film Distributors and the German Video Association.[36]

What were called the first energetic steps to combat video piracy in Spain were taken in 1983. One estimate was that video theft in Spain in 1982 generated revenue of $714 million, five times the amount taken legally. A new Spanish decree had two key elements. One was that henceforth all cassettes were required to have a certificate of age classification, such as theatrical films were given by the Culture Ministry. Those certificates were only issued to distributors who could prove they had the legal rights to handle the items. The second key provision was that all sites where films on video were screened, such as taverns, pubs, and private auditoriums, henceforth had to comply with the standards and regulations applied to film theaters. Violators were subject to fines of as much as $15,000 and the closing of their establishment.[37]

In France in 1983, Culture Minister Jack Lang announced the creation of a permanent committee at the National Cinema Centre in Paris to lead the anti-piracy campaign there. That announcement came a few months after Lang had met in Paris with MPAA president Jack Valenti and vice president S. Frederick Gronich. Also, Lang said he would try to mobilize European action against international piracy and that any proposals he came up with would be coordinated with the U.S. industry's anti-piracy office in Paris.[38]

French police and the Assn. de la Lutte Anti-Piraterie (ALPA) raided a pair of film labs and a theater in the Paris area in 1987, making eight arrests and seizing 2,500 illegally duped tapes. Also seized were 500 video masters, 20 VCRs, and various other items of hardware, according to the MPAA. Action came after a seven-month investigation that was initiated by the MPAA-linked ALPA. Those arrested were charged with breaking copyright laws and faced sentences of three months to two years and/or fines of $1,000 to $18,000 if convicted. Some of the suspects had been previously convicted of the same offense and therefore faced a doubling of those penalties if they were found guilty again.[39]

Europe's audiovisual industry organizations united in 1999 in an unprecedented coalition to propose a four-point anti-piracy plan to the European Union (EU). One of the five industry bodies pushing for the implementation of the plan was the MPA. (The MPAA's foreign lobby arm, the Motion Picture Export Association, MPEA, was renamed the Motion Picture Association, MPA, in 1994.) Firstly, the proposal called for more cooperation between the law enforcement agencies of the 15 EU member states along with stronger and more unified penalties for intellectual property theft. Secondly, it called for the regulation and licensing of all CD and video manufacturing plants. Thirdly it would require the embedding of a source identification code in each product. Fourthly, the proposal called for the EU to tie the entry of a new country into the EU with its protection of intellectual property rights. Piracy, for example, was then rampant in Hungary, Poland, and the Czech Republic, all of which aspired to become EU members.[40]

In Russia, in 1988, it was reported that most videos and films available were pirated copies. Walt Disney was then waging a consumer campaign by holding a film festival as part of its effort to win greater copyright protection.[41]

To protest the unauthorized copying of films onto videocassettes in the Soviet Union, the Hollywood majors agreed in 1991 not to license any more films for showing there. Jack Valenti made the announcement and observed that the illegal copying of movies in the Soviet Union "seems to be beyond any perimeters. There doesn't seem to be anything done about it." Valenti sent a letter to a senior Soviet official demanding tougher laws and better enforcement of existing ones. Soviet officials blamed the problem on the results of private initiatives, all hard to control. However, Valenti said that many of the movie houses that screened illegal copies were run by local government agencies and that the state-owned television had recently aired two Arnold Schwarzenegger pictures without permission from the American studios. Private film parlors showed bootlegged U.S. films for profit while many cinemas in the Soviet Union sold tickets to screenings of illegal videotapes. Said Michael Williams-Jones, distribution executive for a firm that handled Paramount, Universal and MGM product offshore, "they charge people to come in and sit in chairs in the lobby and watch pirated videocassettes." An American studio executive who had recently visited a state-owned cinema in Moscow found videocassettes of *Gone with the Wind* and *Rain Man* being shown in the lobby to paying audiences, explained Valenti. He thought enforcing anti-piracy measures in the Soviet Union should not be difficult: "This is easy. You have a police force. There is a court system in place. There are prosecutors in place."[42]

Some 18 months later, the Hollywood majors decided to lift their embargo on supplying film product to the former Soviet Union. Reportedly, the ban was lifted because the government of two of the biggest republics in the old Soviet Union, Russia and Ukraine, were poised to introduce "effective" copyright legislation.[43]

Yet in 1995, for a little more than $2 each, shoppers at a huge outdoor software and video market in Moscow could choose among *Pulp Fiction*, *Forrest Gump*, *Nell* and many other titles that were not even then available in the U.S. Journalist Michael Specter observed that "there is still no genuine functioning legal system. Intellectual property is a vague, emerging concept that few understand and fewer care about. Copyright laws are flouted brazenly here, and there is almost no film, book, compact disc or computer software that cannot be found for a fraction of what it would cost in the United States." Svetlana Abromovna, senior researcher at the Institute of Civil Law in Moscow who had studied intellectual property rights for 30 years, remarked, "There is a law against this kind of theft, but there are many laws in Russia that nobody takes seriously. There are no penalties." Specter added that nearly every kiosk, stall, store or market in the city sold videocassettes, CDs and computer software at low prices. Approximately 98 percent of those items were thought to be pirated. Steven Metalitz, vice president of the International Intellectual Property Alliance, said, "I think it's worse there now than anywhere in the world." His organization estimated U.S. firms lost nearly $1 billion in revenue (on all items) to Russian pirates. He added, "China and other Asian countries are now finally cleaning up their acts, but it seems like Russia is going in another direction." At that big outdoor market, *Schindler's List*, dubbed in Russian, went for $3. As with most of the dubbed movies, though, one Russian actor recorded all the parts. A Microsoft CD-ROM, Professional Office

Suite, was available at the market for $11—that same week the program was selling in Manhattan for $599.98 at Egghead Software. Late in the previous year, 1994, Russia had signed the Berne Convention but copyright violations were still civil offenses, not then covered by criminal law.[44]

After a series of meetings in 1997 between Russian government leaders and U.S. film industry representatives, Russia promised a higher level of diligence and enforcement in the copyright area. Valenti, chairman and CEO of the Motion Picture Association of America, met with Russian Prime Minister Victor Chernomydrin and other senior government officials. According to Valenti, the result of the talks would be a new commitment to copyright enforcement from Russia's leadership. "I have been negotiating with foreign countries for more than 30 years, and I can't think of a more historic moment than my meeting, lasting for more than 45 minutes with Russian Prime Minister Chernomydrin," boasted Valenti. Russia promised to establish a special unit under the Russian Ministry of the Interior dedicated to fight piracy in the near future. Both the MPA and the FBI had plans to be involved in the set up and training of that unit. One day after his meeting with Chernomydrin, Valenti met with Russia's ministers of the Interior and Justice, as well as with the country's top federal prosecutor. Valenti called Russia's copyright laws acceptable, but enforcement of those measures unacceptable. As of January 1, 1997, copyright infringement was punishable under the country's criminal code. Pirated video in Russia was then said to have about 80 percent of the total market.[45]

In neighboring Poland, pirates were said to be plying their trade "everywhere" in 1991. It was so bad that U.S. Secretary of Commerce Robert A. Mosbacher warned the Polish government in October of that year that until something was done about the pirates, Poland could not count on American investment or trade. An estimated 60 percent of the tapes rented in Poland were pirated, according to Rapid Associates, an organization of Polish authors, producers and distributors. The group had been authorized by the Polish government to investigate and levy fines against video shop owners who rented pirate tapes. Rapid president Krzysztof Teodor Teoplitz said, "The argument that we hear from the pirates is that they are helping the Polish population to make contact with the cultures of the world." In Polish parliamentary elections in 1991, there was a political party that stood in favor of piracy. The platform of Party V—whose members owned VCRs—declared that all cultural goods were the property of the people. To change such thinking Rapid had hired private investigators who checked out video shops in search of illicit cassettes. When they found fakes, the investigators flashed an ID stamped with the insignia of the Polish Interior Ministry and invited the shopkeepers to come down to Rapid's headquarters. "We have negotiations daily with about 30 or more pirates," said Teoplitz. For a tape of a popular film, Rapid estimated the pirate should pay about $200 for every six-month period the illegal tape was in circulation to the person who held the legal license. But if the pirate did not wish to pay, he faced no criminal penalty. Under existing Polish law, the only recourse for a licensed distributor was to file a civil suit. In the wake of Mosbacher's rebuke, Polish Prime Minister Jan Krzysztof Bielecki promised to appoint a team of experts to adapt Polish copyright law to "international standards." The popular computer software program World Perfect 5.1 then sold for about $250 in America and for $6 in Warsaw. Not everyone felt that people in Eastern Europe should be forced to pay Western prices for intellectual property. Stanislaw Kern, executive at Warsaw retailer Hektor Computer, explained, "The average Pole earns about one-tenth what the average American earns. So the prices of software should come down by a factor of ten."[46]

Toward the end of 1992 the Motion Picture Export Association (MPEA) sent two officials to Warsaw in hopes of initiating moves for an industry-wide organization to combat piracy in Poland — said to have the most flagrant home video piracy and illegal television and cable operations in Eastern Europe. Partly that was due to the Polish government being "notoriously" slow in carrying out promised copyright reforms. Tim Kuik, MPEA regional director for European and African anti-piracy operations, contrasted Poland with Hungary, the Czech Republic, Slovakia, and the former East Germany, all of which had anti-piracy organizations supported by the MPEA. "One of our tasks is to encourage a change of mentality. For people in the former Eastern bloc, piracy has been the best way of keeping in touch with Western culture," said Kuik. "So, many people don't understand that it's wrong to copy and distribute cassettes." An operation in Hungary initiated by the MPEA-backed ASVA Foundation netted 13,000 illicit cassettes. About 1,000 court cases were then pending against alleged pirates in the Czech Republic. Penalties, though, were small. The maximum fine in Hungary was $150. Kuik estimated pirates controlled as much as 95 percent of the video market in the former Yugoslavia, 85 percent in Hungary and Poland, and perhaps 50 percent in the Czech Republic.[47]

Three years after the fall of Communism Eastern Europe was a far cry from the distributor's dream some had expected. "The bottom line is not as lucrative as we had originally hoped," said Gary Hodes, Warner director of European sales. "We have revised our expectations and abandoned hopes of turning those markets into another Austria, Switzerland or Norway." One or two weeks after the theatrical release of U.S. blockbusters in Hungary, pirated copies appeared in video stores. In Poland, illicit cassettes frequently were available weeks before theatrical release of the 35m prints. Hodes added that "we're not abandoning [any territory] because, if we did, we would never recover it from the pirates." Video pirates, though, were said to be in decline in the Czech Republic and in Slovakia. "Two years ago we were flooded with [pirate] cassettes," said Michael Malek, of the distributor Interama. That had slowed to a "trickle," he noted, since all the Hollywood majors then released product theatrically and on video. And while cassettes of *Under Siege* and *Universal Soldier* "surfaced soon after their U.S. theatrical debut," the quality was so poor (recorded by video cameras in cinemas, Malek believed) they did not find many buyers. In Hungary, George Mihaly, co-managing director of distributor Intercom, said pirate tapes appeared a week or two after the films premiered theatrically. He had no proof but suspected that copies were made from 35m prints obtained from projectionists.[48]

In the Middle East, the MPAA and United Artists achieved a significant victory when a Turkish court, for the first time, confirmed in 1987 that U.S. studios had a right to obtain copyright protection for their films in the Turkish marketplace. That ruling was handed down in Istanbul against Sistem Video, accused of advertising and distributing pirated tapes of UA's *Rocky IV* before its theatrical release in Turkey. In ruling against Sistem, the court cited Turkey's status as a signatory to the Berne Convention and a new Turkish copyright law that took effect in 1987. MPAA estimates were that piracy in Turkey cost the majors $45 million yearly. Sistem was permanently enjoined from distributing unauthorized *Rocky IV* tapes, ordered to destroy those tapes, and ordered to pay some of UA's court costs. After the new Turkish copyright law had been in effect about six months it was said to have reduced the illegal tapes to "only" 30 percent of the market.[49]

Yet another account, on the same page in the same publication as the above estimate, said the Turkish market was 60 percent controlled by pirates with the Hollywood majors estimated to be losing $50 million annually in Turkey to pirates "so financially and politically strong the government long had been afraid to move against them." Since the new law had been enacted, in the Istanbul area alone, about 14,000 illegal tapes had been confiscated, 310 people had been taken to court, and hundreds of thousands of dollars in fines had been levied. Still, if bootleg tapes were no longer openly displayed on store shelves they were still regularly sold under the counter. Warner Brothers found that all of its titles were available on pirate tapes about ten days after they were released. Masters were smuggled into Turkey via other Middle Eastern countries, dubbed into Turkish, then duplicated and sold by the thousands.[50]

Turkish authorities seized 1,575 allegedly illegal tapes in a June 1990 raid on a video lab in Karamursel that provided cassettes to video stores in the Black Sea region of Turkey. It was the largest raid in Turkish history. Since anti-piracy activities had begun some 2½ years earlier authorities had raided a total of 333 locations and seized 9,020 tapes, according to the MPEA.[51]

In Egypt in 1988, the MPAA was becoming more active where an estimated two million VCRs "play almost nothing but pirated vidtapes." It was hoped that if the MPAA was successful in Egypt in obtaining improved copyright laws, it might prompt other Middle Eastern nations—Saudi Arabia for one—to follow suit. At the time there was no anti-piracy legislation in most countries in that part of the world. MPAA officials were said to believe that to fight piracy, U.S. membership in the Berne Convention was needed. Egypt was a signatory; America was not. Thus, there was a question whether U.S. films could be protected under local copyright laws. However, the American film industry had long been in the forefront of groups fighting against American membership in the Berne Convention.[52]

At the end of 1988 the U.S. put the Middle East on notice it was prepared to impose economic sanctions on all Arab countries unable or unwilling to stamp out movie piracy. That warning was sounded at the Pan-Arab Anti-Piracy Forum in Cairo by U.S. Trade Representative Frederic Gaynor, Richard Owens of the U.S. Patent Office, and Walid Nasser, MPAA anti-piracy director for the Middle East. U.S. economic pressure on piracy nations, Gaynor and Owens stressed, was authorized by the Omnibus Trade Act and multilateral treaties. They gave the President and Congress the power to raise import tariffs, restrict access to the U.S. market, and to remove privileged economic status for developing countries. America's trade strength, both Gaynor and Owens assumed, could be very effective as a piracy deterrent in Arab countries. Attending that anti-piracy forum were industry executives from Egypt, Lebanon, Jordan, Saudi Arabia, Morocco, Iraq, and Kuwait.[53]

The Arab Contractor's Video Club on the banks of the Nile in Cairo, Egypt, was renting cassettes of *Silence of the Lambs* for 50 cents a night in 1991. The movie was not then released for home viewing anywhere. Some Egyptian video retailers portrayed themselves as Robin Hoods, stealing from the rich to provide affordable technology and entertainment to the poor. Even when court cases were brought in Egypt, the maximum fine for unauthorized reproduction of material was the equivalent of about $62. Walid Nasser, the MPEA representative in the Middle East, said that all American films then circulating in Cairo were pirated. They came from a variety of sources; films were taped from broadcast or cable television or illegal copies were made from videos obtained legally at rental shops in Europe or the U.S.[54]

For the first time, in 1992, a prison sentence was handed down in an Egyptian video piracy case. Video distributor Maher Shehata, reputed to be a major Cairo player in the piracy business, got three months in jail, a police closure of his operations, and the prospect of a hefty damage suit in a civil court later on. He was caught for distributing bootleg copies of *Lethal Weapon 2*. Three months in jail was the maximum allowed under Egypt's law on intellectual property.[55]

In a reversal of complaints, the Egyptian Film Producers' Union noted in 1995 that virtually all Arabic pictures in video release in the U.S. were bootleg copies and that America was the world's worst offender in the piracy of Arab-language films. Most of the piracy was reported to be centered in New York, Detroit, and Los Angeles, all of which had large Arab immigrant communities. Egyptian producer Youssef Francis said that on a recent visit to Los Angeles he found all eight of his movies on sale in Arabic specialty video shops—and all pirated. Film producers had complained to the American embassy in Cairo about the piracy, but apparently to little avail. Said a U.S. diplomat, "We tell them to hire an American copyright lawyer." Francis replied, "I don't have the time or money to pursue this problem through [U.S.] legal channels by myself, and neither does any other Egyptian film producer." Yossri Ashmawi, head of Cairo's Karnak International Films, commented that "The Americans are anxious to protect their own interests, but they don't seem to care a damn about anybody else's."[56]

In another part of the world, Latin America, crowds of Cubans lined up day after day at three Havana theaters in 1977 to see the hit movie *Jaws*, dubbed into Spanish. There was, of course, a U.S. ban on trade with Cuba that applied to films as well as to other goods. However, in the case of movies, the law was a "laughing stock," observed journalist David Pauly. He added, "As Premier Fidel Castro boasted to visitors earlier this year, Cuba never buys U.S. films. It simply copies them, in defiance of U.S. copyright laws, or buys someone else's illicit copies."[57]

In a series of raids in Caracas, Venezuela, in 1981, more than 25,000 pirated cassettes of the majors' films were seized by federal police. Authorities acted pursuant to an MPAA (working through the MPEA) obtained court order after a year-long investigation by MPAA lawyers. This was said to be the largest seizure since the inception of the MPAA anti-piracy program in 1975 and the first such action in South America. The scope of the raid could be gauged by noting that the FBI seized a total of 16,000 videocassettes in the U.S. for all of 1980. Police seized the entire inventory of 18

Caracas video retail outlets. The bulk of the illicit material consisted of U.S. majors' product with Spanish subtitles, all transferred from film to videotape and duplicated locally in Caracas. The MPAA had been aware of retail activity in South America for pirated tapes for several years but the Spanish subtitled material first appeared on the market just a year earlier. None of the Hollywood majors had licensed any videotape releases for Venezuela at that time. However, that big raid turned out to be a bust; the courts ruled the raid was illegal on a technicality and all 25,000 seized tapes had to be returned to the pirates.[58]

Video piracy in Venezuela was said to be "rampant" in 1983. Almost any new release could be found in cassette at any department store for as little as $10. When the customer tired of it, he could return it to the seller and for $1.20 exchange it for a different one.[59]

A raid late in 1983 resulted in more than 1,500 illicit tapes being seized from a Caracas vendor. That came at the same time that Paramount and Universal became the first Hollywood majors to distribute their films on video locally. Retail price of those legitimate tapes from the majors was $28; tapes of legitimate independent fare ranged from $13 to $20; pirate tapes cost around $7. Paramount said it had wanted to distribute its tapes through legitimate commercial channels for at least two years but held back "until real anti-piracy efforts were in effect."[60]

More than 2,000 pirated videocassettes of U.S. theatrical films were seized in a multi-city crackdown in 1984 in Venezuela. Titles seized included *Indiana Jones and the Temple of Doom*, *Splash*, and *Moscow on the Hudson*. All were in theatrical release in Venezuela. Besides having material confiscated, numerous video retailers were prompted to sign agreements to remove all pirated cassettes from their stock and "desist forever" from dealing in such illegally obtained product. Also, Venezuelan authorities reported that many additional retailers, fearing similar raids, either shut down or disposed of pirated cassettes. It all led, said the MPAA, to "a purchasing spree of legal product." Among cities hit were Caracas, Valencia, and Barquisimeto. Working with Venezuelan authorities in the effort were Richard Campagna, MPAA Latin American anti-piracy counsel based in New York, and Michael Heuser, MPAA regional director based in Caracas. "They coordinated the entire operation, and participated in the Barquisimeto and Caracas raids together with Dr. Ricardo Antequera Parilli, MPAA's anti-piracy counsel in Venezuela."[61]

Video clubs in Brazil charged members from $5 to $10 a month for the right to borrow almost a film a day. In a 1983 raid at 23 of these clubs in Rio de Janeiro, 1,000 tapes were confiscated, all of which were unauthorized. A few days later, however, Secretary of Federal Income Cesar

Dornelles not only ordered them returned to the clubs but called the club owners to apologize. Dornelles said all of the tapes were "perfectly legal." Needless to say, it was a setback in the fight against piracy.[62]

A more positive result was obtained in a series of raids conducted in 1985 against eight large video clubs in Sao Paulo, Brazil, that were dealing in pirate tapes. All eight clubs were shut down. That action by authorities followed what the MPAA described as "continuous pressure" from the Rio de Janeiro-based Brazilian Video Union, a group comprised of national and international copyright owners.[63]

Brazil's videotape market was said to be 75 to 80 percent controlled by pirates in 1987. There were almost 4,000 video outlets in the country with an estimated 95 percent of them offering illicit product. In terms of shelf space, pirated videos exceeded the legal ones by a margin of five to one. Hollywood's majors blamed the lack of persistent action by Brazil's Federal Police for the high level of piracy.[64]

During the first few years of the 1980s, U.S. satellite signals carrying television programs (including movies) intended for cable television viewers in the U.S. had been intercepted by a growing number of television stations throughout the Caribbean and Central America and broadcast without authorization. In Jamaica, for example, the government-owned broadcaster showed *Poltergeist*, *Missing*, *Rocky III* and other pictures not yet released to Jamaican cinemas. Taken without permission from satellites, the State Department and the majors called it piracy. Others argued the law was unclear in that area. Valenti said "The satellites are being used as instruments of grand theft." According to the MPAA, pirating of U.S. television satellite transmission had taken place in Costa Rica, Honduras, the Bahamas, the Cayman Islands, the Dominican Republic, Haiti, Jamaica, and Belize. Some of those foreign television executives, when contacted, said they would be willing to reimburse American companies for the use of their programs but the Americans were unwilling to enter into agreements. It all started in 1975 when Home Box Office (HBO), the cable network owned by Time, first began distributing programs by satellite. This problem was largely solved when satellite transmissions were finally encoded, or scrambled.[65]

As law enforcement officials and other invited guests looked on in 1992 in Mexico City, video cassettes were piled up on a vacant street—then along came a steamroller that smashed them flat. With that, the government put Mexicans on notice that it planned to crack down on anyone caught making or selling illegal copies of movies, music cassettes, and so on. The message was also meant for Mexico's northern neighbors. With U.S. and Canadian legislatures preparing to vote on the North American Free

Trade Agreement (NAFTA—to include the U.S., Canada, and Mexico), Mexico wanted to alter its reputation as a persistent violator of international agreements on copyrights, patents and other intellectual property.[66]

Yet in 1996 U.S. business was complaining about piracy in Mexico. It caused the Mexican government to respond to the pressure by reviving a high-level committee on piracy that became dormant after meeting once in 1993. The heart of the problem was in Tepito, a Mexico City neighborhood that was home to one of the world's largest bazaars for pirated videos, music cassettes, and software. Hundreds of vendors hawked their wares at this market, which was just a few blocks away from the offices of the top Mexican prosecutor in charge of stopping the pirates and right around the corner from the national headquarters of the police who were supposed to hunt them down. A whole section of Tepito's market was devoted to pirated tapes of movies of varying quality. *Braveheart*, which had been out on video for only one month in the U.S. (mainly for rental shops, since it sold for about $100), was available in Tepito for $2.70. Tim Kuik, MPAA anti-piracy director said, "We felt that NAFTA signalled a level of maturity in Mexico that meant that business conditions would improve. Instead, the level of legitimate distribution was greatly reduced. We began to lose terrain we had already gained." Out of hundreds of cases brought before the anti-piracy prosecutor's office in the previous two years, only six pirates had been convicted, and none received substantial jail terms. Ernesto Soriano, prosecutor for intellectual property crimes, complained, "Our legislation is very benevolent with this type of crime." Accused pirates were immediately released on bail as low as a few dollars and faced fines of less than $150. Also, evidence seized by the police—and necessary for trial—sometimes vanished from police warehouses before the cases reached court. In the six-month period from October 1995 to March 1996, Mexican authorities carried out 333 raids and seized a total of 140,000 alleged illicit tapes.[67]

Another part of the world with plenty of pirate activity was the Far East. In South East Asia at the beginning of the 1980s it was reported that the countries with the greatest piracy problems were Malaysia and Taiwan. Hong Kong was said to be the "cleanest" market in the area. Over 300 pirate outfits in Malaysia had formed their own registered video association to combat moves by legal distributors to gain a foothold in the market. Video rental clubs in Malaysia operated on a subscription basis of $100 for 100 tapes a year. As an inducement, the purchase of a VCR in Taiwan entitled the buyer to five complimentary tapes which could then be exchanged for any of the more than 3,000 titles the stores had available at a dollar a time. "Cassettes, of course, are all illegal copies," stated an account. There had been sporadic police raids in Taiwan when tapes and equipment were confiscated, but the courts usually imposed only minor fines and sometimes returned the erased tapes and equipment to the pirates.[68]

William Nix, an MPAA executive, complained in 1986 that the Far East and the Middle East were the worst areas in the world for piracy. "Every video tape being sold in those two parts of the world, with the exception of Japan and Israel, is a bootleg tape." Some two years earlier the State Department pressured ten developing countries by threatening to take away certain trade benefits for failure to create and enforce intellectual property laws. By 1986 that had prompted a number of nations, including Taiwan and Singapore, to broaden legislation in that area.[69]

While he was on a visit to Tokyo, Japan, Charles Morgan, anti-piracy director for Universal, estimated one-third of the video market in Tokyo was pirated items and that there were 2,500 pirate video shops in the city. With regard to lobbying authorities in Japan to be more vigorous in going after pirates, Morgan said, "table pounding isn't the way to do anything. We have better luck in Japan by humbly beseeching the police to help us."[70]

The first Japanese ever charged with piracy of major U.S. films was convicted by the Tokyo District Court in 1986 and given a suspended sentence of 18 months. According to the charges, Shigeo Akiyama made some $25,000 by illegally copying 900 videotapes of such American pictures as *Rocky IV*, *The Goonies*, and *Commando*. Akiyama sold the pirated tapes to 10 different dealers over a one-year period. Akiyama's sentencing came in the "turbulent wake" left by MPAA president Jack Valenti who came to Japan to meet with police and government officials. Valenti urged them to take rigorous action against movie pirates.[71]

By 1987 Japan was the largest foreign customer for U.S. films but also, said one account, supplied America "with its biggest video piracy headache." MPAA member studios took in $140 million from Japan in 1986, but that group estimated the majors lost some $200 million to $300 million annually to pirates in that market. Urged by the studios to do more in Japan, the MPAA responded by allocating more money to fight piracy in Japan than in any other nation. Over the previous 11 months Valenti had made two trips to Japan with a third planned for a few weeks in the future. At one seminar he was slated to give a talk entitled "Attack the Pirates, Stamp out Pirated Videos." As in other countries, the MPAA worked through a local front group, in this case the Japanese Federation Against Copyright Theft (JFACT). Over the first four months of 1987 the MPAA, through JFACT, investigated more than 1,100 of Japan's video shops. About 17,300 illegal cassettes were seized. Valenti wanted to see laws enacted that made search and seizures easier as well as changes in copyright laws.[72]

Apparently the lobbying efforts worked. MPAA spokesman Mark

Harrad said in 1988 that in Tokyo, the percentage of pirated video titles had been reduced from nearly 100 percent to 40 percent in the space of a couple of years. Later that same year reporter Andrea Adelson said that Hollywood's majors had video rentals of $649 million from Japan in 1987. She estimated the percentage of pirated videos in Japan was then 20 percent, "down from an estimated 80 percent in 1986." American film executives working in Japan had been assigned as investigators (apparently as an extra task) who turned over evidence on video bootleggers to local police.[73]

William Nix, MPAA director of anti-piracy, complained in 1986 that almost every blockbuster movie showed up in Thailand within four days of its opening in American theaters. He added that the first cassette the MPAA had been able to track effectively was *Rocky IV*. It went from the United States to Thailand, where copies with local subtitles were sent to Malaysia and Singapore. From there, said Nix, the cassettes went to Jordan, then to Turkey, where they were re-subtitled in Turkish and sent on to Turkish workers in Germany.[74]

An increase in both film and music piracy prompted six U.S. Senators to write to the Thai ambassador in Washington in 1990 to urge immediate action. That came after the D.C.-based International Intellectual Property Alliance (IIPA) protested the "intolerable and inexcusable situation" faced in Thailand by U.S. film, music, book and computer software industries. Citing the "virtually complete and total failure of the Thai authorities" to enforce anti-piracy statutes, the IIPA urged Secretary of State James Baker, U.S. Trade Representative Carla Hills, and Commerce Secretary Robert Mosbacher to address the issue. While 48 raids had been executed on video pirates in the previous 12 months, not one had resulted in a conviction, and only two had even proceeded to court. Signing that letter were Senators Patrick Moynihan (D.—New York); Dennis DeConcini (D.—Arizona); David Boren (D.—Oklahoma); Bob Packwood (R.—Oregon); John Heinz (R.—Pennsylvania); and Jay Rockefeller (D.—W. Virginia).[75]

Late in 1990 the Bush administration put Thailand on notice that it would consider imposing retaliatory tariffs unless the nation took steps to improve the protection of American copyrights. U.S. Trade Representative Carla Hills announced she was investigating Thailand's copyright enforcement practices. She said: "Unfortunately, we have seen no improvement in Thailand's willingness to shut down the considerable illegal copying of U.S. movies, music, books and computer software or to ensure that U.S. companies obtain prompt and effective redress through Thailand's legal system." Hills acted after receiving a petition from the MPAA, the

International Intellectual Property Alliance, and the Recording Industry Association of America.[76]

In April 1991, the Bush administration placed Thailand and India on the Commerce Department watch list—another formal step in moving toward imposing formal sanctions. New movies like David Lynch's *Wild at Heart*, not then available on video in the U.S., were on sale in Thailand for $4 per tape.[77]

The American film industry filed a major trade complaint against South Korea in 1988, charging that it maintained unfair barriers against U.S. motion picture exports and tolerated piracy of U.S. pictures in its home video market. The complaint, under Section 301 of the Trade Act of 1974, could lead to an investigation, formal charges, and possible retaliation by the U.S. government.[78]

At that time the MPAA estimated 66 countries lacked "adequate protection for intellectual property" and that its member firms were losing $1.2 billion a year to foreign pirates. "The most precious possession we have is copyright. If we can't protect what we own, we don't own anything," said Valenti. According to reporter Andrea Adelson, since 1985, United States officials had successfully pressured many foreign nations into adopting new or tougher laws on illicit copying, sometimes under threat of trade sanctions. However, some countries resisted toughening their laws because doing so could do harm to the local industry. Hollywood majors sometimes initiated direct moves in some countries because U.S. government intervention in those areas had only limited success. Faced with such resistance in South Korea, MCA Inc. (the parent of Universal) was acting directly by trying to enlist local filmmakers to push for stricter copyright enforcement. In return, the studio was offering the local film industry financial backing for new theaters.[79]

Some of the countries in the Far East stole from each other. One Western observer wrote in 1976 that the Pakistani film industry's claim to fame was the "scale and impertinence of its plagiarisation," adding that there was not a hit out of Bombay that was not copied in detail. Each month Pakistani producers and directors traveled to Kabul, Afghanistan, to watch the latest Indian movies, purchase them and later copy them frame by frame in their Pakistani studios. Analyzing the 183 movies produced in Bangladesh between 1972 and 1976, one observer declared that 125 (70 percent) of them were plagiarized. Some were copied from Pakistani hits which had been plagiarized from Indian films. Producers and directors from Bangladesh went to Calcutta where they watched Indian movies and tape-recorded their entire soundtracks. Back in Bangladesh, writers used the soundtracks to create "screenplays," usually by picking the best scenes from several films and putting them together. Sri Lanka was another country where investors saw no reason to risk their money in original Sinhala films when they could copy Indian ones.[80]

Taiwan had 5,173 registered video shops in 1986, and from 1,500 to 3,000 illegal outlets, that handled illicit material. The general manager of a major U.S. distribution firm said that all the legal shops also handled unregistered cassettes in an effort to make up for losses incurred from paying royalties on the legal ones. Another distributor remarked that by the time a U.S. film opened theatrically in Taiwan, a pirated version was already in circulation. His policy was to try and speed release in Taiwan to reduce the damage from the pirated video.[81]

Pressure from the MPAA on Taiwan resulted in a 1989 accord that called for legislative steps to render the unlicensed public screenings of videocassettes illegal in Taiwan, plus other steps, including more raids. The MPAA called the accord "a giant step" in resolving "widespread piracy problems" in Taiwan, if officials followed through on their promises.[82]

Apparently, though, they did not. A year later it was observed that pirates throughout the developing world were setting up their own miniature movie houses using ordinary VCRs. Taiwan had more than 1,000 "MTV parlors," as they were called locally, that screened movies for audiences as small as two or three. The MPEA filed a test case on the "public performance" issue in 1988 against the Crow's Nest MTV parlor in the capital city of Taipei to define Taiwan's copyright protection. While the judge ruled the video parlor's owner was involved in "illegal leasing" of tapes, he sidestepped the public performance question. Not only did the MTV parlor operators fail to obtain licenses for public performances of films, they also used cassettes that were mostly all pirated copies.[83]

Under pressure from the U.S. government, Taiwan's Cabinet approved a four-year plan in 1993 to strengthen protection of foreign copyright. The government was to set up a special bureau under the Economics Ministry to enforce copyright legislation and to help plaintiffs file lawsuits against violators. Also, the ministry agreed to negotiate with Parliament to pass new laws improving copyright protection and to regulate Taiwan's cable-television industry, which then used pirated foreign films.[84]

While video versions of the two *Home Alone* movies had legal sales of about 1,000 copies in Malaysia, an estimated 40,000 bootleg copies of the pair were sold. Pirates there had such a fast and efficient distribution network that cassettes reached rural areas before films finished their initial run in major towns. The National Film Development Corporation (FINAS) regularly carried out raids and made seizures but those efforts were said to have barely scratched the surface. In 1993 FINAS seized product worth $1.15 million, an increase of 50 percent from 1992. While *Jurassic Park* was playing in cinemas, pirates were busy selling videocassettes of the film with Chinese subtitles for $12.[85]

On August 18, 1998, the Indian film community halted work in Bombay as about 5,000 employees of India's film industry took to the streets to protest what they called the government's failure to curb piracy of movies. Several prominent Indian actors took part. K. D. Shorey said, "Our prime releases are viewed in cable homes all over the city the day following their premiere." As the protestors worked their way through the streets, they demonstrated outside the offices of In Cable and Zee TV, the biggest cable firms in the nation and believed to be major players in the piracy business. Government officials gave assurances to the protestors that the Copyright Act would be reinforced and that a special enforcement unit would be set up. In Cable and Zee accused local cable operators of airing pirated movies without their knowledge. Also, cable operators felt the film producers were in no position to cry foul, "being culpable themselves with their plagiarism of songs, themes and ideas taken outright from foreign hits."[86]

A year later several Hollywood majors petitioned the New Delhi High Court accusing two of India's cable companies, In Cable, and Siti Cable, and their distributors, of illegally copying and broadcasting their films. According to the news agency Press Trust of India, the court ordered the police to stop the cable networks from broadcasting the films without the permission of the petitioners.[87]

Martial arts hero Jackie Chan led a contingent of Hong Kong film stars who were demanding tougher penalties against copyright infringement. During the 17th Hong Kong film awards, the director Fruit Chan highlighted the issue (while accepting an award) by jokingly thanking video pirates for not circulating his movie before its premiere. A year earlier Jackie Chan had threatened to leave the territory if intellectual property rights were not strengthened. In May 1998, the Prevention of Copyright Piracy Ordinance went into effect amid U.S. criticism that theft of intellectual property in the territory was getting worse. America was sufficiently upset and Hong Kong was placed on the U.S. Trade Representative's watch list—a move that could ultimately lead to formal trade sanctions.[88]

Walt Disney's animated film *Mulan* made its theatrical debut in Hong Kong on July 9, 1998. Yet more than a week earlier thousands of illegal video compact disc (VCD) copies of the picture, with Chinese subtitles, were for sale in Hong Kong shopping arcades. Lowell Strong, the MPA's Singapore-based director of anti-piracy operations for Asia, complained "Two years ago we had made great progress in eliminating videocassette piracy in Asia.

Then we were hit by VCDs. It's killing us." Hong Kong customs officials made frequent raids on factories and shops, but as fast as one was closed another opened up. A few months earlier the Hong Kong government seized 41 illicit disc production lines and 22 million pirated discs, with a combined street value of $130 million. Also, they arrested a senior customs official for allegedly taking bribes from the syndicate. Reportedly, the Hong Kong film industry had been hard hit by piracy with production cut to about 80 features in 1998, down from 200 a few years earlier. Woody Tsung, chief executive of Hong Kong's Motion Picture Industry Association, said, "Many film projects were aborted because of piracy." A movie on a legal VCD sold for about $20 in Hong Kong, but pirated copies retailed for $2 to $3 each. Pirates could make an illicit disc film for only 35 cents. Much of the output from Hong Kong and Macao pirates (some had moved to those areas after China cracked down on its pirates) was smuggled into China.[89]

On March 17, 1999, all cinemas in Hong Kong closed for the day to protest the flood of illicit movies. An array of local film stars, including Jackie Chan, led a rally of 2,000 people to demand a tougher crackdown on piracy. Woody Tsung complained again about the bad effects piracy had on the local motion picture industry. Just one month earlier Hong Kong was taken off the watch list by the U.S. government after it stepped up efforts to raid factories that produced illegally copied material. Still, film executives in Hong Kong said the former British colony remained one of the worst offenders in Asia for copyright violations. On the day of the protest, the Queen's Theater in central Hong Kong had signs on its box office window apologizing for being closed. It added: "Imagine a city without cinemas. If piracy is allowed to continue, this will be the result." In all of 1998, Hong Kong officials seized 39 million pirated disks and arrested 1,645 people. Watching the demonstration that day was Wu Chun-Keung, a 26-year-old construction worker, who said he could not justify paying $7 for a single movie ticket when he could buy a package of 10 bootleg movies for $12. "It's so cheap that I have to buy them. If they shut down every store, I'll go back to the movie theaters."[90]

The Clinton administration accused China in 1994 of the flagrant piracy of American films, recordings, books, and software, launching an investigation that could lead to heavy trade sanctions if the dispute was not resolved. China was then attempting to gain membership in GATT (General Agreement on Tariffs and Trade). However, the U.S. could keep China out. Mickey Kantor, U.S. Trade Representative, declared, "We will strongly support China accession [to GATT] when they meet the standards" of copyright protection.[91]

At the end of 1994 the Clinton administration got tougher when it warned China it would ban more than $1 billion in Chinese imports beginning in February 1995 unless China's officials took strong steps to control piracy. Kantor explained the U.S. government insisted that China impose stiff penalties against pirates, and provide greater market access in China for American entertainment products. China then permitted only 10 U.S. movies to be imported at one time. Bootleg copies of hit movies such as *The Lion King* and *Jurassic Park* were available for home viewing in China before the videotapes had been released in the U.S. At a Chinese plant in a city north of Hong Kong, a U.S. motion picture industry official found illegal copies of 30 U.S.-made pictures, from *Twins* to *Gone with the Wind.* China should not expect to gain WTO (World Trade Organization — successor to GATT) membership, warned Kantor, while its protection of foreign intellectual property fell "so far below WTO standards." Illegal copies of films such as *Terminator 2: Judgment Day* were showing in thousands of cinemas, added the administration.[92]

Responding to the pressure, Beijing said it had launched a crackdown on pirates, that it had gotten tough. For more than a week the English-language Chinese press had been filled with stories about the government's attempts to rid the country of pirated products. One editorial reported that in a recent three-month period, a force of several thousand officials in 10 towns and provinces launched surprise raids on video and audio markets, netting 258,100 illegally reproduced audio and video laser discs, and 441,400 audio and videotapes. Not everybody believed the official line, though. Reporter Keith Richburg said,"But the reality on the streets suggests that despite the official claims that authorities are getting tough, pirates continue to operate with apparent impunity, and the fakes are as plentiful as ever."[93]

American and Chinese negotiators reached a tentative agreement on February 26, 1995, on the protection of intellectual property, narrowly averting a trade war, minutes past the February 25 deadline when U.S. sanctions on more than $1 billion worth of goods were to kick in. China agreed to become much more serious about conducting raids and seizures and it gave assurances it would seek much stiffer penalties when it prosecuted pirates. Also, the accord provided greater access for U.S. films and recordings to the Chinese market, lifting Chinese quotas on imported movies.[94]

President Clinton and U.S. trade and industry officials all hailed the agreement with China, describing the pact as the most comprehensive and detailed copyright enforcement agreement they had ever negotiated with any country. A major sign that Chinese negotiators were serious was said to be the raids carried out in the previous week against seven of the 29 CD factories that the U.S. had labeled as major pirate facilities. One day before the agreement was signed the Chinese military raided Shenfei, a key plant in Shenzhen that American negotiators had singled out. Deputy U.S. Trade Representative Charlene Barshefsky called Shenfei, which was partly owned by the local government and was toured in 1992 by China's leader Deng Xiaoping, "the most notorious" for making bootleg video and music copies. Barshefsky, chief U.S. negotiator in Beijing, added, "Piracy in China is rampant. But this is a good beginning and a foundation on which we can build." Success of the agreement would depend upon its enforcement by Chinese authorities who, until then, had been inconsistent when it came to Chinese copyright and trademark laws.[95]

A few months later China's State Copyright Administration announced it had fined three companies for pirating various U.S. films. No details were released about the size of the fines levied against the firms.[96]

As of late November 1995, Barshefsky stated that China was falling "far short" on its promises to crackdown on piracy. She warned that unless Beijing "sharply" improved efforts to implement the anti-piracy accord over the coming three months, Washington would consider taking "decisive action." That warning from Barshefsky came after numerous private admonitions during meetings with top Chinese leaders. U.S. Trade Representative Mickey Kantor declared "we will not wait forever as the Chinese government attempts to implement these agreements." Of those seven of 29 factories that closed less than a year earlier, all but one had reopened and U.S. officials believed that most of those plants had resumed pirate activity. Valenti grumbled that since the February 26 accord pirating "had actually increased" in China.[97]

The Supreme People's Court of China announced heavy prison sentences in 1997 in two prominent cases of copyright piracy. Pu Xinghua, former deputy general manager of the Suzhou Baodie Compact Disk Company, was sentenced to 17 years in prison for pirating more than three million video and audio compact disks. Separately, Wang Binyan, former chairman and general manager of Cailing Audio and Video Products in Guangzhou was sentenced to four years for copying over five million video and audio disks. It was all part of an effort to convince the U.S. that China was serious about reducing piracy. In the past, pirates had generally been punished with minor fines or they escaped prosecution altogether because they had ties to China's military and police. Wang's office, for example, was located in a military compound in Guangzhou. Pu was first brought to court on piracy charges in Shanghai in April 1995, but he was let go "with little more than a slap on the wrist." Despite the crackdown efforts, pirate tapes of current movies were still said to be openly available in large cities, though supplies had decreased and prices had risen.[98]

In the downtown area of almost every major Chinese city, observed reporter Seth Faison in 1998, signs were openly displayed on store windows for pirated compact disks of Hollywood movies on sale for less than $2 each. Pirates were distributing their wares "unchecked." *Titanic* had been sold in Shanghai since November 1997, a month before its American theatrical release. "Chinese authorities have essentially given up efforts to prevent the sale of illegally copied videodisks," said Faison. "The open sale of pirated movies signals a failure of the intellectual property rights agreement that China reached with the United States in 1995." Cheng Ching-ming, who monitored piracy in China for the International Federation of Phonographic Industries, commented that "The situation is out of control. For movies, there has been a complete breakdown in enforcement. The authorities seem to have lost all interest in trying to prevent sales." Video compact disks (VCDs) were introduced at trade shows several years earlier but they never caught on in North America and were bypassed by another format, DVDs. A boom in VCDs, however, transformed the electronics industry of China (and some other countries in the region). The same size as music compact disks, VCDs contained up to 70 minutes of a movie on each disk, using two disks for a Hollywood feature. Legitimate VCDs sold in stores in China for $5 to $10 apiece, while pirate VCDs went for $2 or less each. At a downtown Shanghai store called the MusicBox, a sign in the window advertised VCDs for under $2, a price that store retailers readily acknowledged could only mean they were illegal copies. "Of course they're pirated. Otherwise how could we sell them so cheap?" said the MusicBox proprietor. She said she used to keep the pirated VCDs under the counter but since the previous autumn when Shanghai's copyright police had stopped coming around to check she felt no fear and so displayed the items openly.[99]

Somewhat strangely, Jack Valenti responded to Faison's article with a letter to the editor of the *New York Times* in which he contradicted Faison's conclusions and defended China and its efforts to reduce piracy.[100]

Two months after that, in June 1998, President Clinton arrived in China on an official visit. Earlier that same month Chinese authorities cracked down on pirate activities "at least superficially," wrote Faison. When Barshefsky met with reporters in Beijing that month, she tried to deflect concern over piracy by expressing approval of Beijing's crackdown efforts and even argued that China had ceased to be a major exporter of pirated goods, falling well down the list of offending countries. "We have a far bigger problem now with Italy," she said. But industry observers who followed the situation closely claimed the only real change was that the pirates, many of them Taiwan businessmen with histories of organized crime, had moved their operations from the Chinese mainland to Macao, the Portuguese colony slated to revert to Chinese rule in 1999. Faison declared, "So while Chinese and American officials are each claiming victory in rooting out pirates, more illegally copied material is on sale in China than every before." In a very visible display just a couple of weeks before Clinton's arrival, the authorities in several Chinese cities brought out bulldozers to publicly destroy millions of illicit disks. Some 2.8 million disks were destroyed in that one day in the southern city of Guangzhou. The same kind of public display of destroying confiscated pirate movies had also been staged back in 1995, when the important guest was Barshefsky.[101]

Five years after the China-U.S. accord was signed little seemed to have changed. Reporter Craig Smith declared that "piracy is still common." Estimates were that 91 percent of the software used in China in 1999 was stolen, down slightly from 1994. Traffic in pirated copies of movies was still conducted openly in stores where, for example, recent Hollywood hits including *Gladiator* were available for $2 each.[102]

Within a week after the November 17, 2000, release in America of *Dr. Seuss' How the Grinch Stole Christmas*, VCD copies of the film were selling on China's streets (available in both dubbed and not dubbed versions) for about $1.20 each. Around 50 million Chinese families owned video compact disk players (selling for about $70) at the end of 1998. So pervasive was the pirating activity that it was "almost impossible" to sell legitimate movies there, which cost more than double the price of a pirate version. *Titanic* sold 300,000 legitimate copies but pirates sold 20 to 25 million copies. Usually pirates outsold distributors by a margin of 35 to one on a particular film. Most films were available in China within days of their U.S. cinema release. Pirates first recorded films with video cameras in U.S. theaters and then shipped them to China where editors added subtitles or dubbed some of them into Chinese. Then the pirates used computers to enhance the quality and usually made new copies when the movies were officially released on videotape or DVD. Competing pirated versions of the same film often circulated in the market.[103]

7

Conclusion

When the motion picture arrived and started to become popular it debuted in the midst of vaudeville, the most popular form of mass entertainment at the start of the twentieth century. Vaudeville performers regularly stole material from each other with few legal restraints on the practice as the legal code in that area was still being established and interpreted by the courts. Although many of the vaudeville circuits and booking agencies came out publicly against piracy, they were just as likely to turn a blind eye to the practice or to encourage it indirectly because it was often in their financial interests to do so. When material was pirated it was almost always done so at the expense of a copyright holder who was an individual, as opposed to a company. Many of those people did not have the resources to wage a long court battle, even if such an option seemed viable. Instead, to the extent that piracy was limited in vaudeville, it was mainly controlled through performers letting each other know who was stealing from whom and then getting together informally to pressure circuits not to book pirating acts and/or confronting pirating artists and trying to convince or shame them into changing their ways. More formal methods evolved whereby performers could register material with third parties and then arbitration could deal with disputes. The formal legal system was not used often. Nor was the problem of piracy in vaudeville ever solved. Vaudeville withered away altogether in the face of competition from motion pictures and radio.

Up until the early part of the 1910s, piracy in the motion picture industry was largely limited to producer stealing from producer. It remained "in the family" and was pervasive as the industry went through its early growth period. As the industry stabilized and the first of the cartels formed, the member studios set up their own rules and piracy ceased to be an internal problem. Producers no longer stole from other producers. However, by the early part of the 1910s, the film business was very popular and very lucrative. Outsiders got involved in the piracy. There were a lot of physical thefts of films and a lot of gangs operated that duped the stolen prints, often shipping them to offshore destinations. As early as 1919 the Hollywood majors had determined the problem was serious enough that they needed to establish a separate unit, funded by the cartel, to deal exclusively with piracy. Hollywood also turned to the federal government in Washington to demand help in stamping out piracy abroad. Invaluable assistance was provided, especially in the 1920s. Despite the possible benefits from joining the principal international copyright agreement, the Berne Convention, and gaining at least some degree of protection in foreign countries, America refused to sign the agreement, uncomfortable with the European concept of moral rights for the creative talent involved in filmmaking.

Exhibitors joined in stealing from Hollywood around the time of World War I, especially through the practice of bicycling. Sometimes exhibitors cut material from films to reduce the total time of a program, and always argued that they had improved the film. It was a practice that infuriated the creative talent, obviously, but also infuriated the Hollywood majors. Yet in later years, the majors would not care when television mutilated their product. A major difference was that at this early time, Hollywood still sold many of its movies for so many cents per foot. Any cuts reduced the income.

While it battled to save its own copyrighted material, Hollywood blithely stole from others, especially books and plays. Court decisions brought that practice to an end, at least an end to the most egregious cases. Vaudeville material was also stolen for film use. Additionally, copyrighted music was purloined with ASCAP having to wage a long battle to get cinemas to pay a very modest sum for the use of its catalog. When old movies were sometimes reissued, it was a fairly common thing for studios to give them new names and pretend they were really new releases.

With the arrival of talking pictures at the end of the 1920s, the leasing of films to exhibitors quickly changed to percentage leasing whereby the distributor took a certain percentage of the box office dollar, rather than rent the movie on a flat-rate basis. That initiated a new wave of larceny by theaters as they tried to find ways of under-reporting their receipts. It was a problem that plagued Hollywood for decades, resolved only by the majors devoting resources to physically checking box offices and auditing records. Piracy of motion pictures continued through the 1930s but probably reached its lowest ebb during World War II as the transportation of films offshore, legal or not, became next to impossible. Copyright now rested in the hands of huge corporations, and not individuals. The majors, with their vast financial reserves, were quick to use the court system by then to enforce their claims. Over time, copyright law would be subtly rewritten to favor those large firms, and to drastically increase the punishment for those found guilty.

After the war, piracy picked up again both offshore and domestically. As 16m equipment became increasingly popular and available in America, there were more potential customers domestically for illicit films. Although Hollywood initially refused to deal with television, the majors soon changed their minds and started to sell their old libraries to the new medium. That resulted in the wholesale mutilation of movies so they could fit allocated and pre-determined time periods. Lawsuits launched by directors to prevent such butchery confirmed the results from earlier suits started by creative talent — that is, in the U.S., motion picture creative talent had no say whatsoever in what happened to films. They had no moral rights. By the mid 1970s Hollywood appeared to have piracy under control. Of course, it had not been eliminated but it was seemingly a relatively minor problem.

Then Hollywood hit its roughest period as the VCR and the videocassette arrived and became ubiquitous. Piracy increased because the potential market for pirate films expanded dramatically. Offshore, the distinction of being the biggest piracy nation made its way around the globe, stopping in such places as the UK, Italy, and China. Things were almost as bad domestically; pirated tapes turned up in the nation's video stores and in the hands of street peddlers and others. More than at any time in the past, Hollywood established a separate and formal infrastructure to deal with the issue. That varied from establishing front groups in various nations, to setting up its own investigative force to turning more and more to the U.S. government for assistance. As globalization proceeded, Hollywood was able to get the federal government to exert pressure on countries it felt were not doing enough to fight piracy through mechanisms such as the World Trade Organization and its own Omnibus trade bill. Domestically, Hollywood used the FBI more and more as that agency conducted everything from elaborate sting operations to straightforward raids, all at the behest of the Hollywood cartel. In all likelihood, those tactics worked in keeping piracy totals to a reasonable level. While Hollywood has released estimates of its dollar losses to piracy, especially from the late 1970s onward, they have not been reliable; the numbers have been all over the place and probably were highly exaggerated.

As some in the industry have pointed out, much of the piracy that took place was a direct result of Hollywood's own practices. As Hollywood relentlessly hyped a new film that was coming, people all over the world tended to be aware of it to some extent. Yet the cartel still released movies at different times, often months later, in different parts of the world. When Hollywood released a film on video or DVD, it did so months after the theatrical release in each country because of release window policies. Both of these practices created a demand for the product that was not met, and the opportunity for pirates to meet it. Hollywood's pricing of product offshore, while not as high as in North America, was nevertheless often much higher than people in those countries could afford. The issue, of course, was that of trying to impose first world prices on third world countries.

Hollywood had demanded that its copyrights be vigorously respected, even to the extent of badgering other countries to change their laws to something acceptable to the cartel. Yet it all rang hollow when compared to how Hollywood had ignored the copyrights of others, or treated them with disdain. It was a disdain that extended to its own creative talent and even to its own product.

Notes

Chapter 1

1. "Artists' forum." *Variety*, January 13, 1906, p. 11; "Artists' forum." *Variety*, January 27, 1906, p. 11.
2. *Ibid. Variety*, February 3, 1906, p. 11.
3. *Ibid. Variety*, February 10, 1906, p. 10.
4. *Ibid. Variety*, February 3, 1906, p. 11.
5. *Ibid. Variety*, June 22, 1907, p. 7.
6. *Ibid. Variety*, August 17, 1907, p. 7.
7. *Ibid. Variety*, August 17, 1907, p. 7; "Artists' forum." *Variety*, September 5, 1908. p. 11.
8. *Ibid. Variety*, September 5, 1908, p. 11.
9. *Ibid. Variety*, November 14, 1908, p. 9.
10. Advertisement. *Variety*, February 24, 1906, p. 24.
11. *Ibid. Variety*, May 19, 1906, p. 24; *Variety*, September 15, 1906, p. 20.
12. *Ibid. Variety*, December 15, 1906, p. 34; *Variety*, October 7, 1911, p. 25.
13. *Ibid. Variety*, January 19, 1907, p. 25.
14. *Ibid. Variety*, November 1, 1918, p. 25.
15. "The copy act coming." *Variety*, June 30, 1906, p. 4; "Copy act in London." *Variety*, July 20, 1907, p. 6.
16. "Hill chasing pirates." *Variety*, January 5, 1907, p. 7.
17. "To give a copy act." *Variety*, August 18, 1906, p. 4.
18. Advertisement. *Variety*, August 18, 1906, p. 16; *Variety*, October 20, 1906, p. 19.
19. "Karno-Bedini case argued." *Variety*, December 29, 1906, p. 5; "May enjoin 'Around the Clock.'" *Variety*, January 5, 1907, p. 5.
20. "Keith bows to Karno." *Variety*, January 19, 1907, p. 2.
21. "Drew denies infringement charges." *Variety*, September 14, 1907, p. 4.
22. "Eva Tanguay on imitators." *Variety*, March 6, 1909, p. 5.
23. "Admits 'copping' an act." *Variety*, March 6, 1909, p. 5.
24. "36 weeks cancelled for copy act." *Variety*, September 14, 1907, p. 5.
25. "Has act protected." *Variety*, September 21, 1907, p. 6.
26. "After show for piracy." *Variety*, December 12, 1908, p. 6.
27. "Chicago's center for the disposal of 'lifted stuff.'" *Variety*, February 6, 1909, p. 6.
28. "Burlesque manager favors rules against copyists." *Variety*, January 14, 1911, p. 9.
29. "Protection by copyright of original material." *Variety*, January 21, 1911, p. 5.
30. "Orchestra leader offered $4 to steal an act verbatim." *Variety*, February 24, 1912, p. 10.

31. "Copy act consequences made plain in Harrisburg." *Variety*, January 10, 1913, p. 7.
32. "Injustice of copyists exemplified in Barnes' case." *Variety*, November 28, 1913, p. 4.
33. "Protection from 'choosers' uniquely sought by artist." *Variety*, October 15, 1915, p. 5.
34. "Copies everywhere." *Variety*, September 15, 1906, p. 5.
35. "Pirating abroad." *Variety*, May 18, 1907, p. 7.
36. "Another European steal." *Variety*, October 26, 1907, p. 6.
37. "Hymack." (review). *Variety*, January 4, 1908, p. 11.
38. "A 'copy' in England." *Variety*, February 13, 1909, p. 4.
39. "Protection from 'thieves' needed by American acts." *Variety*, July 5, 1912, p. 6.
40. "Hayes cables manuscript to ward off foreign piracy." *Variety*, November 29, 1912, p. 4.
41. "Toby Claude plays copy act in London hall and scores." *Variety*, March 28, 1913, p. 4.
42. "10,000 marks piracy fine for unauthorized 'effect.'" *Variety*, October 17, 1913, p. 4.
43. "The latest copy act." *Variety*, September 28, 1907, p. 3.
44. "*Clipper* still copying." *Variety*, October 5, 1907, p. 3.
45. "The thieving *Dramatic Mirror* caught red-handed with the goods." *Variety*, May 23, 1908, p. 5.
46. "Originality will be protected." *Variety*, December 1, 1906, p. 2.
47. "The White Rats urge protection of originality." *Variety*, May 2, 1908, p. 8.
48. Sime Silverman. "Copy acts." *Variety*, December 12, 1908, pp. 26, 88.
49. "Studying new copyright law." *Variety*, June 12, 1909, p. 9.
50. "'Copy acts' not allowed on Loew's small time." *Variety*, March 26, 1910, p. 8.
51. "World's League of Artists and copy acts passed upon." *Variety*, August 5, 1911, p. 4.
52. "First benefit of copy-act pact at Paris conference." *Variety*, November 4, 1911, p. 4.
53. "German artists' society throws out a copy act." *Variety*, March 9, 1912, p. 4.
54. "Private detective system for 'material-stealers.'" *Variety*, April 24, 1914, p. 7.
55. "Criminal copyright action ended by five in U.S. court." *Variety*, July 10, 1914, p. 3.
56. "'Protected material' dep't. under Variety's direction." *Variety*, February 4, 1916, pp. 5, 13.
57. "Variety's anti-copy pact eliminates Orange Packers!" *Variety*, October 13, 1916, p. 5.
58. John E. DiMeglio. *Vaudeville U.S.A.* Bowling Green, Ohio: Bowling Green University Popular Press, 1973, p. 78.
59. "Variety's anti-copy pact eliminates Orange Packers!" *Variety*, October 13, 1916, p. 5.
60. John E. DiMeglio, op. cit., pp. 75–76, 78.
61. *Ibid.*, p. 78.
62. Bill Smith. *The Vaudevillians*. New York: Macmillan, 1976, p. 10.
63. *Ibid.*, pp. 12, 37, 83–84.
64. Jeanne Thomas Allen. "Copyright and early theater vaudeville, and film competition." In John L. Fell, ed. *Film Before Griffith*. Berkeley: University of California Press, 1983, pp. 182–3.
65. "International copyright through State Department." *Variety*, December 5, 1913, p. 11.
66. "Pittsburgh play pirating grown to be common thing." *Variety*, February 13, 1914, p. 10.
67. "Alleged play pirate nabbed after river and city search." *Variety*, September 10, 1915, p. 11.
68. "Stopping pirating." *Variety*, November 12, 1915, p. 3; "N.Y. play pirate caught." *Variety*, January 28, 1976, p. 10.
69. "Plays are openly pirated by Coast stock producers." *Variety*, September 27, 1923, p. 1.

070. "Canadian piracy of 'Abie' brings fines for offenders." *Variety*, February 17, 1926, pp. 1, 14.

71. "Held on copyright infringement charge." *Variety*, January 6, 1922, p. 3.

Chapter 2

1. Jeanne Thomas Allen. "Copyright and early theater, vaudeville, and film competition." In John L. Fell, ed. *Film Before Griffith*. Berkeley: University of California Press, 1983, p. 176; Kenneth MacGowan. *Behind the Screen*. New York: Delacorte, 1976, p. 90.

2. Andre Gaudreault. "The infringement of copyright laws and its effects (1900–1906)" *Framework* no. 29 (1985): 3–6.

3. Arthur Knight. *The Liveliest Art*. New York: Macmillan, 1957, p. 42.

4. William K. Everson. *American Silent Film*. New York: Oxford, 1978, pp. 101–102.

5. Eileen Bowser. *History of the American Cinema: The Transformation of Cinema 1907–1915*. Vol. 2. New York: Scribner's Sons, 1990, pp. 137–139.

6. "Manufacturers assume control of all moving pictures." *Variety*, January 16, 1909, p. 13.

7. "Secret service for snippers." *Variety*, January 23, 1914, p. 15.

8. "Alleged film flimmers." *Variety*, September 11, 1914, p. 20; "Film crooks." *Variety*, April 16, 1915, p. 17; "Seizing Keystone Chaplins." *Variety*, September 10, 1915, p. 18.

9. "Theft exposes film plot." *Variety*, February 23, 1917, p. 21.

10. "Serious film thefts." *Variety*, March 2, 1917, p. 22.

11. "More film theft arrests." *Variety*, May 11, 1917, p. 29.

12. "Film thefts increasing." *Variety*, September 28, 1917, p. 30.

13. "Dealer pleads guilty to film theft in 1919." *New York Times*, March 24, 1928, p. 29.

14. "Three gem thefts baffling police." *New York Times*, March 31, 1921, p. 17.

15. "Film gyps work Mexico." *Variety*, April 22, 1921, p. 47.

16. "To check piracy of American films." *Variety*, August 17, 1921, p. 19.

17. "United Artists satisfied with clean-up of pirates." *Variety*, December 23, 1921, p. 39.

18. *Ibid*.

19. "Sentenced for film theft." *New York Times*, January 22, 1922, p. 21; "Long jail term for film thieves." *Variety*, February 3, 1922, p. 45.

20. "Film thieves $35,000 coup on the coast." *Variety*, January 27, 1922, p. 45.

21. George Mooser. "Japanese pirates defiant." *Variety*, June 2, 1922, p. 39.

22. "Plot to steal many films frustrated in Los Angeles." *Variety*, January 25, 1923, p. 46.

23. "Robert Miller arrested for theft." *Variety*, March 7, 1919, p. 73.

24. "Statewide probe into thefts." *Variety*, July 4, 1919, p. 47; "Film theft examination." *Variety*, July 4, 1919, p. 47.

25. "Asks $2,000,000 damages." *Variety*, November 21, 1919, p. 64.

26. "Lauds capture of film thieves." *New York Times*, August 22, 1919, p. 2.

27. "$50,000 film theft leads to arrest." *New York Times*, November 11, 1919, p. 17.

28. "Young thieves arrested." *Variety*, December 19, 1919, p. 49.

29. "Film thieves held for grand jury." *Variety*, June 25, 1920, p. 39.

30. "Campaign against film thieves receives impetus at start." *Variety*, May 13, 1921, p. 47.

31. "Held in wholesale film theft charge." *Variety*, January 27, 1922, p. 42.

32. "Duped films in Boston for mail orders." *Variety*, November 16, 1927, p. 9.

33. "Pursue film pirates." *Variety*, March 28, 1934, p. 4; "Stop wholesale 'duping' cry of European movie men." *Variety*, July 10, 1914, p. 18.

34. "Film drama disappears." *New York Times*, January 15, 1919, p. 2.
35. "Pirating going on." *Variety*, September 10, 1915, p. 19.
36. "Duping still continues." *Variety*, June 8, 1917, p. 18.
37. "Film smugglers of the East." *Variety*, March 11, 1925, pp. 31, 34.
38. "Mexican pirates clean up smuggling American films." *Variety*, July 11, 1919, p. 64; "Arrest 3; tell silk theft." *New York Times*, December 10, 1919, p. 8.
39. "Gov't aiding film piracy fight." *Variety*, November 4, 1925, p. 34.
40. "Protection in Palestine." *Variety*, December 16, 1925, p. 31.
41. "Cuba after film pirates." *New York Times*, September 13, 1923, p. 31.
42. "To guard American films." *New York Times*, May 28, 1924, p. 48.
43. "Turkey pirate stopped by Kemal Bey." *Variety*, February 24, 1926, p. 35.
44. "Piracy checked in near East." *Variety*, August 24, 1927, p. 17.
45. "Gigantic film plot exposed in Warsaw." *New York Times*, June 10, 1926, p. 29.
46. "Turkey upholds 'dupe' film." *Variety*, July 21, 1926, pp. 5, 11.
47. "Bold Polish film pirates exhibit Chaplin's *Gold Rush* at Bucharest." *Variety*, October 6, 1926, pp. 40, 46.
48. "*Sea Beast*, *Girl Shy* pirated; shown in China and Greece." *Variety*, January 19, 1927, p. 4.
49. "No protection from Venezuela pirates." *Variety*, March 30, 1927, p. 10.
50. "Pirating film out of N.Y." *Variety*, September 28, 1927, p. 4.
51. Advertisement. *Variety*, February 1, 1908, p. 33; *Variety*, October 24, 1913, p. 30.
52. "Film theft bill up in Washington." *Variety*, January 20, 1922, p. 39.
53. "U.S. probes charge Calif. exhibs smuggle pictures into Mexico." *Variety*, September 9, 1936, p. 6.
54. "Motion picture protected against piracy by Berne convention articles." *Variety*, September 15, 1926, p. 4; Bernard A. Kosicki. "International copyright relations between the American republics." *Variety*, December 15, 1926, pp. 8, 10.
55. "Standing for switching." *Variety*, April 16, 1915, p. 17.
56. "Vigilance against theft." *Variety*, February 21, 1919, p. 73; "Film suspect arrested." *Variety*, February 28, 1919, p. 65.
57. "Organized crusade to stop thievery shows quick results." *Variety*, March 7, 1919, p. 73.
58. "To read sensational charges at open exhibitors' meeting." *Variety*, July 16, 1920, p. 39.
59. "Upstate bicyclers admit guilt; pay up." *Variety*, July 30, 1920, p. 36.
60. "Looking for bicycling." *Variety*, March 26, 1924, p. 18.
61. "Bicycle exhib is nicked $1,589 by film board." *Variety*, May 9, 1928, p. 42.
62. "Bicycling damages for $10,000 against Hildinger Co. by film board." *Variety*, November 7, 1928, p. 20.
63. "Film vandals taken in hand by principal manufacturers." *Variety*, January 16, 1914, p. 17.
64. "Picture director protests against cutting of feature." *Variety*, January 19, 1917, p. 20.
65. "Contracting for no cuts." *Variety*, February 23, 1917, p. 19.
66. "Exhibitors for cutting film may have to pay big penalty." *Variety*, July 9, 1920, p. 29.
67. "May raise movie prices." *New York Times*, August 19, 1924, p. 15.
68. "Title change upheld in Canada." *Variety*, January 19, 1927, p. 13.
69. "Say film infringes on copyright." *Variety*, March 21, 1908, p. 14.
70. Jeanne Thomas Allen, op. cit., p. 185.
71. "Must pay royalties on moving pictures." *New York Times*, May 6, 1908, p. 5.
72. "Blow to moving pictures." *New York Times*, November 14, 1911, p. 13; "Rights of authors vindicated." *New York Times*, November 15, 1911, p. 10.
73. William K. Everson, op. cit., p. 102.

74. David Bordwell, Janet Staiger and Kristin Thompson. *The Classical Hollywood Cinema: Film Style and Mode of Production to 1960*. London: Routledge & Kegan Paul, 1985, pp. 130–131.

75. Anthony Slide. *The American Film Industry: A Historical Dictionary*. Westport, Conn.: Greenwood, 1986, p. 79.

76. "After picture pirates." *Variety*, November 19, 1915, p. 21.

77. "Chaplin copy injunction." *Variety*, October 12, 1917, p. 31; "Chaplin claim assented to." *Variety*, October 19, 1917, p. 25.

78. "Author's protective bureau." *Variety*, February 22, 1918, p. 50.

79. "Authors' League charges mutilation in transference." *Variety*, April 12, 1923, p. 1.

80. "*Feet of Clay* enjoined." *New York Times*, August 21, 1925, p. 8.

81. "Inside stuff on vaudeville." *Variety*, November 4, 1925, p. 3.

82. "Producers are stealing material, says Screen Writers' Guild organ." *Variety*, May 2, 1928, p. 10.

83. "Picture men have 'joker' for the copyright law." *Variety*, February 10, 1912, p. 12; "Fight motion picture men." *New York Times*, February 28, 1912, p. 11.

84. "Urges copyright change." *New York Times*, March 11, 1912, p. 3.

85. Advertisement. *Variety*, February 18, 1921, p. 44.

86. "Music licenses." *Variety*, January 20, 1922, p. 39.

87. "Agitation over 'music tax' started by Frank Rembusch." *Variety*, July 21, 1922, p. 39.

88. "Exhibitors' own music department stand against weekly fee." *Variety*, July 28, 1922, p. 39.

89. "Movie theater men fight Hays groups." *New York Times*, May 23, 1923, p. 5; "May raise movie prices." *New York Times*, August 19, 1924, p. 15.

90. "Publishers win movie music suit." *New York Times*, July 18, 1924, p. 7.

91. "Reissuing old prints." *Variety*, September 11, 1914, p. 20.

92. "Dating films." *Variety*, August 10, 1917, p. 19.

93. "'Reissue' business method corrected by Commission." *Variety*, April 18, 1919, p. 56.

94. "To bar old films under new titles." *New York Times*, August 8, 1922, p. 16; "Fox Film Corporation protest press wire." *New York Times*, August 9, 1922, p. 36.

95. "Federal Trade Commission heard 4,000 film complaints." *Variety*, December 10, 1924, p. 26.

96. "Limits new titles for reissued films." *New York Times*, April 1, 1925, p. 21.

97. "Inside stuff of pictures." *Variety*, November 23, 1927, p. 14.

98. Elliott Forbes. "Here's looking at you, Fred." *Film Comment* 34 (May/June, 1998): 79.

99. "Brings suit to prevent changes in his films." *New York Times*, October 6, 1922, p. 28; "Fairbanks loses film revision suit." *New York Times*, December 9, 1922, p. 11.

Chapter 3

1. "New epidemic of film piracy." *Variety*, August 8, 1933, p. 4.

2. "Bootlegging of feature pix and shorts still a big trade worry." *Variety*, August 26, 1936, p. 3.

3. "Tricks of the 'jack rabbit.'" *Variety*, May 26, 1937, pp. 5, 62.

4. "Jackrabbit scourge up." *Variety*, May 6, 1942, pp. 7, 25; "Gas-tire rationing and wartime biz boom 'jackrabbit' exhibs." *Variety*, September 16, 1942, p. 18.

5. "Air pirate sound effects at no expense." *Variety*, November 15, 1932, p. 7.

6. "Bootleg film ad reels, new gyp." *Variety*, July 12, 1939, p. 4.

7. "Film bootlegging grows." *Variety*, December 20, 1939, p. 3.

8. "Indicts 3 in N.Y. for handling 'hot' films." *Variety*, February 5, 1941, p. 7.

9. Ezra Goodman. "Hollywood's private gumshoes." *New York Times*, December 1, 1940, sec. 10, p. 4.

10. "U.S. probes charge Calif. Exhibs smuggle pictures into Mexico." *Variety*, September 9, 1936, p. 6.

11. "Urge fixed damages in copyright bill." *New York Times*, April 14, 1936, p. 13.

12. "Hold movies need copyright penalty." *New York Times*, April 15, 1936, p. 24.

13. "Film, radio, music trades unite against world copyright union." *Variety*, April 14, 1937, pp. 4, 75; "Immediate ratification of int'l copyright convention urged on U.S." *Variety*, December 1, 1937, p. 11.

14. "Copyright laws traced by Kilroe." *Variety*, December 6, 1944, p. 8.

15. "Movies seek change in copyright pact." *New York Times*, July 11, 1939, p. 17.

16. "Bicycling fines of $500." *Variety*, April 15, 1931, pp. 11, 75.

17. "Bicycling suits to recover $250 or more from Texas indie exhibs are started by Copyright Bureau." *Variety*, July 28, 1931, p. 7; "Bicycling charges filed against Texas exhibs— may have jury edge." *Variety*, August 11, 1931, p. 31.

18. "Copyright infringement by film exhibitor." *Scientific American* 147 (July, 1932): 61.

19. "E. M. Loew claim soaked $3,000 on cycling charge." *Variety*, May 12, 1937, p. 21.

20. "N.Y. copyright suits won by Metro, U." *Variety*, January 10, 1945, p. 11.

21. "Percentage cheaters." *Variety*, April 23, 1930, pp. 5, 20.

22. "Chiseling checkers, besides percentage cheaters, maybe causing dicks to be watchers." *Variety*, May 7, 1930, p. 17

23. "Percentage evil worse." *Variety*, May 14, 1930, pp. 5, 14.

24. "Bicycling fines of $500." *Variety*, April 15, 1931, pp. 11, 75.

25. "House employes gyppers." *Variety*, June 9, 1931, pp. 11, 36

26. "Bicycling charges filed against Texas exhibs— may have jury edge." *Variety*, August 11, 1931, p. 31.

27. "% film checker's hazards." *Variety*, January 8, 1935, p. 7.

28. "Film checking tightens." *Variety*, December 31, 1941, pp. 5, 54.

29. "Consultants in on % pix." *Variety*, March 29, 1944, p. 9.

30. "Tighter gov't b.o. check." *Variety*, April 12, 1944, p. 7.

31. "Films central checking." *Variety*, June 28, 1944, p. 13.

32. "Revenouers may become interested in curbing gypping exhibs on % pix." *Variety*, December 20, 1944, p. 4.

33. "Called 'stool pigeon,' checker awarded 10G damages from exhib." *Variety*, January 10, 1945, p. 11.

34. "5 majors set up own checking bureau." *Variety*, March 7, 1945, p. 9; "Pix checkers bid for Edgar Hoover." *Variety*, July 11, 1945, p. 3.

35. "Distributors backing Ross Federal anew to bolster checking system." *Variety*, October 24, 1945, p. 12.

36. "'Piracy' pact soon due." *Variety*, April 8, 1931, p. 3; "Expect many mix-ups over studios new anti-talent raiding agreement." *Variety*, February 16, 1932, p. 4.

37. "Zanuck's raiding mess." *Variety*, June 13, 1933, pp. 5, 43.

38. "Anti-raiding pact given boot by all three major studios." *Variety*, November 6, 1934, p. 4.

39. "Fox screen deletions." *Variety*, March 4, 1931, pp. 11, 27.

40. "Directors protest editing of pictures by $40 cutters." *Variety*, June 7, 1933, p. 7.

41. "*Lettie Lynton* movie ruled a plagiarism." *New York Times*, January 18, 1936, p. 19.

42. "Authors win suit in Supreme Court." *New York Times*, May 5, 1936, p. 12.

43. "$10,000 verdict in film suit." *New York Times*, March 11, 1938, p. 15; "Tarkington need not go to N.Y. for WB exam." *Variety*, February 22, 1939, p. 6.

44. "Asks 500G damages, claims *Wilson* theft." *Variety*, January 10, 1945, p. 11.

45. Tad Friend. "Copy cats." *New Yorker* 74 (September 14, 1998): 54, 57.

46. Roy Chartier. "A good print is the ultimate in a film's merchandising." *Variety*, January 6, 1937, p. 6.

Chapter 4

1. "Loew's International ties up with DeVry for 16mm foreign markets." *Variety*, December 12, 1945, p. 5.
2. Richard Albarino. "UA goes into narrow gauge." *Variety*, May 25, 1966, pp. 11, 22.
3. "Exhibs applaud Disney Prod.'s move to tighten restraints on 16m films." *Variety*, August 30, 1967, p. 26.
4. "Black market sales of majors' 16m pix exposed." *Variety*, March 13, 1946, pp. 1, 27.
5. "FBI nails sailor bootlegging pix." *Variety*, December 25, 1946, p. 4.
6. "FBI's fine job in bootleg pix K.O." *Variety*, April 26, 1950, p. 2.
7. Hazel Guild. "Fox's fear of 16m piracy bars *Star Wars* from global GI sites." *Variety*, March 21, 1979, p. 51.
8. "U's pirated *Uncle Tom* 25 years old, hot b.o.; court impounds prints." *Variety*, September 10, 1952, pp. 3, 18; "Howard Underwood found guilty of piracy." *Variety*, March 9, 1955, p. 5.
9. "Churches buy bootleg films." *Variety*, November 22, 1961, p. 11.
10. "20th cracks down, closes club showing 16m prints from undisclosed sources." *Variety*, October 26, 1966, p. 13.
11. "8 majors sue Florida firm for pix piracy." *Variety*, June 17, 1970, p. 3.
12. Ronald Gold. "Hang fines on film pirate." *Variety*, April 12, 1972, p. 5.
13. "Print pirate: 'Why am I unpopular?'" *Variety*, April 26, 1972, p. 29.
14. "Tighten noose on pirate-film prints at Middlesex, N.J." *Variety*, August 11, 1971, p. 6; "8 majors crack down on Ala. print pirate." *Variety*, September 1, 1971, p. 4.
15. Robert J. Landry. "Writers' new piracy phobia." *Variety*, March 1, 1972, pp. 5, 24.
16. "Curb Dunnahoo on print piracy." *Variety*, June 7, 1972, p. 22.
17. Joe McBride. "28-yr. renewal failure throws films in public domain and onto ex-pirate's lawful list." *Variety*, August 28, 1974, pp. 5, 28.
18. "FBI apprehends 3 in *Godfather* stolen prints." *Variety*, September 27, 1972, p. 4.
19. "Dirty pictures, dirty pirates; Buckley cites Florida crowd." *Variety*, July 31, 1974, p. 31.
20. "Schools pirate off 16m rentals." *Variety*, June 18, 1975, pp. 7, 30.
21. "U.S. pix behind 'Iron Curtain.'" *Variety*, August 21, 1946, pp. 3, 28.
22. "U.S. asks return of 2 motion picture films diverted in the Soviet for propaganda ends." *New York Times*, January 23, 1951, p. 22.
23. "Hollywood, Soviet style." *New York Times*, January 25, 1951, p. 24.
24. "U.S. film list rises in Russian cinemas." *New York Times*, April 11, 1951, p. 35.
25. "Soviet continues to pirate old U.S. pix." *Variety*, May 21, 1952, p. 3; "Soviet rebuffs U.S. on return of 5 films." *New York Times*, September 22, 1952, p. 19.
26. "Film ties to U.S. sought by Soviet." *New York Times*, March 10, 1956, p. 9.
27. "Pirated U.S. play filmed in Soviet." *New York Times*, March 10, 1961, p. 24.
28. "Mex piracy of Yank scripts seen ending." *Variety*, September 2, 1959, p. 11.
29. "Film pirates irk Mexican pic biz." *Variety*, March 5, 1969, p. 2.
30. "Indonesian exhib pirates pic." *Variety*, June 22, 1966, p. 5; "Recover 850 prints stolen in Indonesia." *Variety*, November 22, 1967, p. 21.
31. "Print piracy, censorship problems in Iran." *Variety*, November 12, 1969, p. 28.
32. "India cracks down on film smuggling." *Variety*, December 3, 1969, p. 22; "Seize prints of pirated Indian pic in So. Africa." *Variety*, April 25, 1973, p. 7.
33. "Turk producers ignore copyright." *Variety*, June 10, 1970, p. 25.
34. Jack Pitman. "Print pirates vex majors." *Variety*, July 8, 1970, p. 31.

35. "Film piracy hits record level in So. Africa market." *Variety*, March 24, 1971, p. 31.
36. "Chaplin wins vs. *Gold Rush* pirate." *Variety*, March 24, 1971, p. 31.
37. "Print theft rising; Sicilians warned." *Variety*, June 30, 1971, p. 34.
38. "Map Interpol vs. pix pirates." *Variety*, March 29, 1972, pp. 1, 88; "U.S.-U.K. team vs. print piracy." *Variety*, October 4, 1972, p. 4.
39. "Trial date nears for 10 defendants in U.K. film bootlegging case." *Variety*, February 7, 1973, p. 29.
40. "Egypt film biz losing 'millions' from smuggling, officials claim." *Variety*, October 17, 1973, p. 21.
41. "Universal copyright convention okayed; films covered in pact." *Variety*, September 14, 1955, pp. 3, 18.
42. "Columbia registers with MPA titles of telepix made by Screen Gems." *Variety*, May 25, 1955, p. 4.
43. "Picking film titles: arduous sport." *Variety*, March 20, 1957, p. 20.
44. "Film 'plagiarism' arouses studios." *New York Times*, August 4, 1961, p. 11.
45. "Spy mania complicates protection of Agent 007 at United Artists." *Variety*, February 16, 1966, p. 11; Paul D. Springer. "Recent decisions ease choice of film titles." *Variety*, January 7, 1970, p. 43.
46. "Majors fighting print piracy with 175G war chest." *Variety*, July 22, 1970, p. 28.
47. "Pro and amateur crooks in 16m pix biz." *Variety*, March 26, 1975, pp. 5, 28.
48. "$20,000,000 gyp of % deals." *Variety*, May 22, 1946, p. 7.
49. "Metro supplementing its checking system" *Variety*, May 22, 1947, p. 7.
50. "Revenouers get co-op from majors checking on chiseling exhibs." *Variety*, May 22, 1946, p. 7.
51. Ira Wit. "Handbook for chiseling exhibs." *Variety*, June 5, 1946, pp. 5, 29.
52. "Exhibs blame film sales." *Variety*, September 25, 1946, pp. 11, 20.
53. "Nomikos' 10 houses sued for phoney % returns." *Variety*, September 25, 1946, pp. 11, 18.
54. "Distribs see Mpls. and Pa. exhibs on % deals." *Variety*, September 25, 1946, p. 11; "Checkers figure exhibs get away with as much as $25,000,000." *Variety*, October 2, 1946, p. 9.
55. Hayden Talbot. "Hypoed grind hours provide lush grosses." *Variety*, October 9, 1946, p. 27.
56. "Aver exhib chiseling spreads." *Variety*, July 9, 1947, pp. 5, 26.
57. "Flats grow with checking curb." *Variety*, October 15, 1947, pp. 9, 20.
58. "Par's %-chiseling suit vs. Brandt may get out-of-court settlement." *Variety*, February 11, 1948, p. 13.
59. "% chiseling probe a new weapon by majors in fighting trust suits." *Variety*, May 5, 1948, p. 4.
60. "Important ruling vs. % chiselers." *Variety*, May 19, 1948, p. 6.
61. "Film checking declines 44%." *Variety*, August 18, 1948, pp. 5, 20.
62. "Exhib %-chiseling on wane." *Variety*, April 13, 1949, pp. 7, 20.
63. "Rodgers to brush % chiselers." *Variety*, November 1, 1950, pp. 5, 23.
64. "10,509 % cases in 1949 probed by law firm." *Variety*, January 31, 1951, p. 5.
65. "200 fraud % suits vs. exhibs." *Variety*, January 24, 1951, pp. 5, 13.
66. "NCA says 'unreasonable' % deals are at root of exhibs' checking trouble." *Variety*, September 2, 1953, pp. 4, 15.
67. "Exhibs burn at claim of checking rental." *Variety*, August 18, 1954, p. 3.
68. "Dix exhibs defending honor." *Variety*, May 1, 1957, p. 25.
69. "Rentals as 'funds in trust.'" *Variety*, June 19, 1957, pp. 3, 7.
70. "Court hits B.O. chiseling." *Variety*, March 9, 1966, p. 7.
71. "Eye on boxoffice larceny." *Variety*, December 3, 1969, pp. 3, 15.
72. "Sharing terms and larceny." *Variety*, August 6, 1969, pp. 5, 51.
73. "Alarmed by sticky-fingered exhibs, NATO to banish 'em, upon conviction." *Variety*, March 3, 1971, p. 5.

74. "Tough recoup from cheats." *Variety*, June 9, 1971, p. 3.
75. "More gripes, more suits, more hisses for those cheating-hearted exhibitors." *Variety*, June 30, 1971, p. 3.
76. "Infra-red checks drive-in." *Variety*, August 30, 1972, p. 7.
77. "Under-reporting now 'crime.'" *Variety*, January 10, 1973, pp. 5, 30.
78. "Tell multiples to stop site switching." *Variety*, August 13, 1975, pp. 3, 22.
79. "Slow pay exhibs speed TV." *Variety*, April 3, 1963, pp. 3, 14.
80. Gene Arneel. "U socks slow-pay exhibs." *Variety*, February 25, 1970, p. 3.
81. "Fox charging exhibs for slow pay." *Variety*, June 24, 1970, p. 3.
82. "Par gets tough on late-pay rentals." *Variety*, October 1, 1975, pp. 3, 38.
83. "Robbery begins on staff." *Variety*, January 15, 1969, p. 7.
84. Gene Arneel. "Theater theft constant." *Variety*, April 1, 1970, pp. 7, 28.
85. "Plots sneak in advertising." *Variety*, August 7, 1957, pp. 3, 22.
86. Murray Horowitz. "TV sugar-'codes' old features." *Variety*, April 17, 1957, pp. 1, 15.
87. "Everybody's rights trampled upon when TV stations mutilate — Woolner." *Variety*, December 8, 1965, p. 5.
88. Robert B. Frederick. "TV kind of film editing escapes Preminger's try for injunction." *Variety*, January 26, 1966, p. 17.
89. A. D. Murphy. "Pix-TV spotlight on how NBC will not 'emasculate' George Stevens' film." *Variety*, February 16, 1966, pp. 1, 23.
90. "Failure of Stevens' suit vs. NBC opens door for TV to carve pix." *Variety*, June 8, 1966, pp. 26, 38.
91. Bill Greely. "Butchery in TV's grindhouse." *Variety*, October 19, 1966, pp. 1, 36.
92. Paul M. Jensen. "TV mutilation of widescreen: Stevens & Preminger's anguish." *Variety*, January 3, 1968, p. 17.
93. "Directors seek 'integrity' proviso on cutting of films sold to TV." *Variety*, May 15, 1968, p. 20.
94. George Ferris III. "Confessions of a movie butcher." *Washington Post*, March 6, 1988, pp. G1, G6–G7.
95. Fred Hift. "Nobody counts the minutes." *Variety*, June 17, 1959, pp. 3, 16.
96. "Doug McClelland on the art of film editing." *Variety*, October 4, 1972, p. 20.
97. "'Moral right' on scissored pix stirs up French." *Variety*, May 11, 1949, p. 13.
98. Robert F. Hawkins. "In Italy: director is all." *Variety*, February 28, 1962, p. 11.
99. "Continual changes in copyright values affect all show biz." *Variety*, November 6, 1957, p. 2.
100. "Director is king in pictures." *Variety*, February 27, 1957, pp. 5, 15.
101. "The importance of the title." *Variety*, April 15, 1959, p. 7.
102. "'Anti-raiding' policy said to be stagnating sales dept. personnel." *Variety*, July 28, 1948, pp. 5, 22.
103. "Phoney film bookkeeping." *Variety*, June 2, 1948, pp. 3, 14.
104. "Keep Broadway believable." *Variety*, March 20, 1968, pp. 3, 17.
105. "$200,000 suit settled." *New York Times*, March 2, 1954, p. 22.
106. "Sam Spade is author's property." *Variety*, November 17, 1954, p. 3.
107. "'Scenes' in ads not on screen." *Variety*, June 19, 1957, p. 27.
108. Louis Calta. "New city rule bars deceptive ad uses of review quotings." *New York Times*, March 23, 1972, p. 50.

Chapter 5

1. "Say all can play cassette." *Variety*, November 4, 1970, p. 5.
2. "Britain's Vidicord shed cassettes' umbilical cord with pix-on-video." *Variety*, December 16, 1970, pp. 1, 70.

3. "Pirates, porn ops not in the groove of videodisk biz." *Variety*, January 24, 1979, pp. 1, 100.

4. Aljean Harmetz. "Sales of movie cassettes for home use rising." *New York Times*, June 27, 1983, pp. A1, B7.

5. "A blank tape for Hollywood." *Newsweek* 143 (January 30, 1984): 57–58; Fred Barbash. "Viewer videotaping of TV programs upheld." *Washington Post*, January 18, 1984, pp. A1, A17.

6. "'It's plain theft' campus profs told as to rampant piracy." *Variety*, August 22, 1979, p. 6.

7. "Video bootleggers: bane of film studios." *New York Times*, October 23, 1982, pp. 41, 43.

8. Steven Prince. *History of the American Cinema: A New Pot of Gold*. New York: Scribner's Sons, 2000, pp. 98–99.

9. "Film, TV piracy: a global probe." *Variety*, December 18, 1974, p. 6.

10. "McDowall films seized in piracy investigation." *Variety*, January 18, 1975, p. 39.

11. "McDowall cleared by U.S. of film piracy connection." *New York Times*, June 3, 1975, p. 25; "Free McDowall, but warn buffs of 'stolen property' entanglements." *Variety*, June 4, 1975, p. 6.

12. Jon Nordheimer. "U.S. and industry fight piracy of films." *New York Times*, June 8, 1975, p. 47.

13. "Crucial print piracy victory." *Variety*, October 1, 1975, p. 48.

14. "Tough federal action drives film pirates underground." *Variety*, September 15, 1976, pp. 6, 32.

15. James Monaco. "Stealing the show: the piracy problem." *American Film* 3 (July/August, 1978): 59; "The film clippers." *Time* 106 (October 22, 1975): 70.

16. "Court reversal makes piracy tough to prove." *Variety*, October 12, 1977, pp. 1, 44.

17. "World-wide war on pix print pirates." *Variety*, February 19, 1975, pp. 5, 30.

18. A. H. Weiler. "Movie security group will hunt for pirates." *New York Times*, February 19, 1975, p. 22.

19. "Nolan, Layhew, FBI alumni head pic war on pirates." *Variety*, March 12, 1975, p. 5.

20. "Piracy requires more MPAA 'eyes.'" *Variety*, March 8, 1978, p. 5.

21. "Quietly adopted warnings: 'film pirates prosecuted.'" *Variety*, October 1, 1975, p. 5.

22. Frank Segers. "Pix pirates face secret weapon." *Variety*, May 26, 1976, pp. 1, 34; "Piracy runs into million-$ losses; strengthen copyright." *Variety*, March 21, 1979, p. 40.

23. "Piracy and privilege: Bel-Air home threat." *Variety*, December 22, 1976, p. 4.

24. "WB offers $5,000 to employees who finger pix pirates." *Variety*, June 1, 1977, p. 1.

25. "NFS offers reward, warns of 'print piracy' danger." *Boxoffice* 111 (August 15, 1977): 10.

26. "$5,000 bounty on film pirate's head." *Variety*, November 9, 1977, p. 7.

27. James Monaco. "Stealing the show: the piracy problem." *American Film* 3 (July/August, 1978): 60–62.

28. Robert Thomas Jr. "Suspect in piracy of films is seized." *New York Times*, February 20, 1975, pp. 1, 38.

29. "Raid on print pirate; title range shock." *Variety*, February 26, 1975, p. 28.

30. "The film clippers." *Time* 106 (October 27, 1975): 70.

31. "Grab pirated cassettes in motels on *Star Wars*, *Jaws* and *Rocky*." *Variety*, September 28, 1977, p. 42.

32. "Federal grand jury in Houston, Tex. indicts 7 in film piracy operation." *Boxoffice* 114 (January 8, 1979): 8.

33. "Pirated films taken in raid in Wichita." *Boxoffice* 113 (June 19, 1978): C4.

34. "Tulsa grand jury issues indictments; five arrested in illegal film sales." *Boxoffice* 114 (January 15, 1979): 7; "Two Philadelphia men arrested for piracy." *Boxoffice* 114 (January 22, 1979): E-1.

35. "FBI seizes tapes, films worth $100,000." *Variety*, September 12, 1979, p. 30.

36. "Theater boothmen as No. 1 'suspects' in piracy of films." *Variety*, July 18, 1979, p. 24.

37. "Labs, booths, buffs feed lifters." *Variety*, March 7, 1979, p. 5.

38. "Thus far, *Alien* not pirated; FBI raps failure to 'encode.'" *Variety*, July 4, 1979, p. 4.

39. Stephen Rebello. "State of siege." *American Film* 9 (May, 1984): 44; William Nix. "New technology hurt and helped global video piracy during 1985." *Variety*, January 8, 1986, pp. 7, 240.

40. William Nix. "New technology hurt and helped global video piracy during 1985." *Variety*, January 8, 1986, pp. 7, 240.

41. David Bollier. "At war with the pirates." *Channels* (New York, N.Y.) 7 (March, 1987): 31, 35; Lawrence Van Gelder. "At the movies." *New York Times*, February 19, 1988, p. C8.

42. "MPAA boosts film piracy kitty." *Variety*, April 23, 1980, p. 7.

43. Stephen Klain. "Will science soon trace pirate lairs?" *Variety*, July 1, 1981, pp. 5, 33.

44. "*Ark* raid tied to Par's upfront anti-piracy ploys." *Variety*, July 1, 1981, pp. 5, 34.

45. David Shribman. "Top-notch lobbyists on tape royalties." *New York Times*, November 24, 1982, p. A20.

46. Jack Valenti. "A film ripoff by the Japanese." *New York Times*, March 6, 1985, p. A23.

47. Ted Clark. "Int'l fests tighten anti-piracy guard." *Variety*, November 24, 1982, pp. 7, 27.

48. Aljean Harmetz. "*Jedi* prints stolen for cassette piracy, movie industry says." *New York Times*, July 9, 1983, pp. 1, 10.

49. Aljean Harmetz. "*Cotton Club* cassettes coded to foil pirates." *New York Times*, April 24, 1985, p. C15.

50. Aljean Harmetz. "Film industry escalates war against pirates." *New York Times*, June 23, 1986, p. C14; David Bollier. "At war with the pirates." *Channels* (New York, N.Y.) 7 (March 7, 1987): 35.

51. Clyde H. Farnsworth. "U.S. eases threats of sanctions." *New York Times*, November 2, 1989, pp. D1, D18.

52. Lorin Brennan. "2d generation video piracy; export assns. move to strike back." *Variety*, January 20, 1988, pp. 159–160.

53. "Soviet copyright plan." *New York Times*, April 20, 1989, p. D7; Irwin Karp. "The copyright renewal trap." *Film Comment* 26 (January/February, 1990): 12–15; Thomas McCarroll. "Whose bright idea?" *Time* 137 (June 10, 1991): 45.

54. Kurt Stanberry. "Piracy of intellectual property." *Society* 27 (September/October, 1990): 35–38.

55. "Law puts muscle behind fight against piracy, limited access." *Variety*, August 31, 1988, p. 3.

56. Clyde H. Farnsworth. "China called top copyright pirate." *New York Times*, April 20, 1989, p. D7.

57. "Sheinburg says piracy is no. 1 industry threat." *Variety*, July 16, 1980, pp. 1, 88.

58. Robert D. McFadden. "New York pornography suspect dies as agents seek him." *New York Times*, February 15, 1980, p. B4; "FBI exposes porno & piracy affinity." *Variety*, February 20, 1980, p. 7.

59. "FBI probe yields 9 indictments: porn, piracy, prostitution link." *Variety*, June 3, 1981, p. 38.

60. "Vid pirate Ewald, pending trial, is nabbed again." *Variety*, October 13, 1982, p. 41.

61. "Windy City laundering reputation as nation's video piracy capital." *Variety*, December 8, 1982, p. 39.

62. "U.S. Attorney says Chicago was major piracy capital, but argues prosecution has eased problems." *Variety*, December 8, 1982, pp. 42, 46.

63. Aljean Harmetz. "*Jedi* prints stolen for cassette piracy, movie industry says." *New York Times*, July 9, 1983, pp. 1, 10.

64. Tom Bierbaum. "Piracy war: slow-win situation." *Variety*, November 13, 1985, pp. 1, 133.

65. David Bollier. "At war with the pirates." *Channels* (New York, N.Y.) 7 (March, 1987): 30.

66. David Pauly. "A scourge of video pirates." *Newsweek* 110 (July 27, 1987): 40–41.

67. "FBI believes it's uncovered biggest piracy setup ever." *Variety*, February 10, 1988, pp. 1, 132; Lawrence Van Gelder. "At the movies." *New York Times*, February 19, 1988, p. C8.

68. Tom Bierbaum. "Piracy raids by FBI, MPAA nab 3,300 vidtapes." *Variety*, March 30, 1988, p. 40.

69. "Check cheating-heart employees." *Variety*, April 13, 1977, p. 5.

70. "U.N. campaign to combat film and recording piracy." *New York Times*, February 21, 1981, p. 15; "Officials seize videotapes." *New York Times*, March 18, 1982, p. D10; "How pirates are plundering the studios." *Business Week*, February 21, 1983, p. 81; Alexander L. Taylor III. "Hollywood war on video pirates." *Time* 121 (June 6, 1983): 44.

71. Tony Seideman. "World vid piracy at $1-bil mark." *Variety*, December 21, 1983, pp. 1, 68.

72. Roger Watkins. "Organized crime now into piracy; global woe ongoing." *Variety*, January 11, 1984, pp. 91, 128; David Bollier, op. cit., p. 30.

73. "MPAA sets meet on global piracy, $2-bil-a-year tix." *Variety*, July 3, 1985, pp. 31, 85; "High-tech tactics slow film piracy." *New York Times*, January 29, 1986, p. C13; "Piracy costly for Hollywood." *New York Times*, March 27, 1989, p. D4; "MPAA reports record-breaking results in 1988's war on global piracy." *Variety*, April 5, 1989, p. 2.

74. Tom Bierbaum. "MPAA claims progress in piracy fight." *Variety*, March 19, 1986, pp. 5, 92.

75. "MPAA turned up antipiracy heat in '86, but burned fewer pirates." *Variety*, April 1, 1987, p. 46.

76. "MPAA says raids on pirates up, convictions down." *Variety*, February 8, 1989, p. 47.

77. "MPAA reports record-breaking results in 1988's war on global piracy." *Variety*, April 5, 1989, p. 2.

78. "FBI alters rules on following up vid piracy cases." *Variety*, December 7, 1988, p. 75.

79. "Government claims U.S. is losing $23-bil revenue to piracy globally." *Variety*, March 16, 1988, p. 76.

80. John Burgess. "Global product piracy may be costing firms billions." *Washington Post*, February 27, 1988, p. B2; Gary M. Hoffman and George T. Marcou. "The costs and complications of piracy." *Society* 27 (September/October, 1990): 26.

81. Peter M. Nichols. "Home video." *New York Times*, December 18, 1998, p. E34.

82. Matt Lake. "Tweaking technology to stay ahead of the film pirates." *New York Times*, August 2, 2001, p. G9.

83. Max Alexander. "New antipiracy laws allow local authorities more power." *Variety*, August 1, 1990, pp. 31, 34.

84. Barry Fox. "Attack on video pirates backfires." *New Scientist* 151 (July 20, 1996): 21.

85. Philip E. Ross. "Cops versus robbers in cyberspace." *Forbes* 158 (September 9, 1996): 134–136.

86. "Format makes rental films disposable." *New York Times*, September 10, 1997, p. D7.

87. "5 companies join in anti-piracy pact." *New York Times*, February 20, 1998, p. D4.

88. "Cinema solution." *Washington Post*, August 11, 1990, p. A20.

89. Morrie Gelman. "FBI raids in Gotham, N.J. crack massive vid operation." *Variety*, February 28, 1990, p. 33.

90. Robert F. Howe. "Fairfax raid nets 50,000 bootleg videos." *Washington Post*, May 7, 1993, pp. A1, A4.
91. "Police announce breakup of pirate videotape ring." *New York Times*, July 8, 1994, p. B5.
92. Linda Wheeler. "U.S. cracks down on video pirates." *Washington Post*, December 7, 1994, p. D3.
93. Ashley Merryman. "Help, police! They've got Pocahontas!" *Washington Post*, July 23, 1995, p. C7.
94. Johnnie L. Roberts. "Buyers beware." *Newsweek* 128 (October 14, 1996): 66–67.
95. David M. Halbfinger. "Stalking the video pirates." *New York Times*, March 10, 1998, p. B4.
96. Linda Lee. "Bootleg videos: piracy with a camcorder." *New York Times*, July 7, 1997, pp. D1, D6.
97. *Ibid.*
98. "Officials say Brooklyn raid cracks bootleg video ring." *New York Times*, November 10, 1997, p. B3.
99. "5 are accused of video piracy after detectives raid factory." *New York Times*, February 20, 1998, p. B8.
100. David M. Halbfinger, op. cit., pp. B1, B4.
101. *Ibid.*
102. Kit R. Roane. "Police smash piracy ring for video, arresting 43." *New York Times*, May 6, 1998, p. B4.
103. Will Tusher. "U.S. losses to global piracy fall 25% in '89, per Valenti." *Variety*, January 10, 1990, p. 13; Faye Rice. "How copycats steal billions." *Fortune* 123 (April 22, 1991): 158; Thomas McCarroll. "Whose bright idea?" *Time* 137 (June 10, 1991): 44.
104. Rex Weiner. "Video pirates find rough seas abroad." *Variety*, May 9, 1994, p. C86; David Halbfinger, op. cit., p. B1; "Comment: piracy." *Wall Street Journal*, August 9, 2001, p. A10.
105. Tom Bierbaum. "Anti-piracy raids on the rise but they make little impact on $1-billion loss." *Variety*, April 4, 1990, p. 37.
106. Lawrence Van Gelder. "At the movies." *New York Times*, February 22, 1991, p. C12.
107. Marc Berman. "Stormy seas for pirates in 1991 video crackdown." *Variety*, January 27, 1992, pp. 19–20; Adam Sandler. "MPAA reports banner year for nabbing pirates." *Variety*, February 13, 1995, p. 24.
108. Philip E. Ross. "Cops versus robbers in cyberspace." *Forbes* 158 (September 9, 1996): 135.
109. Anita Hamilton. "Next on the Net: pirated movies." *Time* 153 (March 15, 1999): 73.
110. Marc Graser. "Cyber-challenged not likely to pirate pix." *Variety*, June 7, 1999, p. 4.
111. Steve Wilson. "On-line piracy turns from music to movies." *New York Times*, July 29, 1999, pp. G1, G6.
112. Marc Graser and Paul Sweeting. "Get ready for piracy.com." *Variety*, November 1, 1999, pp. 1, 107.
113. John C. Dvorak. "Piracy panic." *Forbes* 164 (November 29, 1999): 230.
114. Jack Valenti. "There's no free Hollywood." *New York Times*, June 21, 2000, p. A23.
115. "Now playing: Hollywood vs. the Internet." *New York Times*, June 25, 2000, sec. 4, p. 16.
116. Lee Gomes. "Now, the 'Napsterization' of movies." *Wall Street Journal* (east. ed.) July 17, 2000, pp. B1, B7.
117. Matt Richtel. "Movie and record companies sue a film trading site." *New York Times*, July 21, 2000, p. C2.
118. Amy Harmon. "Free speech rights for computer code?" *New York Times*, July 31, 2000, pp. C1, C6.

119. John Sullivan. "Judge halts program to crack DVD film codes." *New York Times*, August 18, 2000, pp. C1, C5.

120. Amy Harmon. "Copyright office backs ban on code-breaking software." *New York Times*, October 30, 2000, p. C16.

121. Amy Harmon. "Internet services must help fight online movie pirates, studios say." *New York Times*, July 30, 2001, p. C4.

122. Rick Lyman. "Hollywood, an eye on piracy, plans movies for a fee online." *New York Times*, August 17, 2001, pp. A1, C3.

123. Steve Toy. "Borrow music from old films gotta pay original musicians." *Variety*, January 28, 1976, p. 7.

124. Stephen Klain. "Rule *West Story Side* shorted in UA 'package.'" *Variety*, October 24, 1979, pp. 1, 6.

125. Tad Friend. "Copy cats." *New Yorker* 74 (September 14, 1998): 54.

126. *Ibid.*, pp. 55–56.

127. Kim Masters. "Paramount opens books." *Washington Post*, February 5, 1990, pp. B1, B4; John H. Richardson, "Judge in Buchwald suit may order Paramount to open its books." *Washington Post*, August 7, 1990, pp. E1–E2.

128. John H. Richardson. "Contract unfair to Buchwald, court says." *Washington Post*, December 22, 1990, pp. D1, D10.

129. Irvin Molotsky. "Colored movies ruled eligible for copyright." *New York Times*, June 20, 1987, p. 9.

130. David F. Prindle. *Risky Business: the Political Economy of Hollywood*. Boulder, Colorado: Westview, 1993, p. 140.

131. Andrew L. Yarrow. "New hearing is held on coloring movies." *New York Times*, September 9, 1988, p. C3.

132. "Final say over films at issue." *New York Times*, March 4, 1988, p. C18; Elliott Forbes. "Here's looking at you, Fred." *Film Comment* 34 (May/June, 1998): 80.

133. Steve Pond. "Final cut: waiting on the last word." *Washington Post*, February 21, 1995, p. D7.

Chapter 6

1. "Crucial print piracy victory." *Variety*, October 1, 1975, p. 48.

2. "Indict David Barnes, Frank Zichella." *Variety*, February 8, 1978, p. 30; "David Barnes admits pic piracy; *Star Wars*, others to So. Africa." *Variety*, April 5, 1978, p. 18.

3. Oliver Barlet. *Decolonizing the Gaze*. London: Zed, 2000, p. 48; David Pauly. "The film pirates." *Newsweek* 90 (October 17, 1977): 90.

4. "*Zhivago*, *GWTW* among pirate videocassettes seized in Australia." *Variety*, February 3, 1982, p. 37.

5. David Stratton. "UIP's Williams-Jones: 'piracy is numero uno woe down under.'" *Variety*, November 9, 1983, pp. 39, 41.

6. "Aussies squeezing vid pirates; police raids hit various areas." *Variety*, June 26, 1985, p. 84.

7. "Aussie video pirates facing rougher waters in '89." *Variety*, April 26, 1989, p. 161.

8. Ted Clark. "Mob organizes global pix piracy." *Variety*, April 27, 1977, pp. 1, 33.

9. "Interpol to fight film pirate gangs." *Variety*, June 22, 1977, pp. 1, 100.

10. "Interpol told to track down film pirates." *Variety*, July 27, 1977, pp. 1, 77.

11. "Interpol plans to help stamp out film piracy." *Boxoffice* 111 (September 19, 1977): 6.

12. "*Rocky*, *Star Wars* hottest films in pirate hit parade." *Variety*, March 15, 1978, pp. 2, 110.

13. Ted Clark. "Europe thought 'natural' pirate roost as videocassette technology spreads." *Variety*, October 25, 1978, p. 7.

14. Ted Clark. "Tighten screws on pix pirates, but some countries are still lax in applying full weight of law." *Variety*, May 9, 1979, p. 502.
15. "Indict 15 in Rome for pirating films." *Variety*, June 27, 1979, pp. 2, 82.
16. Inge Hanson. "Sweden cracks cassette pirated catalog of 534 feature titles." *Variety*, June 27, 1979, p. 41.
17. Hazel Guild. "U.S. distribs suffer heavy rent losses on theatricals as pirates use cassettes for giant ripoff." *Variety*, February 20, 1980, pp. 6, 36.
18. Bert Baker. "Britain's piracy plague: day-&-date release Rx?" *Variety*, May 12, 1982, p. 413.
19. "Pirates flood U.K. with *E.T.* vidprints beat Xmas release." *Variety*, September 8, 1982, pp, 87–88.
20. "Piracy case gags MPEA press meet." *Variety*, October 13, 1982, p. 41.
21. "Anglo-U.S. task force set up to kill U.K. piracy, 'save' biz." *Variety*, October 27, 1982, pp. 3, 35.
22. "Homevideo shifts gears, keeps rolling." *Variety*, January 12, 1983, pp. 191, 198.
23. R. E. T. Birch. "Piracy's growth in U.K. spawns org to wage war." *Variety*, January 12, 1983, pp. 191, 198.
24. "How pirates are plundering the studios." *Business Week*, February 21, 1983, p. 81.
25. "British seeking to curb video piracy." *New York Times*, July 3, 1983, p. 31.
26. Robert Murphy. "Off the back of a van." *Sight & Sound* 54 (no. 2, 1985): 78–79; "Effective gains made by FACT vs. U.K. pirates." *Variety*, January 23, 1985, pp. 41, 44.
27. Aljean Harmetz. "Film industry escalates war against pirates." *New York Times*, June 23, 1986, p. C14.
28. "Dishing up a pirate." *Variety*, May 20, 1987, p. 82.
29. "Scottish vid bootleggers nabbed by the MPAA." *Billboard*, July 5, 1997, p. 60.
30. "Illegal film biz booming in Italy: pix turning up on TV, elsewhere." *Variety*, October 6, 1982, pp. 61, 82.
31. "Vid pirates and legal operations share Italian biz about 50/50." *Variety*, October 14, 1987, p. 152.
32. "MPAA's anti-pirates targeting Med basin and Mideast markets." *Variety*, February 24, 1988, pp. 224, 234.
33. Heidi R. Klaimitz. "Piracy cuts deep as vid biz fights back." *Variety*, July 24 1995, p. 62.
34. John Tagliabue. "Fakes blot a nation's good names." *New York Times*, July 3, 1997, pp. D1, D3.
35. Hazel Guild. "German pirate cassettes of *E.T.* said to earn twice legal entries." *Variety*, February 16, 1983, p. 46.
36. Hazel Guild. "Major crackdown in Germany scores pirated-tape bonanza." *Variety*, April 24, 1985, pp. 63, 68.
37. Peter Besas. "Spain cracks down on homevid piracy, a $714-mil business." *Variety*, September 14, 1983, pp. 1, 98.
38. Ted Clark. "France leads anti-piracy thrust for EEC, under Lang's baton." *Variety*, December 21, 1983, pp. 5, 32.
39. "Crackdown on piracy around the world reported by MPAA." *Variety*, July 15, 1987, pp. 34, 36.
40. Erich Boehm. "Industry orgs pitch EU on new antipiracy plan." *Variety*, March 8, 1999, p. 24.
41. Andrea Adelson. "Entertainment industry adds anti-piracy tricks." *New York Times*, November 22, 1988, p. D8.
42. Keith Bradsher. "Hollywood bars films to protest Soviet piracy." *New York Times*, June 12, 1991, pp. C13, C26.
43. Don Groves and Hugh Fraser. "Majors to end embargo on CIS." *Variety*, December 7, 1992, pp. 47, 90.

44. Michael Specter. "Latest films for $2: video piracy booms in Russia." *New York Times*, April 11, 1995, p. A3.
45. Tom Birchenough. "Valenti visit jump-starts Russian anti-piracy fight." *Variety*, July 28, 1997, pp. 9, 14–15.
46. Blaine Harden. "Polish copyright pirates peril U.S. trade ties." *Washington Post*, October 21, 1991, pp. A1, A14.
47. Don Groves. "Polish pirates put on alert." *Variety*, December 7, 1992, pp. 47, 49.
48. Don Groves. "Too quiet on the Eastern front." *Variety*, January 18, 1993, pp. 1, 95.
49. "UA MPAA claim win over Turkish pirates." *Variety*, October 7, 1987, pp. 3, 32; "With Turkish pirate count down film distribs and HV cozy up as Yanks reenter the business." *Variety*, February 24, 1988, p. 224.
50. "MPAA's anti-pirates targeting Med basin and Mideast markets." *Variety*, February 24, 1988, pp. 224, 234.
51. "Piracy raid yields record vid catch in Turkey." *Variety*, June 27, 1990, p. 47.
52. "MPAA's anti-pirates targeting Med basin and Mideast markets" *Variety*, February 24, 1988, pp. 224, 234.
53. Hank Werba. "U.S. warns Arabs to get it together on film/vid piracy." *Variety*, December 28, 1988, pp. 1, 4.
54. William E. Schmidt. "A third-world rule on video: copy it and sell it." *New York Times*, August 18, 1991, pp. 1, 12.
55. Peter Warg. "Egypt jails vid distribber for piracy." *Variety*, May 18, 1992, pp. 41–42.
56. Peter Warg. "Filmmakers cry foul, charge U.S. with piracy." *Variety*, March 6, 1995, p. 50.
57. David Pauly. "The film pirates." *Newsweek* 90 (October 17, 1977): 90, 95.
58. "18 'pirate dens' raided in Caracas' defendants can't flee land; nab record 25,000 tapes, mostly U.S." *Variety*, September 9, 1981, pp. 3, 42; "Home video growing in face of piracy." *Variety*, March 30, 1983, p. 53.
59. "Piracy clobbers Venezuela b.o." *Variety*, March 30, 1983, p. 53.
60. Stephen Klain. "MPAA hits Caracas pirates on copyright." *Variety*, December 21, 1983, pp. 5, 32.
61. "2,000-plus tapes seized, agreements inked in Venezuela." *Variety*, October 17, 1984, p. 39.
62. "Brazil minister's negative decision clobbers fight against vid piracy." *Variety*, March 30, 1983, p. 53.
63. "Sao Paulo raids clubs; MPAA promotes Stott." *Variety*, January 23, 1985, pp. 41, 44.
64. "Brazil's legal HV biz thriving despite pirates' 75-80% grasp." *Variety*, March 25, 1987, p. 146.
65. Peter Kerr. "Foreign 'piracy' of TV signals stirs concern." *New York Times*, October 13, 1983, pp. A1, C26.
66. Tod Robberson. "Mexico puts software pirates on notice." *Washington Post*, March 6, 1993, p. A25.
67. "As piracy grows in Mexico, U.S. companies shout foul." *New York Times*, April 20, 1996, p. 34.
68. "Some nations fight vid pirates, others let Jolly Roger unfurl." *Variety*, October 13, 1982, p. 41.
69. "High-tech tactics slow film piracy." *New York Times*, January 29, 1986, p. C13.
70. Aljean Harmetz. "Film industry escalates war against pirates." *New York Times*, June 23, 1986, p. C14.
71. Jim Hardiman. "Japanese court convicts pirate for first time." *Variety*, December 17, 1986, pp. 1, 100.
72. "Japan & U.S. link up to curb pirates." *Variety*, September 23, 1987, p. 90.
73. Lawrence Van Gelder. "At the movies." *New York Times*, February 19, 1988, p. C8; Andrea Adelson. "Entertainment industry adds anti-piracy tricks." *New York Times*, November 21, 1988, p. D8.

74. Aljean Harmetz. "Film industry escalates war against pirates." *New York Times*, June 23, 1986, p. C14.

75. Dennis Wharton. "Senators get tough on Thais over piracy." *Variety*, June 13, 1990, p. 4.

76. "U.S. tells Thailand to improve protection of U.S. copyrights." *Washington Post*, December 25, 1990, p. D3.

77. Thomas McCarroll. "Whose bright idea?" *Time* 137 (June 10, 1991):45.

78. Clyde H. Farnsworth. "U.S. film industry assails Seoul's curbs." *New York Times*, September 17, 1988, pp. 35–36.

79. Andrea Adelson. "Entertainment industry adds anti-piracy tricks." *New York Times*, November 21, 1988, p. D8.

80. John A. Lent. *The Asian Film Industry*. London: Christopher Helm, 1990, pp. 256, 266, 268.

81. *Ibid.*, pp. 79-80.

82. "MPAA hails accord with Taiwanese on piracy." *Variety*, May 31, 1989, p. 45.

83. Gary M. Hoffman and George T. Marcou. "The costs and complications of piracy." *Society* 27 (September/October, 1990): 27.

84. "Taiwan moves on copyrights." *New York Times*, June 28, 1993, p. D2.

85. Baharudin Latif and Don Groves. "Video pirates still loom large in country." *Variety*, August 22, 1994, p. 37.

86. Jesse McKinley. "Footlights." *New York Times*, August 19, 1998, p. E1; Arti Mathur. "Bollywood unites for piracy protest." *Variety*, August 24, 1998, p. 13.

87. "Indian cable dispute." *New York Times*, July 8, 1999, p. C3.

88. Davena Monk. "Chan throws weight behind antipiracy fight." *Variety*, June 22, 1998, p. 55.

89. Andrew Tanner. "Tech-savvy pirates." *Forbes* 162 (September 7, 1998): 162, 164.

90. Mark Landler. "Politics and pop mix in film piracy protest in Hong Kong." *New York Times*, March 18, 1999, p. C4.

91. Peter Behr. "U.S. blasts China on copyright violations." *Washington Post*, July 1, 1994, p. F2.

92. Peter Behr. "U.S. threatens Chinese over pirated movies, CDs." *Washington Post*, January 1, 1995, pp. A27, A33.

93. Keith B. Richburg. "Despite 'crackdown,' bootlegs rife on Chinese streets." *Washington Post*, February 11, 1995, p. A18.

94. Steven Mufson. "Trade war averted by U.S., China." *Washington Post*, February 26, 1995, pp. A1, A28.

95. Seth Faison. "U.S. and China sign accord to end piracy of software, music recordings and film." *New York Times*, February 27, 1995, pp. A1, D6; Martha M. Hamilton and Steven Mufson. "Clinton hails accord with China on trade." *Washington Post*, February 27, 1995, pp. A1, A16.

96. "Copying U.S. films brings China fines." *New York Times*, May 23, 1995, p. D22.

97. Paul Blustein. "U.S. warns China to step up efforts against piracy." *Washington Post*, November 30, 1995, p. B13; David E. Sanger. "U.S. reopens trade dispute, saying China ignores piracy." *New York Times*, December 1, 1995, pp. D1, D15.

98. Seth Faison. "China jails audio and movie disk pirates." *New York Times*, April 17, 1995, p. D18.

99. Seth Faison. "China turns a blind eye to pirated disks." *New York Times*, March 28, 1998, pp. D1–D2.

100. "China's pirated disks." *New York Times*, April 3, 1998, p. A26.

101. Seth Faison. "Chinese cracking down on the pirating of CD's." *New York Times*, June 24, 1998, p. A10.

102. Craig S. Smith. "Piracy a concern as the China trade opens up." *New York Times*, October 5, 2000, p. W1.

103. Craig S. Smith. "A tale of piracy: how the Chinese stole the Grinch." *New York Times*, December 12, 2000, p. A3.

Bibliography

Advertisement. *Variety*, February 24, 1906, p. 24.
_____. *Variety*, May 19, 1906, p. 24.
_____. *Variety*, August 18, 1906, p. 16.
_____. *Variety*, September 15, 1906, p. 20.
_____. *Variety*, October 20, 1906, p. 19.
_____. *Variety*, December 15, 1906, p. 34.
_____. *Variety*, January 19, 1907, p. 25.
_____. *Variety*, February 1, 1908, p. 33.
_____. *Variety*, October 7, 1911, p. 25.
_____. *Variety*, October 24, 1913, p. 30.
_____. *Variety*, February 18, 1921, p. 44.
Adelson, Andrea. "Entertainment industry adds anti-piracy trials." *New York Times*, November 21, 1988, p. D8.
"Admits 'copping' an act." *Variety*, March 6, 1909, p. 5.
"After picture pirates." *Variety*, November 19, 1915, p. 21.
"After show for piracy." *Variety*, December 12, 1908, p. 6.
"Agitation over 'music tax' started by Frank Rembusch." *Variety*, July 21, 1922, p. 39.
"Air pirates sound effects at no expense." *Variety*, November 15, 1932, p. 7.
"Alarmed by sticky-fingered exhibs, NATO to banish 'em, upon conviction." *Variety*, March 3, 1971, p. 5.
Albarino, Richard. "UA goes into narrow gauge." *Variety*, May 25, 1966, pp. 11, 22.
Alexander, Max. "New antipiracy laws allow local authorities more power." *Variety*, August 1, 1990, pp. 31, 34.
"Alleged film flimmers." *Variety*, September 11, 1914, p. 20.
"Alleged play pirate nabbed after river and city search." *Variety*, September 10, 1915, p. 11.
"Anglo-U.S. task force set up to kill U.K. piracy, 'save' biz." *Variety*, October 27, 1982, pp. 3, 35.
"Another European steal." *Variety*, October 26, 1907, p. 6.
"Anti-raiding pact given boot by all but three major studios." *Variety*, November 6, 1934, p. 4.
"Anti-raiding policy said to be stagnating sales dept. personnel." *Variety*, July 28, 1948, pp. 5, 22.
"*Ark* raid tied to Par's upfront anti-piracy ploys." *Variety*, July 1, 1981, pp. 5, 34.
Arneel, Gene. "Theater theft constant." *Variety*, April 1, 1970, pp. 7, 28.
_____. "U socks slow-pay exhibs." *Variety*, February 25, 1970, p. 3.
"Arrest 3; tell silk theft." *New York Times*, December 10, 1919, p. 8.
"Artists' forum." *Variety*, January 13, 1906, p. 11.
_____. *Variety*, January 27, 1906, p. 11.

______. *Variety*, February 3, 1906, p. 11.
______. *Variety*, February 10, 1906, p. 10.
______. *Variety*, June 22, 1907, p. 7.
______. *Variety*, August 17, 1907, p. 7.
______. *Variety*, September 5, 1908, p. 11.
______. *Variety*. November 14, 1908, p. 9.
"As piracy grows in Mexico, U.S. companies shout foul." *New York Times*, April 20, 1996, p. 34.
"Asks 500G damages, claims *Wilson* theft." *Variety*, January 10, 1945, p. 11.
"Asks $2,000,000 damages." *Variety*, November 21, 1919, p. 64.
"Aussie video pirates facing rougher waters in '89." *Variety*, April 26, 1989, p. 161.
"Aussies squeezing vid pirates; police raids hit various areas." *Variety*, June 26, 1985, p. 84.
"Authors' League charges mutilation in transference." *Variety*, April 12, 1923, p. 1.
"Author's protective bureau." *Variety*, February 22, 1918, p. 50.
"Authors win suit in Supreme Court." *New York Times*, May 5, 1936, p. 12.
"Aver exhib chiseling spreads." *Variety*, July 9, 1947, pp. 5, 26.
Baker, Bert. "Britain's piracy plague: day-&-date release Rx?" *Variety*, May 12, 1982, p. 413.
Barbash, Fred. "Viewer videotaping of TV programs upheld." *Washington Post*, January 18, 1984, pp. A1, A17.
Barlet, Oliver. *Decolonizing the Gaze*. London: Zed, 2000.
Behr, Peter. "U.S. blasts China on copyright violations." *Washington Post*, July 1, 1994, p. F2.
______. "U.S. threatens Chinese over pirated movies, CDs." *Washington Post*, January 1, 1995, pp. A27, A33
Berman, Marc. "Stormy seas for pirates in 1991 video crackdown." *Variety*, January 27, 1992, pp. 19–20.
Besas, Peter. "Spain cracks down on homevid piracy, a $714-mil business." *Variety*, September 14, 1983, pp. 1, 98.
"Bicycle exhib is nicked $1,589 by film board." *Variety*, May 9, 1928, p. 42.
"Bicycling charges filed against Texas exhibs – may have jury edge." *Variety*, August 11, 1931, p. 31.
"Bicycling damages for $10,000 against Hildinger Co. by film board." *Variety*, November 7, 1928, p. 20.
"Bicycling fines of $500." *Variety*, April 15, 1931, pp. 11, 75.
"Bicycling suits to recover $250 or more from Texan indie exhibs are started by Copyright Bureau." *Variety*, July 28, 1931, p. 7.
Bierbaum, Tom. "Anti-piracy raids on the rise but they make little impact on $1-billion loss." *Variety*, April 4, 1990, p. 37.
______. "MPAA claims progress in piracy fight." *Variety*, March 19, 1986, pp. 5, 92.
______. "Piracy raids by FBI, MPAA nab 3,300 vidtapes." *Variety*, March 30, 1988, p. 40.
______. "Piracy war: slow-win situation." *Variety*, November 13, 1985, pp. 1, 133.
Birch, R. E. T. "Piracy's growth in U.K. spawns org to wage war." *Variety*, January 12, 1983, pp. 191, 198.
Birchenough, Tom. "Valenti visit jump-starts Russian anti-piracy fight." *Variety*, July 28, 1997, pp. 9, 14–15.
"Black market sales of majors' 16m pix exposed." *Variety*, March 13, 1946, pp. 1, 27.
"A blank tape for Hollywood." *Newsweek* 143 (January 30, 1984): 57–58.
"Blow to moving pictures." *New York Times*, November 14, 1911, p. 13.
Blustein, Paul. "U.S. warns China to step up efforts against piracy." *Washington Post*, November 30, 1995, p. B13.
Boehm, Erich. "Industry orgs pitch EU on new antipiracy plan." *Variety*, March 8, 1999, p. 24.
"Bold Polish film pirates exhibit Chaplin's *Gold Rush* at Bucharest." *Variety*, October 6, 1926, pp. 40, 46.

Bollier, David. "At war with the pirates." *Channels* (New York, N.Y.) 7 (March, 1987): 28–31+.
"Bootleg film ad reels, new gyp." *Variety*, July 17, 1939, p. 4.
"Bootlegging of feature pix and shorts still a big trade worry." *Variety*, August 26, 1936, p. 3.
Bordwell, David, Janet Staiger and Kristin Thompson. *The Classical Hollywood Cinema: Film Style and Mode of Production to 1960*. London: Routledge & Kegan Paul, 1985.
Bowser, Eileen. *History of the American Cinema: the Transformation of Cinema, 1907–1915*, vol. 2. New York: Scribner's Sons, 1990.
Bradsher, Keith. "Hollywood bars films to protest Soviet piracy." *New York Times*, June 12, 1991, pp. C13, C26.
"Brazil minister's negative decision clobbers fight against vid piracy." *Variety*, March 30, 1983, p. 53.
"Brazil's legal HV biz thriving despite pirates' 75–80% grasp." *Variety*, March 25, 1987, p. 146.
Brennan, Lorin. "2d generation video piracy: export assns. move to strike back." *Variety*, January 20, 1988, pp. 159-160
"Brings suit to prevent changes in his films." *New York Times*, October 6, 1922, p. 28.
"Britain's Vidicord sheds cassettes' umbilical cord with pix-on-video." *Variety*, December 16, 1970, pp. 1, 70.
"British seeking to curb video piracy." *New York Times*, July 3, 1983, p. 31.
Burgess, John. "Global product piracy may be costing firms billions." *Washington Post*, February 27, 1988, p. B2.
"Burlesque manager favors rules against copyists." *Variety*, January 14, 1911, p. 9.
"Called 'stool pigeon,' checker awarded 10G damages from exhib." *Variety*, January 10, 1945, p. 11.
Calta, Louis. "New city rule bars deceptive ad uses of review quotings." *New York Times*, March 23, 1972, p. 50.
"Campaign against film thieves receives impetus at start." *Variety*, May 13, 1921, p. 47.
"Canadian piracy of 'Abie' brings fines for offenders." *Variety*, February 17, 1926, pp. 1, 14.
"Chaplin claim assented to." *Variety*, October 19, 1917, p. 25.
"Chaplin copy injunctions." *Variety*, October 12, 1917, p. 31.
"Chaplin wins vs. *Gold Rush* pirate." *Variety*, March 24, 1971, p. 31.
Chartier, Roy. "A good print is the ultimate in a film's merchandising." *Variety*, January 6, 1937, p. 6.
"Check cheating-heart employees." *Variety*, April 13, 1977, p. 5.
"Checkers figure exhibs get away with as much as $25,000,000." *Variety*, October 2, 1946, p. 9.
"Chicago's center for the disposal of 'lifted stuff.'" *Variety*, February 6, 1909, p. 6.
"China's pirated disks." *New York Times*, April 3, 1998, p. A26.
"Chiseling checkers, besides percentage cheaters, maybe causing dicks to be watchers." *Variety*, May 7, 1930, p. 17.
"Churches buy bootleg films." *Variety*, November 22, 1961, p. 11.
"Cinema solution." *Washington Post*, August 11, 1990, p. A20.
Clark, Ted. "Europe thought 'natural' pirate roost as videocassette technology spreads." *Variety*, October 25, 1978, p. 7.
_____. "France leads anti-piracy thrust for EEC, under Lang's baton." *Variety*, December 21, 1983, pp. 5, 32.
_____. "Int'l fests tighten anti-piracy guard." *Variety*, November 24, 1982, pp. 7, 27.
_____. "Mob organizes global pix piracy" *Variety*, April 27,1977, pp. 1, 33.
_____. "Tighten screws on pix pirates, but some countries are still lax in applying full weight of Law." *Variety*, May 9, 1979, p. 502.
"Clipper still copying." *Variety*, October 5, 1907, p. 3.
"Columbia registers with MPA titles of telepix made by Screen Gems." *Variety*, May 25, 1955, p. 4.

"Comment: piracy." *Wall Street Journal*, August 9, 2001, p. A10.
"Consultants in on % pix." *Variety*, March 29, 1944, p. 9.
"Continual changes in copyright values affect all show biz." *Variety*, November 6, 1957, p. 2.
"Contracting for no cuts." *Variety*, February 23, 1917, p. 19.
"Copies everywhere." *Variety*, September 15, 1906, p. 5.
"The copy act coming." *Variety*, June 30, 1906, p. 4.
"Copy act consequences made plain in Harrisburg." *Variety*, January 10, 1913, p. 7.
"Copy act in London." *Variety*, July 20, 1907, p. 6.
"Copy acts." *Variety*, December 12, 1908, pp. 26, 88.
"Copy acts not allowed on Loew's small time." *Variety*, March 26, 1910, p. 8.
"A 'copy' in England." *Variety*, February 13, 1909, p. 4.
"Copying U.S. films brings China fines." *New York Times*, May 23, 1995, p. D22.
"Copyright infringement by film exhibitor." *Scientific American* 147 (July, 1932): 61.
"Copyright laws traced by Kilroe." *Variety*, December 6, 1944, p. 8.
"Court hits B.O. chiseling." *Variety*, March 9, 1966, p. 7.
"Court reversal makes piracy tough to prove." *Variety*, October 12, 1977, pp. 1, 44.
"Crackdown on piracy around the world reported by MPAA." *Variety*, July 15, 1987, pp. 34, 36.
"Criminal copyright action ended by fine in U.S. court." *Variety*, July 10, 1914, p. 3.
"Crucial print piracy victory." *Variety*, October 1, 1975, p. 48.
"Cuba after film pirates." *New York Times*, September 13, 1923, p. 31.
"Curb Dunnahoo in print piracy." *Variety*, June 7, 1972, p. 22.
"Dating films." *Variety*, August 10, 1917, p. 19.
"David Barnes admits pic piracy; *Star Wars*, others to So. Africa." *Variety*, April 5, 1978, p. 18.
"Dealer pleads guilty to film theft in 1919." *New York Times*, March 24, 1928, p. 29.
DiMeglio, John E. *Vaudeville U.S.A.* Bowling Green, Ohio: Bowling Green University Popular Press, 1973.
"Director is king in pictures." *Variety*, February 27, 1957, pp. 5, 15.
"Directors protest editing of pictures by $40 cutters." *Variety*, June 7, 1932, p. 7.
"Directors seek 'integrity' proviso in cutting of films sold to TV." *Variety*, May 15, 1968, p. 20.
"Dirty pictures' dirty pirates; Buckley cites Florida crowd." *Variety*, July 31, 1974, p. 31.
"Dishing up a pirate." *Variety*, May 20, 1987, p. 82.
"Distribs sue Mpls. and Pa. exhibs on % deals." *Variety*, September 25, 1946, p. 11.
"Distributors backing Ross-Federal anew to bolster checking system." *Variety*, October 24, 1945, p. 12.
"Dix exhibs defending honor." *Variety*, May 1, 1957, p. 25.
"Doug McClelland on the art of film editing." *Variety*, October 4, 1972, p. 20.
"Drew denies infringement charges." *Variety*, September 14, 1907, p. 4.
"Duped films in Boston for mail orders." *Variety*, November 16, 1927, p. 9.
"Duping still continues." *Variety*, June 8, 1917, p. 18.
Dvorak, John C. "Piracy panic." *Forbes* 164 (November 29, 1999): 230.
"E. M. Loew chain soaked $3,000 on cycling charge." *Variety*, May 12, 1937, p. 21.
"Effective gains made by FACT vs. U.K. pirates." *Variety*, January 23, 1985, pp. 41, 44.
"Egypt film biz losing 'millions' from smuggling, officials claim." *Variety*, October 17, 1973, p. 21.
"8 majors crack down on Ala. print pirate." *Variety*, September 1, 1971, p. 4.
"8 majors sue Florida firm for pix piracy." *Variety*, June 17, 1970, p. 3.
"18 'pirate dens' raided in Caracas; defendants can't flee land; nab record 25,000 tapes." *Variety*, September 9, 1981, pp. 3, 42.
"Eva Tanguay on imitators." *Variety*, March 6, 1909, p. 5.
Everson, William K. *American Silent Film*. New York: Oxford, 1978.
"Everybody's rights trampled upon when TV stations mutilate — Woolner." *Variety*, December 8, 1965, p. 5.

"Exhib %-chiseling on wane." *Variety*, April 13, 1949, pp. 7, 20.
"Exhibitors for cutting film may have to pay big penalty." *Variety*, July 9, 1920, p. 29.
"Exhibitors' own music department stand against weekly fee." *Variety*, July 28, 1922, p. 39.
"Exhibs applaud Disney Prod.'s move to tighten restraints on 16m films." *Variety*, August 30, 1967, p. 26.
"Exhibs blame film sales." *Variety*, September 25, 1946, pp. 11, 20.
"Exhibs burn at claim of checking rental." *Variety*, August 18, 1954, p. 3.
"Expect many mix-ups over studios new anti-talent raiding agreement." *Variety*, February 16, 1932, p. 4.
"Eye on boxoffice larceny." *Variety*, December 3, 1969, pp. 3, 15.
"Failure of Stevens' suit vs NBC opens door for TV to carve pix." *Variety*, June 8, 1966, pp. 26, 38.
"Fairbanks loses film revision suit." *New York Times*, December 9, 1922, p. 11.
Faison, Seth. "China jails audio and movie disk pirates." *New York Times*, April 17, 1997, p. D18.
_____. "China turns a blind eye to pirated disks." *New York Times*, March 28, 1993, pp. D1–D2.
_____. "Chinese cracking down on the pirating of CD's." *New York Times*, June 24, 1998, p. A10.
_____. "U.S. and China sign accord to end piracy of software, music recordings and films." *New York Times*, February 27, 1995, pp. A1, D6.
Farnsworth, Clyde H. "China called the top copyright pirate." *New York Times*, April 20, 1989, p. D7.
_____. "U.S. eases threats of sanctions." *New York Times*, November 2, 1989, pp. D1, D18.
_____. "U.S. film industry assails Seoul's curbs." *New York Times*, September 17, 1988, pp. 35–36.
"FBI alters rules on following up vid piracy cases." *Variety*, December 7, 1988, p. 75.
"FBI apprehends 3 in *Godfather* stolen prints." *Variety*, September 27, 1972, p. 4.
"FBI believes it's uncovered biggest piracy setup ever." *Variety*, February 10, 1988, pp. 1, 132.
"FBI exposes porno & piracy affinity." *Variety*, February 20, 1980, p. 7.
"FBI nails sailor bootlegging pix." *Variety*, December 25, 1946, p. 4.
"FBI probe yields 9 indictments: porn, piracy, prostitution links." *Variety*, June 3, 1981, p. 38.
"FBI seizes tapes, films worth $100,000." *Variety*, September 12, 1979, p. 30.
"FBI's fine job in bootleg pix K.O." *Variety*, April 26, 1950, p. 2.
"Federal grand jury in Houston, Tex. indicts 7 in film piracy operation." *Boxoffice* 114 (June 8, 1979): 8.
"Federal Trade Commission heard 4,000 film complaints." *Variety*, December 10, 1924, p. 26.
"*Feet of Clay* enjoined." *New York Times*, August 21, 1925, p. 8.
Ferris III, George. "Confessions of a movie butcher." *Washington Post*, March 6, 1988, pp. G1, G6–G7.
"$50,000 film theft leads to arrest." *New York Times*, November 11, 1919, p. 17.
"Fight motion picture men." *New York Times*, February 28, 1912, p. 11.
"Film bootlegging grows." *Variety*, December 20, 1939, p. 3.
"Film checking declines 44%." *Variety*, August 18, 1948, pp. 5, 20.
"Film checking tightens." *Variety*, December 31, 1941, pp. 5, 54.
"The film clippers." *Time* 106 (October 27, 1975): 70.
"Film crooks." *Variety*, April 16, 1915, p. 17.
"Film drama disappears." *New York Times*, January 15, 1919, p. 2.
"Film gyps work Mexico." *Variety*, April 22, 1921, p. 47.
"Film piracy hits record level in So. Africa market." *Variety*, March 24, 1971, p. 31.
"Film pirates irk Mexican pic biz." *Variety*, March 5, 1969, p. 2.
"Film 'plagiarism' arouses studios." *New York Times*, August 4, 1961, p. 11.

"Film, radio, music trades write against World Copyright Union." *Variety*, April 14, 1937, pp. 4, 75.
"Film smugglers of the East." *Variety*, March 11, 1925, pp. 31, 34.
"Film suspect arrested." *Variety*, February 28, 1919, p. 65.
"Film theft bill up in Washington." *Variety*, January 20, 1922, p. 39.
"Film theft examination." *Variety*, July 4, 1919, p. 47.
"Film thefts increasing." *Variety*, September 28, 1917, p. 30.
"Film thieves held for grand jury." *Variety*, June 25, 1920, p. 39.
"Film thieves $35,000 coup on the coast." *Variety*, January 27, 1922, p. 45.
"Film ties to U.S. sought by Soviet." *New York Times*, March 10, 1956, p. 9.
"Film, TV piracy: a global probe." *Variety*, December 18, 1974, p. 6.
"Film vandals taken in hand by principal manufacturers." *Variety*, January 16, 1914, p. 17.
"Films central checking." *Variety*, June 28, 1944, p. 13.
"Final say over films at issue." *New York Times*, March 4, 1988, p. C18.
"First benefit of copy-act pact at Paris conference." *Variety*, November 4, 1911, p. 4.
"5 are accused of video piracy after detectives raid factory." *New York Times*, February 20, 1998, p. B8.
"5 companies in anti-piracy pact." *New York Times*, February 20, 1998, p. D4.
"5 majors set up own checking bureau." *Variety*, March 7, 1945, p. 9.
"$5,000 bounty on film pirate's head." *Variety*, November 9, 1977, p. 7.
"Flats grow with checking curb." *Variety*, October 15, 1947, pp. 9, 20.
Forbes, Elliott. "Here's looking at you, Fred." *Film Comment* 34 (May/June, 1998): 78–81.
"Format makes rental films disposable." *New York Times*, September 10, 1997, p. D7.
Fox, Barry. "Attack on video pirates backfires." *New Scientist* 151 (July 20, 1996): 21.
"Fox charging exhibs for slow pay." *Variety*, June 24, 1970, p. 3.
"Fox Film Corporation protests press wire." *New York Times*, August 9, 1922, p. 36.
"Fox screen deletions." *Variety*, March 4, 1931, pp. 11, 27.
Frederick, Robert B. "TV kind of film editing escapes Preminger's try for injunction." *Variety*, January 26, 1966, p. 17.
"Free McDowall, but warn buffs of 'stolen property' entanglements." *Variety*, June 4, 1975, p. 6.
Friend, Tad. "Copy cats." *New Yorker* 74 (September 14, 1998): 51+.
"Gas-tire rationing and wartime biz boom 'jackrabbit' exhibs." *Variety*, September 16, 1942, p. 18.
Gaudreault, Andre. "The infringement of copyright laws and its effects (1900–1906)." *Framework* no. 29 (1985): 2–14.
Gelman, Morrie.; "FBI raids in Gotham, N.J. crack massive pirate vid operation." *Variety*, February 28, 1990, p. 33.
"German artists' society throws out a copy act." *Variety*, March 9, 1912, p. 4.
"Gigantic film plot exposed in Warsaw." *New York Times*, June 10, 1926, p. 29.
Gold, Ronald. "Hang fines on film pirate." *Variety*, April 12, 1972, p. 5.
Gomes, Lee. "Now, the 'Napsterization' of movies." *Wall Street Journal*, July 17, 2000, pp. B1, B7, eastern edition.
Goodman, Ezra. "Hollywood's private gumshoes." *New York Times*, December 1, 1940, sec. 10. p. 4.
"Government claims U.S. is losing $23-bil revenue to piracy globally." *Variety*, March 16, 1988, p. 76.
"Gov't aiding film piracy fight." *Variety*, November 4, 1925, p. 34.
"Grab pirated cassettes in motels of *Star Wars, Jaws* & *Rocky*." *Variety*, September 28, 1977, p. 42.
Graser, Marc. "Cyber-challenged not likely to pirate pix." *Variety*, June 7, 1999, p. 4.
_____, and Paul Sweeting. "Get ready for piracy.com." *Variety*, November 1, 1999, pp. 1, 107.
Greely, Bill. "Butchery in TV's grindhouse." *Variety*, October 19, 1966, pp. 1, 36.
Groves, Don. "Polish pirates put on alert." *Variety*, December 7, 1992, pp. 47, 49.

_____. "Too quiet on the Eastern front." *Variety*, January 18, 1993, pp. 1, 95.
_____, and Hugh Fraser. "Majors to end embargo on CIS." *Variety*, December 7, 1992, pp. 47, 90.
Guild, Hazel. "Fox's fear of 16m piracy bans *Star Wars* from global GI sites." *Variety*, March 21, 1979, p. 51.
_____. "German pirate cassettes of *E.T.* said to earn twice legal entries." *Variety*, February 16, 1983, p. 46.
_____. "Major crackdown in Germany scores pirated-tape bonanza." *Variety*, April 24, 1985, pp. 63, 68.
_____. "U.S. distribs suffer heavy rent losses on theatricals as pirates use cassette for giant ripoff." *Variety*, February 20, 1980, pp. 6, 36.
Halbfinger, David M. "Stalking the video pirates." *New York Times*, March 10, 1998, pp. B1, B4.
Hamilton, Anita. "Next on the Net: pirated movies." *Time* 153 (March 15, 1999): 73.
Hamilton, Martha M. and Steven Mufson. "Clinton hails accord with China on trade." *Washington Post*, February 27, 1995, pp. A1, A16.
Hanson, Inge. "Sweden cracks cassette pirated catalog of 534 feature titles." *Variety*, June 27, 1979, p. 41.
Harden, Blaine. "Polish copyright pirates peril U.S. trade ties." *Washington Post*, October 21, 1991, pp. A1, A14.
Hardiman, Jim. "Japanese court convicts pirate for first time." *Variety*, December 17, 1986, pp. 1, 100.
Harmetz, Aljean. *Cotton Club* cassettes coded to foil pirates." *New York Times*, April 24, 1985, p. C15.
_____. "Film industry escalates war against pirates." *New York Times*, June 23, 1986, p. C14.
_____. *Jedi* prints stolen for cassette piracy, movie industry says." *New York Times*, July 9, 1983, pp. 1, 10.
_____. "Sales of movie cassettes for home use rising." *New York Times*, June 27, 1983, pp. A1, B7.
Harmon, Amy. "Copyright office backs ban on code-breaking software." *New York Times*, October 30, 2000, p. C16.
_____. "Free speech rights for computer code?" *New York Times*, July 31, 2000, pp. C1, C6.
_____. "Internet services must help fight online movie pirates, studios say." *New York Times*, July 30, 2001, p. C4.
"Has act protected." *Variety*, September 21, 1907, p. 6.
Hawkins, Robert F. "In Italy: director is all." *Variety*, February 28, 1962, p. 11.
"Hayes cables manuscript to ward off foreign piracy." *Variety*, November 29, 1912, p. 4.
Hoffman, Gary M. and George T. Marcou. "The costs and complications of piracy." *Society* 27 (September/October, 19990): 25-34.
"Hold movies need copyright penalty." *New York Times*, April 15, 1936, p. 24.
"Hollywood, Soviet style." *New York Times*, January 25, 1951, p. 24.
"Homevideo growing in face of piracy." *Variety*, March 30, 1983, p. 53.
"Homevideo shifts gears, keeps rolling." *Variety*, January 12, 1983, pp. 191, 198.
Horowitz, Murray. "TV sugar-'codes' features." *Variety*, April 17, 1957, pp. 1, 15.
"House employes gyppers." *Variety*, June 9, 1931, pp. 11, 36.
"How pirates are plundering the studios." *Business Week*, February 21, 1983, p. 81.
"Howard Underwood found guilty of piracy." *Variety*, March 9, 1955, p. 5.
Howe, Robert F. "Fairfax raid nets 50,000 bootleg videos." *Washington Post*, May 7, 1993, pp. A1, A4.
"Held in wholesale film theft charge." *Variety*, January 27, 1922, p. 42.
"Held on copyright infringement charge." *Variety*, January 6, 1922, p. 3.
Hift, Fred. "Nobody counts the minutes." *Variety*, June 17, 1959, pp. 3, 16.
"High-tech tactics slow film piracy." *New York Times*, January 29, 1986, p. C13.
"Hill chasing pirates." *Variety*, January 5, 1907, p. 7.

"Hymack." (review). *Variety*, January 4, 1908, p. 11.
"Illegal film biz booming in Italy: pix turning up on TV, elsewhere." *Variety*, October 6, 1982, pp. 61, 82.
"Immediate ratification of int'l copyright convention urged on U.S." *Variety*, December 1, 1937, p. 11.
"The importance of the title." *Variety*, April 15, 1959, p. 7.
"Important ruling vs. % chiselers." *Variety*, May 19, 1948, p. 6.
"India cracks down on film smuggling." *Variety*, December 3, 1969, p. 22.
"Indian cable dispute." *New York Times*, July 8, 1999, p. C3.
"Indict David Barnes, Frank Zichella." *Variety*, February 8, 1978, p. 30.
"Indict 15 in Rome for pirating films." *Variety*, June 27, 1979, pp. 2, 82.
"Indicts 3 in N.Y. for handling 'hot' films." *Variety*, February 5, 1941, p. 7.
"Indonesian exhib pirates pic." *Variety*, June 22, 1966, p. 5.
"Infra-red checks drive-ins." *Variety*, August 30, 1972, p. 7.
"Injustice of copyists exemplified in Barnes' case." *Variety*, November 28, 1913, p. 4.
"Inside stuff of pictures." *Variety*, November 23, 1927, p. 14.
"Inside stuff on vaudeville." *Variety*, November 4, 1925, p. 3.
"International copyright through State Department." *Variety*, December 5, 1913, p. 11.
"Interpol plans to help stamp out film piracy." *Boxoffice* 111 (September 19, 1977): 6.
"Interpol to fight film pirate gangs." *Variety*, June 22, 1977, pp. 1, 100.
"Interpol told to track down film pirates." *Variety*, July 27, 1977, pp. 1, 77.
"'It's plain theft' campus profs told as to rampant piracy." *Variety*, August 22, 1979, p. 6.
"Jackrabbit scourge up." *Variety*, May 6, 1942, pp. 7, 25.
"Japan & U.S. link up to curb pirates." *Variety*, September 23, 1987, p. 90.
Jensen, Paul M. "TV mutilation of widescreen: Stevens & Preminger's anguish." *Variety*, January 3, 1968, p. 17.
"Karno-Bedini case argued." *Variety*, December 29, 1906, p. 5.
Karp, Irwin. "The copyright renewal trap." *Film Comment* 26 (January/February, 1990): 12–15.
"Keep Broadway believable." *Variety*, March 20, 1968, pp. 3, 17.
"Keith bows to Karno." *Variety*, January 19, 1907, p. 2.
Kerr, Peter. "Foreign 'piracy' of TV signals stirs concern." *New York Times*, October 13, 1983, pp. A1, C26.
Klaimitz, Heidi R. "Piracy cuts deep as vid biz fights back." *Variety*, July 24, 1995, p. 62.
Klain, Stephen. "MPAA hits Caracas pirates on copyright." *Variety*, December 21, 1983, pp. 5, 32.
_____. "Rule West Side Story shorted in UA 'package.'" *Variety*, October 24, 1979, pp. 1, 6.
_____. "Will science soon trace pirate lairs?" *Variety*, July 1, 1981, pp. 5, 33.
Knight, Arthur. *The Liveliest Art*. New York: Macmillan, 1957.
Kosicki, Bernard A. "International copyright relations between the American republics." *Variety*, December 15, 1926, pp. 8, 10.
"Labs, booths, buffs feed lifters." *Variety*, March 7, 1979, p. 5.
Lake, Matt. "Tweaking technology to stay ahead of the film pirates." *New York Times*, August 2, 2001, p. G9.
Landler, Mark. "Politics and pop mix in film piracy protest in Hong Kong." *New York Times*, March 18, 1999, p. C4.
Landry, Robert J. "Writers' new piracy phobia." *Variety*, March 1, 1972, pp. 5, 24.
"The latest copy act." *Variety*, September 28, 1907, p. 3.
Latif, Baharudin and Don Groves. "Video pirates still loom large in country." *Variety*, August 22, 1994, p. 37.
"Lauds capture of film thieves." *New York Times*, August 22, 1919, p. 2.
"Law puts muscle behind fight against piracy, limited access." *Variety*, August 31, 1988, p. 3.
Lee, Linda. "Bootleg videos: piracy with a camcorder." *New York Times*, July 7, 1997, pp. D1, D6.

Lent, John A. *The Asian Film Industry*. London: Christopher Helm, 1990.
"*Lettie Lynton* movie ruled a plagiarism." *New York Times*, January 18, 1936, p. 19.
"Limits new titles for reissued films." *New York Times*, April 1, 1925, p. 21.
"Loew's International ties up with DeVry for 16mm foreign markets." *Variety*, December 12, 1945, p. 5.
"Long jail terms for film thieves." *Variety*, February 3, 1922, p. 45.
"Looking for 'bicycling.'" *Variety*, March 26, 1924, p. 18.
Lyman, Rick. "Hollywood, an eye on piracy, plans movies for a fee online." *New York Times*, August 17, 2001, pp. A1, C3.
MacGowan, Kenneth. *Behind the Screen*. New York: Delacorte, 1965.
"Majors fighting print piracy with 175G war chest." *Variety*, July 22, 1970, p. 28.
"Manufacturers assume control of all moving pictures." *Variety*, January 16, 1909, p. 13.
"Map 'Interpol' vs. pix pirates." *Variety*, March 29, 1972, pp. 1, 88.
Masters, Kim. "Paramount opens books." *Washington Post*, February 5, 1990, pp. B1, B4.
Mathur, Arti. "Bollywood unites for piracy protest." *Variety*, August 24, 1998, p. 13.
"May enjoin 'Around the Clock.'" *Variety*, January 5, 1907, p. 5.
"May raise movie prices." *New York Times*, August 19, 1924, p. 15.
McBride, Joe. "28-year renewal failure throws film in public domain, and onto ex-pirate's lawful list." *Variety*, August 28, 1974, pp. 5, 28.
McCarroll, Thomas. "Whose bright idea?" *Time* 137 (June 10, 1991): 44–46.
"McDowall cleared by U.S. of film piracy connection." *New York Times*, June 3, 1975, p. 25.
"McDowall films seized in piracy investigation." *Variety*, January 18, 1975, p. 39.
McFadden, Robert D. "New York pornography suspect dies as agents seek him." *New York Times*, February 15, 1980, p. B4.
McKinley, Jesse. "Footlights." *New York Times*, August 19, 1998, p. E1.
Merryman, Ashley. "Help, police! They've got Pocahontas!" *Washington Post*, July 23, 1995, p. C7.
"Metro supplementing its checking system." *Variety*, May 22, 1946, p. 7.
"Mex piracy of Yank scripts seen ending." *Variety*, September 2, 1959, p. 11.
"Mexican pirates clean up smuggling American films." *Variety*, July 11, 1919, p. 64.
Molotsky, Irvin. "Colored movies ruled eligible for copyright." *New York Times*, June 20, 1987, p. 9.
Monaco, James. "Stealing the show: the piracy problem." *American Film* 3 (July/August, 1978): 56–67.
Monk, Davena. "Chan throws weight behind anti-piracy fight." *Variety*, June 22, 1998, p. 55.
Mooser, George. "Japanese pirates defiant." *Variety*, June 2, 1922, p. 39.
"'Moral right' on scissored pix stirs up French." *Variety*, May 11, 1949, p. 13.
"More film theft arrests." *Variety*, May 11, 1917, p. 29.
"More gripes, more suits, more hisses for those cheating-hearted exhibitors." *Variety*, June 30, 1971, p. 3.
"Motion picture protected against piracy by Berne Convention article." *Variety*, September 15, 1926, p. 4.
"Movie theater men fight Hays group." *New York Times*, May 23, 1923, p. 5.
"Movies seek change in copyright pact." *New York Times*, July 11, 1939, p. 17.
"MPAA boosts film piracy kitty." *Variety*, April 23, 1980, p. 7.
"MPAA hails accord with Taiwanese on piracy." *Variety*, May 31, 1989, p. 45.
"MPAA reports record-breaking result in 1988's war on global piracy." *Variety*, April 5, 1989, p. 2.
"MPAA says raids on pirates up, convictions down." *Variety*, February 8, 1989, p. 47.
"MPAA sets meet on global piracy, $2-bil-a-year tix." *Variety*, July 3, 1985, pp. 31, 85.
"MPAA turned up anti-piracy heat in '86, but burned fewer pirates." *Variety*, April 1, 1987, p. 46.
"MPAA's anti-pirates targeting Med basin and Mideast markets." *Variety*, February 24, 1988, pp. 224, 234.

Mufson, Steven. "Trade war averted by U.S., China." *Washington Post*, February 26, 1995, pp. A1, A28.
Murphy, A. D. "Pix-TV spotlight on how NBC will not 'emasculate' George Stevens' film." *Variety*, February 16, 1966, pp. 1, 23.
Murphy, Robert. "Off the back of a van." *Sight & Sound* 54 (no. 2, 1985): 78–79.
"Music licenses." *Variety*, January 20, 1922, p. 39.
"Must pay royalties on moving pictures." *New York Times*, May 6, 1908, p. 5.
"NCA says 'unreasonable' % deals are at root of exhibs' checking trouble." *Variety*, September 2, 1953, pp. 4, 15.
"New epidemic of film piracy." *Variety*, August 8, 1933, p. 4.
"NFS offers reward, warns of 'print piracy' danger." *Boxoffice* 111 (August 15, 1977): 10.
Nichols, Peter M. "Home video." *New York Times*, December 18, 1998, p. E34.
Nix, William. "New technology hurt and helped global video piracy during 1985." *Variety*, January 8, 1986, pp. 7, 240.
"No protection from Venezuela pirates." *Variety*, March 30, 1927, p. 10.
"Nolan, Layhew, FBI alumni head pic war on pirates." *Variety*, March 12, 1975, p. 5.
"Nomikos' 10 houses sued for phoney % returns." *Variety*, September 25, 1946, pp. 11, 18.
Nordheimer, Jon. "U.S. and industry fight piracy of films." *New York Times*, June 8, 1975, p. 47.
"Now playing: Hollywood vs. the Internet." *New York Times*, June 25, 2000, sec. 4, p. 16.
"N.Y. copyright suits won by Metro, U." *Variety*, January 10, 1945, p. 11.
"N.Y. play pirate caught." *Variety*, January 28, 1916, p. 10.
"Officials say Brooklyn raid cracks bootleg video ring." *Variety*, November 10, 1997, p. B3.
"Officials seize videotapes." *New York Times*, March 18, 1982, p. D10.
"Orchestra leader offered $4 to steal an act verbatim." *Variety*, February 24, 1912, p. 10.
"Organized crusade to stop thievery shows quick results." *Variety*, March 7, 1919, p. 73.
"Originality will be protected." *Variety*, December 1, 1906, p. 2.
"Par gets tough on late-pay rentals." *Variety*, October 1, 1975, pp. 3, 38.
"Par's %-chiseling suit vs. Brandt may get out-of-court settlement." *Variety*, February 11, 1948, p. 13.
Pauly, David. "The film pirates." *Newsweek* 90 (October 17, 1977): 90, 95.
_____. "A scourge of video pirates." *Newsweek* 110 (July 27, 1987): 40–41.
"Percentage cheaters." *Variety*, April 23, 1930, pp. 5, 20.
"% film checker's hazards." *Variety*, January 8, 1935, p. 7.
"% chiseling probe a new weapon by majors in fighting trust suits." *Variety*, May 5, 1948, p. 4.
"Percentage evil worse." *Variety*, May 14, 1930, pp. 5, 14.
"Phoney film bookkeeping." *Variety*, June 2, 1948, pp. 3, 14.
"Picking film titles: arduous sport." *Variety*, March 20, 1957, p. 20.
"Picture director protests against cutting of feature." *Variety*, January 19, 1917, p. 20.
"Picture men have 'joker' for the copyright law." *Variety*, February 10, 1912, p. 12.
"Piracy and privilege: Bel-Air home threat." *Variety*, December 22, 1976, p. 4.
"Piracy case gags MPEA press meet." *Variety*, October 13, 1982, p. 41.
"Piracy checked in near East." *Variety*, August 24, 1927, p. 17.
"Piracy clobbers Venezuela b.o." *Variety*, March 30, 1983, p. 53.
"Piracy costly for Hollywood." *New York Times*, March 27, 1989, p. D4.
"Piracy pact soon due." *Variety*, April 8, 1931, p. 3.
"Piracy raid yields record vid catch in Turkey." *Variety*, June 27, 1990, p. 47.
"Piracy requires more MPAA 'eyes.'" *Variety*, March 8, 1978, p. 5.
"Piracy runs into million-$ losses, strengthen copyright." *Variety*, March 21, 1979, p. 40.
"Pirated films taken in raid in Wichita." *Boxoffice* 113 (June 19, 1978): C4.
"Pirated U.S. play filmed in Soviet." *New York Times*, March 10, 1961, p. 24.
"Pirates flood U.K. with *E.T.* vidprints beat Xmas release." *Variety*, September 8, 1982, pp. 87–88.

"Pirates, porn ops not in the groove of videodisk biz." *Variety*, January 24, 1979, pp. 1, 100.
"Pirating abroad." *Variety*, May 18, 1907, p. 7.
"Pirating films out of N.Y." *Variety*, September 28, 1927, p. 4.
"Pirating going on." *Variety*, September10, 1915, p. 19.
Pitman, Jack. "Print pirates vex majors." *Variety*, July 8, 1970, p. 31.
"Pittsburgh play pirating grown to be common thing." *Variety*, February 13, 1914, p. 10.
"Pix checkers bid for Edgar Hoover." *Variety*, July 11, 1945, p. 3.
"Plays are openly pirated by Coast stock producers." *Variety*, September 17, 1923, p. 1.
"Plot to steal many films frustrated in Los Angeles." *Variety*, January 25, 1923, p. 46.
"Plots sneak in advertising." *Variety*, August 17, 1957, pp. 3, 22.
"Police announce breakup of pirate videotape ring." *New York Times*, July 8, 1994, p. B5.
Pond, Steven. "Final cut: waiting on the last world." *Washington Post*, February 21, 1995, p. D7.
Prince, Stephen. *History of the American Cinema: A New Pot of Gold*. New York: Scribner's Sons, 2000.
Prindle, David F. *Risky Business: the Political Economy of Hollywood*. Boulder, Colorado: Westview, 1993.
"Print piracy, censorship problems in Iran." *Variety*, November 12, 1969, p. 28.
"Print pirate: 'Why am I unpopular?'" *Variety*, April 26, 1972, p. 29.
"Print theft rising; Sicilians warned." *Variety*, June 30, 1971, p. 34.
"Private detective system for 'material-stealers!'" *Variety*, April 24, 1914, p. 7.
"Pro & amateur crooks in 16m pix biz." *Variety*, March 26, 1975, pp. 5, 28.
"Producers are stealing material, says Screen Writers' Guild organ." *Variety*, May 2, 1928, p. 10.
"'Protected material' dep't under Variety's direction." *Variety*, February 4, 1916, pp. 5, 13.
"Protection by copyright of original material." *Variety*, January 21, 1911, p. 5.
"Protection from 'choosers' uniquely sought by artists." *Variety*, October 15, 1915, p. 5.
"Protection from 'thieves' needed by American acts." *Variety*, July 5, 1912, p. 6.
"Protection in Palestine." *Variety*, December 16, 1925, p. 31.
"Publishers win movie music suit." *New York Times*, July 18, 1924, p. 7.
"Pursue film pirates." *Variety*, March 28, 1913, p. 4.
"Quietly adopted warnings: 'film pirates prosecuted.'" *Variety*, October 1, 1975, p. 5.
"Raid on print pirate; title range shock." *Variety*, February 26, 1975, p. 28.
Rebello, Stephen. "State of siege." *American Film* 9 (May, 1984): 40–45.
"Reissue business method corrected by Commission." *Variety*, April 18, 1919, p. 56.
"Reissuing old prints." *Variety*, September 11, 1914, p. 20.
"Rentals as 'funds in trust.'" *Variety*, June 19, 1957, pp. 3, 7.
"Revenouers may become interested in curbing gypping exhib on % pix." *Variety*, December 20, 1944, p. 4.
Rice, Faye. "How copycats steal billions." *Fortune* 123 (April 22, 1991): 157–158+.
Richardson, John H. "Contract unfair to Buchwald, court says." *Washington Post*, December 22, 1990, pp. D1, D10.
_____. "Judge in Buchwald suit may order Paramount to open its books." *Washington Post*, August 7, 1990, pp. E1–E2.
Richburg, Keith B. "Despite crackdown, bootlegs rife on Chinese streets." *Washington Post*, February 11, 1995, p. A18.
Richtel, Matt. "Movie and record companies sue a film trading site." *New York Times*, July 21, 2000, p. C2.
"Rights of authors vindicated." *New York Times*, November 15, 1911, p. 10.
Roane, Kit R. "Police smash piracy ring for videos, arresting 43." *New York Times*, May 6, 1998, p. B4.
Roberson, Tod. "Mexico puts software pirates on notice." *Washington Post*, March 6, 1993, p. A25.
"Robbery begins on staff." *Variety*, January 15, 1969, p. 7.

"Recover 850 prints stolen in Indonesia." *Variety*, November 22, 1967, p. 21.
"Robert Miller arrested for theft." *Variety*, March 7, 1919, p. 73.
Roberts, Johnnie L. "Buyers beware." *Newsweek* 128 (October 14, 1996): 66–67.
"*Rocky*, *Star Wars* hottest films in pirate hit parade." *Variety*, March 15, 1978, pp. 2, 110.
"Rodgers to brush % chiselers." *Variety*, November 1, 1950, pp. 5, 23.
Ross, Philip E. "Cops versus robbers in cyberspace." *Forbes* 158 (September 9, 1996): 134–139.
"Sam Spade is author's property." *Variety*, November 17, 1954, p. 3.
Sandler, Adam. "MPAA reports banner year for nabbing pirates." *Variety*, February 13, 1995, p. 24.
Sanger, David E. "U.S. reopens trade dispute, saying China ignores piracy." *New York Times*, December 1, 1995, pp. D1, D15.
"Sao Paulo raids clubs; MPAA promoter Stott." *Variety*, January 23, 1985, pp. 41, 44.
"Say all can play cassette." *Variety*, November 4, 1970, p. 5.
"Say film infringes on copyright." *Variety*, March 21, 1908, p. 14.
"'Scenes' in ads not on screen." *Variety*, June 19, 1957, p. 27.
Schmidt, William E. "A third-world rule on video: copy it and sell it." *New York Times*, August 18, 1991, pp. 1, 12.
"Schools pirate off 16m rentals." *Variety*, June 18, 1975, pp. 7, 30.
"Scottish vid bootleggers nabbed by the MPAA." *Billboard*, July 5, 1997, p. 60.
"Secret service for snippers." *Variety*, January 23, 1914, p. 15.
Segers, Frank. "Pix pirates face secret weapon." *Variety*, May 26, 1976, pp. 1, 34.
"*Sea Beast*, *Girl Shy* pirated; shown in China and Greece." *Variety*, January 19, 1927, p. 4.
Seideman, Tony. "World vid piracy at $1-bil mark." *Variety*, December 21, 1983, pp. 1, 68.
"Seize prints of pirated Indian pic in So. Africa." *Variety*, April 25, 1973, p. 7.
"Seizing Keystone Chaplins." *Variety*, September 10, 1915, p. 18.
"Sentenced for film theft." *New York Times*, January 22, 1922, p. 21.
"Serious film thefts." *Variety*, March 2, 1917, p. 22.
"Sharing terms and larceny." *Variety*, August 6, 1969, pp. 5, 51.
"Sheinburg says piracy is no. 1 industry threat." *Variety*, July 16, 1980, pp. 1, 88.
Shribman, David. "Top-notch lobbyists on tape royalties." *New York Times*, November 24, 1982, p. A20.
"Slow pay exhibs speed TV." *Variety*, April 3, 1963, pp. 3, 14.
Smith, Bill. *The Vaudevillians*. New York: Macmillan, 1976.
Smith, Craig S. "Piracy a concern as the China trade opens up." *New York Times*, October 5, 2000, p. W1.
_____. "A tale of piracy: how the Chinese stole the Grinch." *New York Times*, December 12, 2000, p. A3.
"Some nations fight vid pirates, others let Jolly Roger unfurl." *Variety*, October 13, 1982, p. 41.
"Soviet continues to pirate old U.S. pix." *Variety*, May 21, 1952, p. 3.
"Soviet copyright plan." *New York Times*, April 20, 1989, p. D7.
"Soviet rebuffs U.S. on return of 5 films." *New York Times*, September 22, 1952, p. 19.
Specter, Michael. "Latest films for $2: video piracy boom in Russia." *New York Times*, April 11, 1995, p. A3.
Springer, Paul D. "Recent decisions each choice of film titles." *Variety*, January 7, 1970, p. 43.
"Spy mania complicates protection of Agent 007 at United Artists." *Variety*, February 16, 1966, p. 11.
Stanberry, Kurt. "Piracy of intellectual property." *Society* 22 (September/October, 1990): 35–40.
"Standing for switching." *Variety*, April 16, 1915, p. 17.
"Statewide probe into thefts." *Variety*, July 4, 1919, p. 47.
"Stop wholesale 'duping' cry of European movie men." *Variety*, July 10, 1914, p. 18.
"Stopping pirating." *Variety*, November 12, 1915, p. 3.

Stratton, David. "UIP's Williams-Jones: 'piracy is numero uno woe down under.'" *Variety*, November 9, 1983, pp. 39, 41.
"Studying new copyright law." *Variety*, June 12, 1909, p. 9.
Sullivan, John. "Judge halts program to crack DVD film codes." *New York Times*, August 18, 2000, pp. C1, C5.
Tagliabue, John. "Fakes blot a nation's good names." *New York Times*, July 3, 1997, p. D1, D3.
"Taiwan moves on copyrights." *New York Times*, June 28, 1993, p. D2.
Tanner, Andrew. "Tech-savvy pirates." *Forbes* 162 (September 7, 1998): 162+.
"Tarkington need not go to N.Y. for WB exam." *Variety*, February 22, 1939, p. 6.
Talbot, Hayden. "Hypoed grind hours provide lush grosses." *Variety*, October 9, 1946, p. 27.
Taylor, Alexander L., III. "Hollywood's war on video pirates." *Time* 121 (June 6, 1983): 44.
"Tell multiples to stop site switching." *Variety*, August 13, 1975, pp. 3, 22.
"$10,000 verdict in film suit." *New York Times*, March 11, 1938, p. 15.
"10,000 marks piracy fine for unauthorized 'effect.'" *Variety*, October 17, 1913, p. 4.
"10,509 % cases in 1949 probed by law firm." *Variety*, January 31, 1951, p. 5.
"Theater boothmen as No. 1 'suspects' in piracy of films." *Variety*, July 18, 1929, p. 24.
"Theft exposes film plot." *Variety*, February 23, 1917, p. 21.
"The thieving *Dramatic Mirror* caught red-handed with the goods." *Variety*, May 23, 1908, p. 5.
"36 weeks cancelled for copy act." *Variety*, September 14, 1907, p. 5.
Thomas, Robert, Jr. "Suspect in piracy of film is seized." *New York Times*, February 20, 1975, pp. 1, 38.
"Three gem thefts baffling police." *New York Times*, March 31, 1921, p. 17.
"Thus far, *Alien* not pirated; FBI raps failure to 'encode.'" *Variety*, July 4, 1979, p. 4.
"Tighten noose on pirate-film prints at Middlesex, N.J." *Variety*, August 11, 1971, p. 6.
"Tighten gov't B.O. check." *Variety*, April 12, 1944, p. 7.
"Title change upheld in Canada." *Variety*, January 19, 1927, p. 13.
"To bar old films under new titles." *New York Times*, August 8, 1922, p. 16.
"To check piracy of American films." *Variety*, August 17, 1921, p. 19.
"To give a copy act." *Variety*, August 18, 1906, p. 4.
"To guard American films." *New York Times*, May 28, 1924, p. 48.
"To read sensational charges at open exhibitors' meeting." *Variety*, July 16, 1920, p. 39.
"Toby Claude plays copy act in London hall and scores." *Variety*, March 28, 1913, p. 4.
"Tough federal action drives film pirates underground." *Variety*, September 15, 1976, pp. 6, 32.
"Tough recoup from cheats." *Variety*, June 9, 1971, p. 3.
Toy, Steve. "Borrow music from old films gotta pay original musicians." *Variety*, January 28, 1976, p. 7.
"Trial date nears for 10 defendants in U.K. film bootleg case." *Variety*, February 7, 1973, p. 29.
"Tricks of the 'jack rabbit.'" *Variety*, May 26, 1937, pp. 5, 62.
"Turk producers ignore copyright." *Variety*, June 10, 1970, p. 25.
"Turkey pirate stopped by Kemal Bey." *Variety*, February 24, 1926, p. 35.
"Turkey upholds 'dupe' film." *Variety*, July 21, 1926, pp. 5, 11.
Tusher, Will. "U.S. losses to global piracy fell 25% in '89, per Valenti." *Variety*, January 10, 1990, p. 13.
"$20,000,000 gyp on % deals." *Variety*, May 22, 1946, p. 7.
"20th cracks down, closes club showing 16m prints from undisclosed sources." *Variety*, October 26, 1966, p. 13.
"200 fraud % suits vs. exhibs." *Variety*, January 24, 1951, pp. 5, 13.
"$200,000 suit settled." *New York Times*, March 2, 1954, p. 22.
"Two Philadelphia men arrested for piracy." *Boxoffice* 114 (January 22, 1979): E-1.

"2,000-plus tapes seized, agreements inked in Venezuela." *Variety*, October 17, 1984, p. 39.
"UA, MPAA claim win over Turkish pirates." *Variety*, October 7, 1987, pp. 3, 32.
"U.N. campaign to combat film and recording piracy." *New York Times*, February 21, 1981, p. 15.
"Under-reporting now 'crime.'" *Variety*, January 10, 1973, pp. 5, 30.
"United States satisfied with clean-up of pirates." *Variety*, December 23, 1921, p. 39.
"Universal copyright convention okayed; films covered in pact." *Variety*, September 14, 1955, pp. 3, 18.
"Upstate bicyclers admit guilt; pay up." *Variety*, July 30, 1920, p. 36.
"Urge fixed damages in copyright bill." *New York Times*, April 14, 1936, p. 13.
"Urges copyright change." *New York Times*, March 11, 1912, p. 3.
"U's pirated *Uncle Tom* 25 years old, hot b.o.; court impounds prints." *Variety*, September 10, 1952, pp. 3, 18.
"U.S. asks return of 2 motion picture films diverted in the Soviet for propaganda ends." *New York Times*, January 23, 1951, p. 22.
"U.S. Attorney says Chicago was major piracy capital, but argues prosecution has eased problems." *Variety*, December 8, 1982, pp. 42, 46.
"U.S. film list rises in Russian cinemas." *New York Times*, April 11, 1951, p. 35.
"U.S. pix behind 'Iron Curtain.'" *Variety*, August 21, 1946, pp. 3, 28.
"U.S. probes charge Calif. exhibs smuggle pictures into Mexico." *Variety*, September 9, 1936, p. 6.
"U.S. tells Thailand to improve protection of U.S. copyrights." *Washington Post*, December 25, 1990, p. D3.
"U.S.-U.K. team vs. print piracy." *Variety*, October 4, 1972, p. 4.
Valenti, Jack. "A film ripoff by the Japanese." *New York Times*, March 6, 1985, p. A23.
_____. "There is no free Hollywood." *New York Times*, June 21, 2000, p. A23.
Van Gelder, Lawrence. "At the movies." *New York Times*, February 19, 1988, p. C8.
_____. "At the movies." *New York Times*, February 22, 1991, p. C12.
Variety's anti-copy pact eliminates Orange Packers." *Variety*, October 13, 1916, p. 5.
"Vid pirate Ewald, pending trial, is nabbed again." *Variety*, October 13, 1982, p. 41.
"Vid pirates and legal operations share Italian biz about 50/50." *Variety*, October 14, 1987, p. 152.
"Video bootleggers: bane of film studios." *New York Times*, October 23, 1982, pp. 41, 43.
"Vigilance against theft." *Variety*, February 21, 1919, p. 73.
Warg, Peter. "Egypt jails vid distribber for piracy." *Variety*, May 18, 1992, pp. 41–42.
_____. "Filmmakers cry foul, charge U.S. with piracy." *Variety*, March 6, 1995, p. 50.
Watkins, Roger. "Organized crime now into piracy; global woe ongoing." *Variety*, January 11, 1984, pp. 91, 128.
"WB offers $5,000 to employees who finger pix pirates." *Variety*, June 1, 1977, p. 1.
Weiler, A. H. "Movie security group will hunt for pirates." *New York Times*, February 19, 1975, p. 22.
Weiner, Rex. "Video pirates find rough seas abroad." *Variety*, May 9, 1994, p. C86.
Werba, Hank. "U.S. warns Arabs to get it together on film/vid piracy." *Variety*, December 28, 1988, pp. 1, 4.
Wharton, Dennis. "Senators get tough on Thais over piracy." *Variety*, June 13, 1990, p. 4.
Wheeler, Linda. "U.S. cracks down on video pirates." *Washington Post*, December 7, 1994, p. D3.
"The White Rates urge protection of originality." *Variety*, May 2, 1908, p. 8.
Wilson, Steve. "On-line piracy turns from music to movies." *New York Times*, July 29, 1999, pp. G1, G6.
"Windy City laundering reputation as nation's video piracy capital." *Variety*, December 8, 1982, p. 39.
Wit, Ira. "Handbook for chiseling exhibs." *Variety*, June 5, 1946, pp. 5, 29.

"With Turkish pirate count down film distribs and HV cozy up as Yanks reenter the business." *Variety*, February 24, 1988, p. 224.
"World's League of Artists and copy acts passed upon." *Variety*, August 5, 1911, p. 4.
"World-wide war on pix print pirates." *Variety*, February 19, 1975, pp. 5, 30.
Yarrow, Andrew L. "New hearing is held on coloring movies." *New York Times*, September 9, 1988, p. C3.
"Young thieves arrested." *Variety*, December 19, 1919, p. 49.
"Zanuck's raiding mess." *Variety*, June 13, 1933, pp. 5, 43.
"*Zhivago*, *GWTW* among pirate vidcassettes seized in Australia." *Variety*, February 3, 1982, p. 37.

Index